# Sunset of the Raj

# Sunset of the Raj –

# Fall of Singapore 1942

## Cecil Lee

The Pentland Press Limited
Edinburgh • Cambridge • Durham

First published in 1994 by
The Pentland Press Ltd.
1 Hutton Close
South Church
Bishop Auckland
Durham

ISBN 1 85821 134 4

Typeset by CBS, Felixstowe, Suffolk
Printed and bound by Antony Rowe Ltd., Chippenham

*To Graham,*
*Susan, John*
*and Jack*

# *Acknowledgments*

I wish to thank for their kind assistance and advice Dr Christopher Dowling and Messrs Philip Reid and R Suddaby of the Imperial War Museum.

I also wish to thank those who were my friends during the course of this work and gave me advice, assistance or encouragement.

Donald Chadwick; the late Sir William Goode GCMG; Donald Hare; the late R. O. Jenkins MC; Tony Mills MCS; Tony Lock CBE, MCS; the late Colonel Brian Montgomery MBE; the late A. W. Porter; the late C. A. Parkinson; Lincoln Page; J. T. Rea CMG, MCS; Ailsa Turner; Major Alexander Wylde; Colin Wiggins; and the late P. O. Wickens, who read through my first draft in 1971 and made valuable suggestions. I also wish to thank the late Brigadier W. R. Selby DSO, who commanded the Gurkha Brigade during the campaign with distinction, and who lent me his war diary and with whom I have had valuable discussions.

Many of the foregoing were fellow POWs with me on the Burma–Siam railway.

# Contents

## List of Photographs
On pages 136–145

*Japanese troops mopping up in Kuala Lumpur during the advance through Malaya.*

*A column of smoke from burning oil tanks rises above the deserted streets of Singapore.*

*A civilian casualty who was killed by a bomb splinter during a Japanese air attack on Singapore.*

*Lieutenant-General Percival and his party carrying the Union Jack on their way to surrender Singapore to the Japanese, 15 February 1942.*

*Japanese Troops parading near Battery Rd, Singapore.*

# List of Maps

# *Foreword*

It will be seen that the Preface to this work is dated 1971. I completed the original manuscript at that time but for various reasons it was not published. Now, with infirmities of age and failing sight, I have enlisted the aid of my son Graham to publish it with certain revisions and additions from material which has appeared since that date.

I have to confess that a spur to my efforts to publish this work arises from a recrudescence of some wild and wilful aspersions on the expatriate community of which I was then a junior member. Recently one writer even stated that the whole of the white community decamped to Australia and New Zealand from Singapore at the first sign of difficulty! While one student of recent history wrote of "A handful of imperial rulers in white ducks or khaki drill...whose energies had been unsprung...by a social round lubricated by an excess of gin slings and stengahs..." etc. etc.

The "imperial rulers" were in fact the excellent Civil Service, the definitive history of which was published in 1983 by an American, the late Professor Heussler, entitled *A Completion of Stewardship – the Malayan Civil Service 1942-1957*. It suffices to refute such absurdities.

For the rest there was the commercial community which consisted of traders, planters, tin miners, etc., and there were the police and various Government services such as the Public Works Department, Health, Agriculture, and so on.

The loss of the battleships *Prince of Wales* and *Repulse* and the rapid military collapse in Malaya resulting in the fall of Singapore gave the British public its greatest shock of the war, apart perhaps from Dunkirk.

The Press were out for blood and there was talk of "whisky-swilling planters". A war correspondent, Ian Morrison, later killed in Korea, published in 1942 a critical book, *Malayan Postscript*. He stated he met only one specimen who deserved this description. I knew one planter, a jovial fellow named Bill Harvey who was in a party of four (three planters and one Australian) who stayed behind the Japanese lines after the capitulation and did valuable work. They were finally caught and imprisoned in Pudu gaol, Kuala Lumpur. The Japanese decreed that anyone trying to escape would be executed. Despite this, these four men made the attempt and were caught, brought back to Pudu gaol, and then after being ordered to dig their own graves were beheaded at Cheras cemetery. The horror of that final scene haunts me to this day.

This account, however, is not meant to be an apology for my fellow expatriates (most of whom are now dead). We had our share of faults and blame but this work is dedicated to those whom I knew (and under whom I served), and whose friendship I enjoyed. Amongst these I take this opportunity of mentioning:

Colonel G. D. A. Fletcher OBE, MC, a director of my firm, Harrisons Barker & Co. Ltd. as it then was. During the latter part of World War I he commanded a brigade. He formed the Local Defence Volunteers in Selangor.

R. O. Jenkins MC, planting adviser to Harrisons Barker, who was seriously wounded in August, 1918 on the Western Front whilst in acting command of his battalion of Royal Welch Fusiliers.

Colonel W. M. James MC, DCM, who was in command of the Selangor Battalion of Volunteers. He had been in the Artist Rifles in World War I, which was the first territorial battalion to land in France in 1914.

His second in command was Major A. Arbuthnott MBE. He was a regular gunner in World War I, but was cruelly wounded, losing an arm and sustaining other severe injuries. So he left the Army, qualified as a chartered accountant and came out to Malaya after the war. He was a director of a company of accountants and rubber estate agents, and latterly a member of the Selangor Legislative Council. These two and others stayed behind after the Japanese surrender in 1945, although not fit, to assist in repatriating the Tamil labourers sent up to work on the Siam Railway.

Sir William Goode GCMG, the last Governor of Singapore, was, at the time of the landings, Assistant Director of Civil Defence. As soon as his work ended, on the Japanese reaching the Island, he left to rejoin the Singapore Volunteers as a corporal, was taken prisoner on the capitulation and worked for most of the war on the Burma-Siam Railway. On his death, Mr Lee Kuan Yew paid a notable tribute to Bill Goode. Gerald Hawkins MCS, served in World War I as an officer in the Gloucestershire Regiment. Although in Australia on leave when war broke out he hurried back to serve as Quartermaster in Dalforce, a guerilla group hastily set up by J. Dalley of the police. He was much loved by all Malayans.

I must mention also my old friend "G", A. S. Gispert, an accountant, who was in command of "A" (M.G.) Company of the Selangor Battalion of the Federated Malay States Volunteer Force, who was on leave from his job when the Japanese War broke out. As soon as he could get back he did but by then Kuala Lumpur had been evacuated and his old command disbanded. He enlisted as a lieutenant in command of the mortar platoon of the Argyll and Sutherland Highlanders who had been much depleted. I saw him briefly when attached to the Argylls on the rearguard at Johore Bahru, but on the second night after the Japanese landings "G" was killed when his platoon was overrun in the night at Bukit Timah. So died a man who took a grave risk to fulfil a moral obligation. Incidentally he had started the Hash House Harriers which has since the war spread throughout the world, and has now some 500 branches – a fitting memorial to my old friend.

These are the sort of men I recall. There were many others. I wish to dedicate this work to them and also to members of the races in Malaya who suffered so grievously. My Malayalee clerk, Mr P. K. Menon, was cruelly murdered during the occupation. I used to take him in my car on audits to rubber estates, and he was always unobtrusively quiet; seldom could I get him to speak.

Above all I regard this work as a homage to Malaya and its peoples, whose hospitality I enjoyed for many years before and after World War II. I loved its great stretches of jungle-clad hills, its pungent scented coastline with coconut palms bordering the long sandy beaches, the serpentine rivers past little Malay *kampongs* with their orchards of bananas and papayas, the rice fields and plantations of rubber, coconut and oil palms. I took as much time as I could from my office in Kuala Lumpur to visit all this with my friends. Kuala Lumpur when I first went there in 1934 was a fascinating little colonial town, where the muddy rivers Klang and Gombak joined by the mosque outside my office window and Malay fisherman cast their nets in the thick silty yellow waters.

Chance or fate sent me to Malaya heedless of the happiness I would derive from those golden years before the war, and so to that sunny country I owe an immeasurable debt.

C. H. Lee
April 1993

# *Preface*

This is an account of the events in Malaya in two short months in 1941–1942 and of the background and principal personalities involved. I have written at some length on these men: Brooke-Popham, Duff Cooper, Percival, Wavell, and Shenton Thomas, the Governor, for on their actions or inaction the fate of Malaya then depended. I have tried not to intrude my own judgments but to submit to those I regard as worthy of respect. A list of books consulted is shown, but my main indebtedness is to the *Official Histories* of the British and Australian Armies and to Compton Mackenzie's moving history of the Indian Army, *Eastern Epic*, supplemented by some firsthand accounts of those who participated. Above all, there is the supplementary account which Major General W. S. Kirby, principal author of the British *Official History*, wrote shortly before his death – *Singapore: The Chain of Disaster* – published in 1971. As the eminent military historian, Michael Howard, has written: "One man who did know was the official historian, Major-General S. Woodburn Kirby, and he knew a great deal more than he could, in his official capacity, reveal. But in the short time left to him between the completion of his official work and his death, he wrote his own account: one which is as frank as it is authoritative."

My account is of the Army, for the circumstances were such that it had to fight almost alone, though this is not to disparage the gallant but unavailing sacrifices of the Navy and Air Force.

As an insignificant observer and participant in some of the story of Malaya, my excuse for writing is that it is a subject that has been of absorbing interest to me ever since those days; how and why did it happen? I am in fact getting off my chest a subject which has made me a bore to my friends and acquaintances! In such humble capacity as I served I do attempt from memory to reflect some of the atmosphere and sentiments of the time.

I was angered when I read that a *Daily Express* correspondent, who was evacuated from Singapore before it fell, wrote in those frenetic days:

> With a few exceptions the white civilian population evinced no interest in the war whatsoever, except at the breakfast table when papers, reporting news from the battle front of Russia and North Africa, gave them something exciting to chatter about.

I would not wish to assert I was any exception but readers must judge for themselves if this and many other judgments just after the event were valid. Since these events the Empire has passed away, and the climate of opinion is different, but as one who was privileged to witness and fortunate to survive those times I have attempted to record my impressions.

C. H. Lee
September 1971

# Introduction

## by Graham Lee

In 1889, Rudyard Kipling stayed at Singapore for a while on his way from India to California. While there he began to formulate the English imperial dream that was to grow until it became the centre of his life in middle age – "the army of a dream"[1] as he called it. By the early part of this century Kipling, long before most of his fellow-citizens, realised how fragile the imperial structure was. This awareness or belief may at least partly explain the intensity of his fears and zeal for the imperialist cause. To buttress against the potential danger from Germany Kipling wanted a strong alliance with France and the United States. He did not see Japan as a threat. It had established itself as a naval power in 1905 after the destruction of the Russian Far Eastern Fleet at Tsushima, but not until Japanese expansionism in China in the early thirties could Japan be seen as a real, rather than potential, challenge to British power. Kipling's opinion was that "Japan is a great people... Mercifully she has been denied the last touch of firmness in her character that would enable her to play with the whole round world."[1] In 1889 such a view may have been excusable, but much of the British public, if they had any at all, held a similar view fifty years later. So did many figures in government and military circles. Nevertheless fear of Japanese potency could not be said to be absent from British government thinking. In 1922 the Washington Naval Treaty limited the tonnage of Japanese battleships to three-fifths that in the Royal and United States Navies, and in 1923 the

---

[1] Angus Wilson, *The Strange Ride of Rudyard Kipling,* p. 137.

decision was taken to develop Singapore as a naval base capable of accommodating and servicing a large fleet. It was not finally completed until 1940, but over the intervening years Singapore was transformed into a clear and vivid symbol of British power and naval strength by government propaganda. Nor was the symbol without content, for with its fortifications and four airfields it would provide the nucleus of an effective scheme of protection for not only Malaya and Borneo, but also the coasts of India, Ceylon, Australia and New Zealand; if, that is, it were home to a suitable fleet and air force contingent.

By 1936, when the Washington Naval Treaty expired and the Japanese Government refused to agree to any more restrictions on its naval power, Britain faced more threatening developments in Europe that became increasingly frightening. The Baldwin and Chamberlain Governments could not but be aware how thinly stretched were Britain's resources to protect all those large areas of the globe painted red. Much of the population was pacifist, the French even more so, and the United States in an isolationist mood. No wonder appeasement of the Axis powers seemed so inviting a policy when Britain's governors doubted that the people had either the will or the strength to defy them, while they knew some in their own ranks supported, or at least tolerated, the growing strength of Fascism.

By the end of 1940, all Kipling's worst fears were realised. France was defeated. Britain was at war, alone. In the United States President Roosevelt was covertly friendly but Congress still neutral. Churchill, a *bête noire* of Kipling's because of his social policies in the Liberal government of 1906-1914, was leader of his empire, desperate to entice the United States into the war as an ally. Singapore was a naval base without a fleet. None could be spared. The Royal Navy was stretched tight from the Atlantic to the Mediterranean. The British public may have believed in "Fortress Singapore" but Churchill and his naval staff could see its weaknesses only too plainly. However Churchill was obsessed with reinforcing the defence of Egypt and the Suez Canal against imminent Axis attack. And even if Japanese militarism was still in full flood, some of the British military hoped its energies would remain directed against China or expand westwards against the Soviet Union, and believed that there would be insufficient capacity and enthusiasm left over to mount an attack on Britain's Far Eastern territories.

The Admiralty was nervous. In early 1941 the First Sea Lord, Admiral of the Fleet Sir Dudley Pound, was in favour of encouraging the United States to base part of its Pacific fleet at Singapore, which in concert with a British force would be a great deterrent to any potential Japanese aggression. "If there is only one fleet in the Pacific at Hawaii, it is doubtful whether the pressure on the Japanese will be sufficient to deter them from their land operations to the southward," Pound wrote to Churchill on February 13th.[2]

But the US government showed no signs of wanting, or at least wishing to be seen as wanting, to prop up Britain's empire in the east. Americans' hidden sense of guilt for their own brand of imperialism made them especially sensitive about Britain's more open, if weaker, empire. Churchill had become annoyed with the Navy for pressing their US counterparts, risking the alienation of the Roosevelt administration and Churchill's efforts to bring the United States into the war against Germany, his naturally predominant foreign policy preoccupation.

On February 17th, Churchill wrote to Pound: "I do not see why, even if Singapore was captured, we could not protect Australia by basing a fleet on Australian ports."[3] This ended one avenue of progress for the Admiralty and demonstrated Churchill's ambivalence over the military value of Singapore; the Navy henceforward concentrated on trying to find a viable fleet that could be sent there. They were also concerned about the Air Force strength in Malaya. Admiral Tom Phillips, the Vice-Chief of Naval Staff and a confidant of Pound, had a reputation for belittling the importance of air strength for naval protection, but in April he pleaded for Hurricane fighters to be sent to Malaya instead of the

---

[2] Admiralty Papers – ADM 205/10
[3] ADM 116/4877

inferior Brewster Buffaloes, American-designed but a model rejected by the USAF. However Churchill and the Air Staff considered the Buffaloes adequate for their task. Not for the first time would the Japanese Air Force be underestimated, but the greater ease of obtaining spare parts for the Buffaloes from the United States also came into the RAF's calculations.

From 18th November 1940 Air Chief Marshal Sir Robert Brooke-Popham became Commander-in-Chief, Land and Air Forces, Far East. He was often vociferous in his contempt for Japanese prowess in general and their Air Force in particular. That he was sixty-two and had already retired from the RAF once, in 1937, might not have mattered (after all Churchill was older) if he had shown more understanding of the factors at work in the Far East and more determination to deal with them. Admittedly his command was framed as co-ordinator rather than as generalissimo and did not cover the Navy, but he has been accused of not having pressed the RAF earlier and strongly enough to fulfil its commitments to the defence of Malaya, preferring to accept Whitehall's judgment, itself prejudiced by Churchill's focus on the Middle East.

One of his first ideas was to reinforce Hong Kong. Churchill vetoed this, seeing that if Singapore was exposed and vulnerable, Hong Kong was many times more so. But if Sir Robert was guilty of complacency he was not more culpable than many of his superiors in Whitehall who still believed or hoped that war in the East was impossible.

In July 1941 Japan occupied French Indo-China, hitherto under the control of France's Vichy Government; thus it gained a naval base at Camranh Bay, and airfields which brought their Air Force within striking range of most parts of Malaya, and even of Singapore, although the military authorities did not know this owing to wrong intelligence about the flying ranges of Japanese bombers. In August Sir Robert responded to this move by supporting a report of Lieutenant-General Percival, the Land Forces Commander, demonstrating how inadequate the defences of Malaya were on land, in the sea and in the air.

In September the responsibility was to some extent lifted from Sir

Robert's shoulders as a member of the government close to Churchill, Duff Cooper, was sent out to Singapore to investigate the situation. His enquiries and conferrals were complete at the end of October; their unhurried course seemed to indicate no great urgency. It was concluded that war with Japan was still unlikely at least for a few months, due to the imminent arrival of the monsoon, which brings very inclement weather to the South China Sea and the Gulf of Siam. There was a sort of belief in Admiral Monsoon which would, like General Winter in another theatre of war, bring valuable relief to the weaker force. In addition it was recommended that one or more battleships should be sent to Singapore. Hopefully these would fulfil several purposes military and political: provide an effective naval force in Singapore, deter the Japanese, assuage Australian demands for greater protection and increase popular morale both in Britain and Malaya. The urgency for action should have been racked up another notch when General Tojo, the militarist Minister of War, succeeded the milder Prince Konoye as Japanese Prime Minister on 14th October.

Meanwhile since August the replacement had been considered of Brooke-Popham by a younger man with more up-to-date war experience. Is the implication that the High Command had not taken the possibility of war seriously when he was appointed in November 1940? For if they did, presumably they should have appointed a more talented commander with greater battlefield experience then. In November 1941, a few weeks before Japan attacked Malaya, Brooke-Popham became aware of the lack of confidence in him. This must have had a detrimental influence on his morale in those vital weeks. In the end the start of hostilities forestalled his immediate replacement. Last-minute changes were also afoot on the naval side: Vice-Admiral Sir Geoffrey Layton, the Naval Commander, was superseded on 3rd December by Admiral Sir Tom Phillips, confidant of Pound and former favourite of Churchill who called him "the Cocksparrow" because of his diminutive height and fearlessness in expressing his opinion. His supporters thought him very knowledgeable and intelligent. He was unimpressive physically, dour, volatile but very hard working, conscientious, clever but often opinionated with a short man's aggressiveness. His detractors, among whom there were admirals who resented his rapid promotion and who regarded him as somewhat of a political admiral, considered him a theorist who refused to accept inconvenient facts, too clever by half, lacking in experience at handling a fleet in wartime – "all brains and no body". In contrast Layton was very experienced in command, in the North Sea and in the Norwegian campaign in the early part of the war. However Phillips had shown both courage and good judgement in persistently opposing the ill-fated expedition to Greece. If he had prevailed, some of the ships saved could have been sent to Singapore. Churchill did not forgive him for being right this time and he fell from favour.

Phillips was to be in command of a substantial fleet named Force Z: the aircraft-carrier *Indomitable*; battle cruiser *Repulse*, an elderly but powerful ship; and the battleship *Prince of Wales,* in the most modern King George V class, the latest thing in battleship design, brand new. The aircraft-carrier ran aground in November and had to be docked for repairs in Norfolk, Virginia. As a consequence, air protection of Force Z was limited to the six squadrons of Buffaloes which might have other calls on their services when the Navy needed them. *Prince of Wales* was so new that the crew had too little time to practise their anti-aircraft gunnery while *Repulse*, being of First World War vintage, was ill-armoured against air attack and had rudimentary anti-aircraft gunnery. Two such large ships also needed destroyer defence against submarine attack. Only four were available and that was considered the very minimum needed for their protection.

Pound and the Admiralty were united in arguing against the dispatch of Force Z but to no avail. Churchill was convinced that the Force could tip the balance towards Japan remaining peaceful towards Britain. He assumed that if there was war it would be joined soon enough by US Navy ships from Pearl Harbor. He deluded himself that *Prince of Wales* could act as the sort of very dangerous lone ranger that the German battleship *Tirpitz* was to British convoys in the Atlantic. The press was encouraged to build up the *Prince of Wales* as a terrifying image of naval might; it was even held to be unsinkable in some quarters. Churchill may have come to believe the propaganda he encouraged. But he must have realised at some level that as a naval force, Force Z was very vulnerable; however in the end political considerations overrode military ones.

On 28th November Brooke-Popham reported to London that a military build-up in Indo-China indicated an imminent invasion of Thailand. He had always assumed that if the Japanese attacked, they would land in Southern Thailand using it as a launching pad for an assault on Malaya. The contingency plan codenamed "Matador" was that British land forces would invade Thailand (which desperately wanted to stay neutral) to forestall the Japanese landings. In his report Brooke-Popham played down the danger to Malaya, emphasising how the low-lying ground of the Kra Isthmus, where the Japanese were expected to land, would be waterlogged in the monsoon season and thus bog down their advance. This supposed effect of the monsoon like others proved to be much exaggerated. However he must have considered the position serious, for the Governor of Singapore and Malaya, Sir Shenton Thomas, proclaimed a State of Emergency on 1st December. Force Z seemed to have failed as a deterrent even before it arrived in Singapore the following day to play its other potential role, to disrupt any Japanese landings. Phillips had arrived on 30th November and took over as Fleet Commander on 3rd December. It seems that neither Brooke-Popham, nor anybody else, apprised Phillips of the imminent crisis, for on the 4th he set off for a conference with Admiral Hart, Commander-in-Chief, US Asiatic Fleet, in Manila, dispatched *Repulse* to Darwin on a goodwill visit to Australia and gave the go-ahead for repairs to be made to *Prince of Wales*. It was strange behaviour if he did believe in the imminence of an attack. Perhaps he was to some extent hypnotized by the arrival of Force Z. *Prince of Wales* had performed a triumphal circuit of Singapore Island and received a tumultuous reception from the European population. It seems especially odd in that the Chiefs of Staff in London must have been aware of the probability of invasion since, on 5th December, they gave Brooke-Popham freedom to implement plan "Matador" if Japan invaded Malaya, Dutch East Indies or Thailand, or if it were necessary to forestall a Japanese landing in Southern Thailand or Malaya. The United States had committed itself to supporting Britain in this event. Churchill regarded this agreement as a great step forward in his goal of bringing the United States into the war on Britain's side. Then there would soon be a US fleet if Singapore were lost; the immense gain of having the United States as an ally would have been achieved. One would have thought that on Phillips' arrival, Brooke-Popham would have asked him to have his fleet set out on patrol in the Gulf of Siam or at least to be ready for sailing. Instead it was inert or dispersed while the British in Malaya and Singapore still luxuriated in the reassurance that the arrival of Force Z had given them. Anglo-Dutch air reconnaissance began on the 3rd December, either a sign that Brooke-Popham took the Japanese threat seriously or a precaution he could not resist. Only two days after he received his, perhaps unwelcome, freedom of action in the case of Matador, Japanese convoys and fleet escorts were sighted heading towards the Gulf. It was a lucky break, as the reconnaissance aircraft was at the extreme limit of its range and the weather was very cloudy and rainy and visibility was poor. That Phillips was taken by surprise by this news is vividly illustrated by the fact that further delay was caused in his return to Singapore by the dispersal of the crew of his Catalina flying boat around Manila on sight-seeing trips. If he had felt a sense of urgency, surely they would have been ordered to be standing by in a state of readiness.

Brooke-Popham was now in a very difficult position. The problem with Matador was that Britain had never obtained the compliance in the plan of the Thai government who were anxious not to upset the Japanese. Whitehall had continually emphasized the policy of doing nothing to precipitate a war with Japan. Violation of Thai neutrality would provide Japan with a *casus belli* and it was a possibility that the ship movements were a Japanese ruse to spark off just such a violation. He also knew that diplomacy with the United States was still continuing. It must have entered his head that a wrong move might start the war with Japan with the British billed as aggressor and the United States dissociating itself from the action. And he, Brooke-Popham, would probably be the scapegoat.

As it was calculated that Matador would take some 36 hours to implement, a quick decision was imperative. It could be argued that a great commander would have taken a calculated risk, relied on his intuition and all the signs pointing to Japanese intentions being warlike and launched plan Matador. Brooke-Popham put the Army and Air Force on alert but he decided not to take what was more a political than a military gamble. On the 7th December he ordered further reconnaissance. By the evening three sightings showed Japanese convoys heading south towards the coast of southern Thailand and northern Malaya. Brooke-Popham and Phillips conferred later that evening. The former was still hesitant. But by now it was too late for Matador. Shortly after the end of the meeting the Japanese landings had begun. Brooke-Popham's predisposition to believe that war with Japan was unlikely, and that Britain's military prowess was superior to that of any other nation, had veiled his intelligence and eroded his will. Even the monsoon had turned out to be a Japanese ally, making aerial reconnaissance more difficult.

Phillips was aware of Pound's and the Admiralty's opposition to the formation of Force Z and must have been acutely aware of the weaknesses of his force. At about 1.00 a.m. on 8th December news reached Singapore that the landings in northern Malaya were taking place. RAF bombers attacking under a brilliant tropical moon caused considerable damage to Japanese ships but the landing was not prevented. Simultaneously, hardly opposed, other landings were occurring in Thailand. A few hours before, in response to an Admiralty enquiry asking him what he proposed to do about the Japanese convoys in the Gulf of Siam, Phillips stated that he proposed to intervene with his fleet, co-ordinating his attack with the RAF.

*Introduction*

Accounts of what happened in the High Command at Singapore in the early morning of the 8th are confused and contradictory. Probably two meetings were held which Brooke-Popham, Phillips, Sir Shenton Thomas, the Governor and Air Vice-Marshal Pulford, the Air Officer Commanding, and various others attended – either one or both. Phillips stated that if the survival of his force was paramount, then it was advisable to withdraw westwards. (Vice-Admiral Layton, though reputedly a fire-eater, thought that this was the only option. But he was not invited to the meetings.) He, Phillips, was concerned about the threat from enemy submarines. The Asdic detection system in his few destroyers was unreliable, particularly in tropical waters. He was not so worried about torpedo bombers because he thought the bad monsoon weather would impede their efficiency. The Admiralty had received an intelligence report that Japanese bombers were much more efficient than expected, and of a longer range than previously thought. An intimation of this was received when an air raid interrupted the deliberations. By some error, a copy of this report was lying unread on a desk in Singapore; it never reached Phillips, unlike the two squadrons of Japanese torpedo bombers of latest design just arrived in Indo-China.

He surmised that, though risky, an attack on the Japanese invasion fleet, using speed and surprise, could succeed. The Governor cautioned against a naval attack without air support. Pulford stressed the poor performance of his fighters and the lack of training of his pilots in a naval protection role. Aware of the evaporation of plan Matador, and with no comprehensive strategy of offensive to put in its place, Brooke-Popham saw an attack by Force Z as the only way to repel or disrupt an invasion.

Phillips had already prepared a cable to London of his intention to attack. Brooke-Popham's opinion must have hardened his resolve, and no cable came from the Admiralty querying his judgment or countermanding his decision, except an oblique one received when Force Z was already at sea referring to the report about Japanese torpedo bombers he had never seen. Yet plenty occurred between the early morning and early evening of the 8th, when Force Z left port, to give him pause.

The air raid itself told him that the range of Japanese bombers was greater than he thought, as at that time the nearest point of operation was Indo-China and hitherto current intelligence made such a raid impossible. It now looked likely that by the time Force Z reached the waters off Southern Thailand where the bulk of troops were expected to disembark the landings would probably be completed, or at least largely so. As time went on Pulford's estimates of the fighter support that he could give were rapidly decreasing. As the fleet prepared to sail out of Singapore, he reported to Phillips that owing to the disruption of the RAF's northern airfields there was less and less prospect of air support the further north he sailed. Finally he signalled to the departing fleet: "Regret fighter support impossible." By then it was evident that the Japanese air force was rapidly establishing itself on the two airfields in Southern Thailand, increasing the potential threat to Force Z as the rationale for the expedition decreased. Why did not Phillips change his mind before it was too late?

Meanwhile in Whitehall there did not seem to be a great sense of urgency, or the inactivity indicated an onset of paralysis through despair. Simultaneously with the news of the invasion of Malaya came that of the destruction of both the US Pacific fleet at Pearl Harbor and of the strategy of Anglo-American naval co-operation in the Far East. At a meeting between Churchill and service chiefs in the evening of 9th December (London time) what to do about the failure of the naval deterrent policy was discussed. Churchill was in favour of withdrawing Force Z to rendezvous with the remnant of the US Pacific fleet. But no decision was made that day. By then Phillips and the crews of *Prince of Wales* and *Repulse* were steaming hurriedly towards destruction.

In London they knew of Phillips' intentions but his plan was not even, it appears, on the agenda. But Churchill may have blenched at taking the decision, even knowing it right, to withdraw Force Z from Singapore and endure the public outcry at the smashing of the image that his own government had so sedulously and lovingly created. To Phillips, prime representative of the prestige of the Royal Navy in the Far East, the reputation of the *Prince of Wales* was now a shirt of Nessus which he could not tear off without also eviscerating the hopes of the British inhabitants of Malaya in general, and the armed forces in particular. The abandonment of Singapore, as a withdrawal of Force Z would be interpreted, would be tantamount to an admission of defeat at the outset of the campaign. Phillips must have recognized that Churchill would have been reluctant to protect him over so unpopular a decision; better to gamble on Japanese mistakes and the alliance with Admiral Monsoon and have a chance of retaining his reputation and the honour of the Navy. Maybe pride, combined with the obstinate streak that he was reputed to have, the reluctance to abandon ideas decomposed by new evidence, had its influence; or he could not withstand being infected by Brooke-Popham's complacency over supposed Japanese deficiencies or the enthusiasm for action of junior officers and crew. After all, he could not be expected to foresee that the Japanese invasion would be so efficient in every way. As the fleet left Singapore, a few senior naval officers looked on with gloomy forebodings, maybe deepened by the vivid symbolism of a tropical sunset. How many of them would have been strong enough to resist the swift currents sweeping Phillips along to defeat?

Churchill's orders later on when it was infinitely clearer that the defence of Singapore was hopeless do him much less honour. On 21st January Churchill cabled to General Wavell, the then Commander-in-Chief; "I want to make it absolutely clear that I expect... no question of surrender to be entertained until after protracted fighting among the ruins of Singapore city."*

Just before this message, Churchill had considered abandoning Singapore, as he judged it impossible to hold onto both the island and Burma; but the vigorous objections of the Australian government in favour of trying to retain Singapore forced his hand. On 10th February when the Japanese had overrun most of the island and five days before

---

* Andrew Gilchrist, *Malaya 1941*, p.158.

lack of water and the threat of massive casualties in Singapore city itself forced a capitulation, Churchill cabled to Wavell: "There must be at this stage no thought of saving the troops or of sparing the civilian population. The battle must be fought to the bitter end at all costs. Commanders and senior officers must die with the troops. The honour of the British Empire is at stake."*

This is cruel in its futility, the fruit of an atavistic urge to send scapegoats to slaughter to assuage defeat. It is also hypocritical when contrasted to Churchill's ambivalent attitude to the port before the Japanese invasion. Behind this was there not the fear that his own reputation was at stake if he had to admit to the British public what he knew himself – that their hopes over Singapore had all along been built on warm soft tropical mud?

---

* W. S. Churchill, *The Second World War*, IV, pp.87-88.

# CHAPTER I

## Malaya

Malaya had little impact on the British public and may be said to have been "discovered" by them when the chain of disaster which ended in the fall of Singapore on 15th February 1942 hit them a terrible blow at a time they thought the worst was over. Its history and its peoples were known only to the *cognoscenti*; the literary art of Joseph Conrad and Somerset Maugham had conveyed to a wider audience something of the romance and flavour of the Golden Chersonese and Spice Islands, but to most Singapore was known only as the bastion of our defences in the Far East. The shock was deep. Writing his diary, that acute and sensitive observer, Harold Nicholson, expressed the feeling after the fall:

> This Singapore surrender has been a terrific blow to all of us. It is not merely the immediate dangers which threaten in the Indian Ocean and the menace to our communications with the Middle East. It is the dread that we are only half-hearted in fighting the war whole-hearted. It is even more than that. We intellectuals must feel, that in all these years we have derided the principles of force upon which our Empire is built. We undermined confidence in our own formula. The intellectuals of 1780 did the same.

An examination of the facts may help to decide something of the truth of this immediate reaction, and how far these reflections were fair and

1

judicious.

"Malaya" is a convenient word to cover a conglomerate colonial administration headed by one man, the Governor of the Straits Settlements and High Commissioner of the Federated and Unfederated Malay States. Of the Straits Settlements, Penang and Province Wellesley were acquired in 1787-1800, Singapore in 1819, and Malacca in 1824. The protectorate and federation of the Malay States of Selangor, Perak, Negri Sembilan and Pahang were processes that began in 1874 and continued until 1895. The Unfederated Malay States of Johore, Kedah, Perlis, Kelantan and Trengganu received protection and the establishment of British Advisers, as opposed to "Residents" in the Federation, during the period 1909-1914.

The man principally responsible for extending British dominion in the Malay Peninsula, pacifying Perak after a brief campaign and laying the foundation for the protectorates over the other Malay States, was the Governor at that time, Sir William Jervois, whose initiative was looked upon with disfavour by the Prime Minister of the day, Benjamin Disraeli, and the Colonial Secretary, Lord Carnarvon, until it was successful. Disraeli gave little thought to that country which in his letters he referred to as "Malay-land" and where some seventy years later the death-knell would be sounded of that great Empire which roused and inspired his flamboyant and romantic imagination.

We will attempt to describe Malaya briefly at the climax of the period of colonial calm in 1941. The whole country is about the size of England. A central spine of jungle-clad hills and mountains runs down the peninsula and peters out in Johore in the south, where the mainland is divided from the island of Singapore by a strait varying in width from five thousand to about six hundred yards at a causeway where road and rail cross to the island. On the west of the main range there were the roads and the substantial development of tin mines and rubber estates. On the east communications and development were sparse. A network of roads in the west was a strategic and tactical advantage to an invader, and rendered defence difficult. Lateral communication across the main

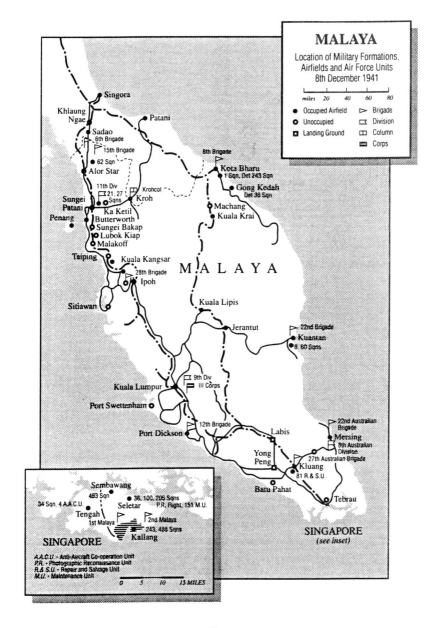

**MALAYA**

Location of Military Formations,
Airfields and Air Force Units
8th December 1941

miles 20 40 60 80

- ● Occupied Airfield ▷ Brigade
- ○ Unoccupied ⊏ Division
- ▣ Landing Ground ⊞ Column
- ▬ Corps

Singora
Khlaung Ngae
Patani
Sadao
6th Brigade
15th Brigade
62 Sqn
Alor Star
8th Brigade
Kota Bharu
1 Sqn, Det 243 Sqn
11th Div
Krohcol
21, 27 Sqns
Kroh
Gong Kedah
Det 36 Sqn
Sungei Patani
Ka Ketil
Machang
Kuala Krai
Penang
Butterworth
Sungei Bakap
Lubok Kiap
Malakoff
Taiping
Kuala Kangsar
M A L A Y A
28th Brigade
Ipoh
Kuala Lipis
Sitiawan
Jerantut
22nd Brigade
Kuantan
8, 60 Sqns
9th Div
III Corps
Kuala Lumpur
Port Swettenham
12th Brigade
Labis
22nd Australian Brigade
Mersing
8th Australian Division
27th Australian Brigade
Port Dickson
Yong Peng
Kluang
81 R.& S.U.
Batu Pahat
Tebrau
SINGAPORE
(see inset)

Sembawang
453 Sqn
36, 100, 205 Sqns
34 Sqn, 4 A.A.C.U.
Seletar
P.R. Flight, 151 M.U.
Tengah
1st Malaya
2nd Malaya
243, 488 Sqns
Kallang
SINGAPORE
A.A.C.U. - Anti-Aircraft Co-operation Unit
P.R. - Photographic Reconnaissance Unit
R.& S.U. - Repair and Salvage Unit
M.U. - Maintenance Unit
0 5 10 15 MILES

3

range was, however, confined to the railway and two roads across the mountain passes.

The population at the time was approximately as follows:

| Malays | - | 2,250,000 |
| Chinese | - | 2,250,000 |
| Indians | - | 75,000 |
| Eurasians | - | 19,000 |
| Europeans | - | 30,000 |

with the Chinese more concentrated in the towns and particularly in Singapore, Malacca & Penang; Indian and Chinese workers on estates and tin mines; and the Malays, in government service in the main, constituting the rural peasantry.

The tropical climate, mild though monotonous, is healthy but not invigorating, especially for the European. Robust physical exercise was generally considered necessary to keep fit and maintain faculties alert, but as the years go on, of course, of this one is less and less capable. The retiring age was considered to be about 55 in this enervating atmosphere. With the advent of rubber planting and tin mining in the early part of the century, and with Sir Malcolm Ross's researches into malaria, the country developed and prospered; and on the whole, compared anyway to many other parts of the world, happiness and prosperity in those days was fairly widely diffused.

Both by natural preference and policy, particularly between the World Wars, the Government stretched its protecting hand over the easy-going Malays, happy to enjoy the even tenor of their ways. By contrast the British commercial classes inclined to the hard-working, hard-headed, thrusting Chinese, who increasingly dominated the economic scene.

Politically the fragmentation of the peninsula was a disadvantage and with the growing Japanese menace drawn to the magnet of Singapore, and Malaya's rubber and tin, unification was desirable. The efforts of Governor Sir Cecil Clementi for union were ill received and resisted by

4

the powerful commercial classes, European, Chinese, and Indian. In fact, recognition of this need came significantly and solely with the creation of Malaya Army Command in 1922, embracing the Straits Settlements and the Federated and Unfederated Malay States.

So it may be said that life went by placidly and monotonously until on 8th December 1941 Malaya was struck by a Japanese thunderbolt.

The tangled story of our defence strategy in the years after the First World War; how the Singapore base was started, was stopped, was resumed; the controversy between the big gun and the aircraft; all has been told many times. We start with the situation as it was when on the fall of France the Japanese threat became real and acute, and first describe some of the principal personalities concerned in the Malayan scene; those who had the misfortune of trying to make the best of our manifold weaknesses in the Far East whilst Great Britain was fighting for its life in the West.

About the time the calamities we will relate were falling on Malaya, there died in England one of the great pioneers of British rule in Malaya, Sir Hugh Clifford. In the old club at Kuala Lipis, capital of the attractive jungle state of Pahang, there was to be seen before the war a fading photograph of Clifford as a young man in the 1880s when he was making his name to become Resident of Pahang, to return later to Malaya as Governor and High Commissioner. To those who knew him by repute and had read his stories of old Malaya, such as *The Further Side of Silence*, this piece of news in that December of 1941 struck a sad chord, the passing away of this old pioneer as if he knew what was to be the fate of his beloved Malaya and that an entrancing past was being swept away by barbarians – no longer the "sweet, just boyish master". This may be an idealistic fantasy but to some of us who had enjoyed the hospitality of this delightful country and its people such were the sentiments.

# CHAPTER II

## The Army Commanders In Malaya

Michael Howard expresses an often forgotten truth in his description of the French General Chanzy in the closing stages of the Franco-Prussian War:*

> He had already shown himself an inspiring leader in the attack, but his full genius was to show itself in the patience, resolution, and fighting capacity with which he led his armies in unbroken retreat, in the dead of winter, for seven terrible weeks. Chanzy deserves better of his country than many of the names which glitter on the roll of Marshals of France; but it is habitual for nations to give exaggerated glory to generals who lead them to victory, and to forget those whose talents merely stave off or mitigate defeat.

Malaya and its mountainous difficulties certainly needed such a commander at this hour.

If we go back to the pre-war years, as a preliminary to considering the problems of General Percival in the conduct of the Malayan campaign we find a figure who later fulfilled his promise and demonstrated his quality in the defence of Malta in the worst period of its peril. In August

---

* M. Howard, *The Franco-Prussian War*, p. 383.

1936, Major-General Dobbie was appointed General Officer Commanding in Malaya, and during the north-eastern monsoon of 1936–7, soon after his arrival, he instituted exercises which showed that not only were landings on the east coast possible at this time of the year but also more probable as bad visibility would hamper air reconnaissance. In November 1937, with Colonel A. E. Percival, as he then was, as his Chief Staff Officer, he forwarded to the War Office a prescient forecast of the course and methods of a Japanese attack. He predicted the acquisition first of advance bases in Siam and Indo-China, and landings at Singora and Patani in Southern Siam, and at Kota Bahru in Malaya, and advances down the main road and railway to capture Singapore from the north, exactly as took place.

In July 1938 he warned of the danger of a landing further south at Mersing in Johore and proposed defences from the Johore River through Kota Tinggi towards Kulai on the main trunk road, and then south-westwards to Pontian Besar on the west coast in order to provide a defensible perimeter sufficiently wide to protect Singapore Island and the base. He obtained the necessary sanction and work started along the Johore River from Kota Tinggi westwards.

In August 1939 Dobbie was succeeded by Major-General L. V. Bond, as his normal tour had been completed. Bond allowed the work instituted by Dobbie to lapse. He accepted and realised the attack would come from the north, but the absence of adequate forces to defend Malaya seems to have tended to paralyse thought and action. Much energy was consumed in controversy with his air force counterpart, Air Vice-Marshal Babington, who was a strong advocate of air defence, although the means were also lacking and likely to remain so, and who was pressing for the defence of the northern airfields in Kedah and Kelantan and Pahang at Kuantan, for which Bond just had not the resources. The logic of Bond's abandonment of the defences started by Dobbie in Johore is unclear.

Bond is described by Kirby, who knew him, as "although a man of sterling worth and character, was lacking in personality, kept himself aloof and was inclined to exercise control from his office chair. He seldom, if ever, studied his problems on the spot."* It is of interest to recall that in 1922, when an instructor at the senior officers' school in India, he published a vehement attack on Captain Liddell-Hart's new theories on tank warfare, stigmatising them as "flapdoodle of the most misleading kind", thus acquiring as a footnote to military history an enduring but unenviable fame. In his memoirs Liddell-Hart somewhat caustically comments on this incident that the Japanese demonstrated in Malaya the effectiveness of armoured penetration which Bond dismissed as impracticable.

There is a further incident that reveals something of Bond's mind. In April 1941 Colonel G. T. Wards, military attaché in Tokyo, gave a lecture in Singapore and warned that the Japanese possessed a first-class fighting machine and deprecated the delusions on their prowess he had encountered on his visit to Singapore. Bond rose at the conclusion of his address and to his astonishment declared that this was "in no way a correct appreciation of the situation" and that "you can take it from me we have nothing to fear from them." When afterwards in private Colonel Wards tackled Bond and remonstrated, he replied to the effect that "we must not discourage the chaps and we must keep their spirits up."†

In July 1940, Bond's civilian counterpart, C. A. Vlieland, the Secretary of Defence, Malaya, produced a military appreciation that is as vivid in its prescience as Bond's vision was opaque. Vlieland saw correctly that the key to victory or defeat in the peninsula lay in the north-western plains around Alor Star and how important it was to use intelligently the local knowledge of experienced European civilians rather than absorb them into the general mass of the armed forces. The memorandum is worth quoting extensively because of its clarity on the important issues. From the last paragraph, one can surmise that one of the reasons that he produced it was out of frustration with Bond's inactivity during his

---

* General S. W. Kirby, *Singapore: The Chain of Disaster*, p. 41.
† Op. cit. p. 74.

period of stewardship from August 1939 to April 1941. Failure to take the initiative in improving Malaya's land defences in this critical period must have had a strong propellant effect towards the ultimate result.

## APPRECIATION BY THE SECRETARY OF DEFENCE, MALAYA  JULY 1940

18. I maintain that, if the enemy once succeeded in driving us out of the north-western plains, complete disaster would follow inevitably. Not only should we lose Malaya, including Singapore, but the Japanese would be well on their way to achieving their whole grand design.

19.     That is my conclusion because there is no area south of the plains of Kedah, Province Wellesley and Krian which offers anything like the same advantages to the defence. I believe it is an accepted military maxim that close country favours the attacker and, if we fail to hold the invader in the finest large open area in the whole country, how can we hope to stop him further south? Especially as the balance of forces must move progressively against us. Kedah offers us the facilities for defence in great depth with extended fields of fire and optimum use of air power, especially in the virtual defiles by which the enemy would have to debouch onto the open plain.

20. If we were forced back out of Kedah and northern Perak, I think the only area where a considerable stand could be made is in the vicinity of Kampar and I should expect a distinct battle there. But I do not think it would be a success for us. It seems to me too certain that we should be forced to withdraw by a threat to the left rear of our positions via the Telok Anson-Bidor road since by that time, the enemy would be in a position to make landings on the west coast.

21. South of the Kampar area I do not think there would be any prospect of stopping the enemy's progress.

22. It has been suggested from time to time that we should go over the frontier into Siam to meet the enemy and I believe plans have been made for such a move. It would of course be admirable if, as General Frazer suggested, we held Lower Siam. But we don't and I see little point in plans to go in at the eleventh hour. H.M.G. would never agree to our doing so until the very last moment and I don't see how we could expect to do better on inevitably unprepared ground in Siam than on our own side of the frontier, where the open country is naturally favourable to the defence and we can do anything we think desirable in the way of preparing positions, satellite landing grounds, supplementary roads, "hards", etc.

23. It seems to me that work of this kind should be put in hand without delay, but there is no sign of it as far as I am aware. What exactly should be done is of course a matter for the Service professionals, but it seems to me, as a civilian who is at least familiar with the terrain, that it would not be difficult to make northern Kedah into a modern equivalent of a "fortress" which Singapore most emphatically is not.*

This appreciation must surely have been prepared as background for the Governor's memorandum of the same month to the Colonial Office and which was a response to the March meeting of the Cabinet Overseas and Defence Committee. In it he states that without considerably enhanced air power Singapore will fall. Writing to the Colonial Office a month before, Dill, the Chief of the Imperial General Staff, showed both the growing awareness of the Japanese danger to Singapore and the government's impotence to resist it. "... Developments in Europe which have reduced the availability of an adequate British force for the Far East make the security of Singapore a matter for grave anxiety."†

---

* Liddell Hart Archive, quoted in Louis Allen, *Singapore 1941–1942*, pp. 292-293.
† PREM 3/168/3, 3/168/7B; CAB 21/2625/9C

Replying a month after the fall of France, it is not surprising that Sir Shenton's conclusions show that he shares that anxiety to an acute extent. "The present policy has been in force for years and is, broadly speaking, that Singapore must hold out until the Fleet can be sent to relieve it. The period before relief was laid down originally, I think, as only 30 days, but it has now been lengthened until it is now 90 days, and not so very long ago six months was suggested.

"Therefore, whereas the time at the disposal of the enemy was originally regarded as limited, it is now very much the reverse. We now know (and so does he) that he would have plenty of time to come through to Singapore from any part of the Malay Peninsula."

Air Chief Marshal Brooke-Popham arrived as Commander-in-Chief in November 1940, and unfortunately shared Bond's misconceptions about the Japanese, based, it seems, on the intelligence reports from the War Office in London, and also the Far Eastern Intelligence Bureau; but he came to the conclusion Bond was inadequate for the post and accelerated his replacement, in May 1941, by Lieutenant-General A. E. Percival. At the same time Air Vice-Marshal Pulford replaced Babington whose term had ended.

Percival had been, as we have said, Dobbie's principal staff officer in 1936–8. At the time of his appointment he was commanding the 44th Division in England. He had not entered the Army through the traditional channels of Sandhurst or Woolwich; like some others who attained high rank in the 1939–45 War, Field Marshal Slim being the most famous, he was a volunteer from civilian life in 1914. He distinguished himself on the Western Front, rose to command a battalion and for a time a brigade, and was awarded the DSO and Bar (in operations in North Russia in 1919) and MC. He remained in the Army after the war, passed through the Staff College with distinction, and for the major part of his time was on staff appointments, culminating in the post of Brigadier General Staff with General Dill's I Corps in France. Dill clearly had a high opinion of him, and he may be regarded as very much a "Dill" man. He was later for a short time Vice-CIGS under him at the War Office before being sent to command 44th Division. In a note to the CIGS (General Sir Alan Brooke) after the fall of Singapore the Director of Military Operations (Major-General Kennedy) wrote:

> The bulk of our army is still untried... Too many Officers have been, and are being, promoted to high command because they are proficient in staff work, because they are good trainers, because they are agreeable or because they are clever talkers...*

Unlike his III Corps commander, Lieutenant General Sir Lewis Heath, who had considerable experience of active command of troops including command of the 5th Indian Division at the capture of Keren in Eritrea, Percival was *par excellence* a staff officer with only a comparatively brief experience as divisional commander in the UK.

Percival faced a daunting task; shortages of staff and of troops, in fact of every military commodity he needed, and where the means were available fate and circumstances, the quirks of personalities, the strict control of the War Office and Treasury, seemed bent on denying them to him. War Office and Treasury control refused him an adequate staff, and the differing pay structure of the British and Indian establishment inhibited the flexibility of transfers which might have assisted him.

Perceiving the imperative need for training, he sought by every means to improve training at the expense of work on defences, and was frustrated at every turn. Labour locally was not lacking but was required for rubber and tin production. Where the local government could have helped, but failed to do so, was in prohibiting the now ever-growing programmes of replanting of rubber with new material, which, however desirable for the future of the industry, was at that time using labour required for defence works, airfield construction, etc. All his desperate efforts to find alternatives in India and Hong Kong foundered on the rocks of War Office and Treasury control of pay rates which was quite

---

* P. 198.

unrealistic. The incomprehensible fact has to be recorded that it was not until 31st January 1942 that London gave the Malayan authorities a free hand on labourers' wages. The means were there, and the rubber planters and tin miners and the members of the Public Works Department were men who, given the right lead, could have been of incomparable benefit in solving Percival's problems in constructing defence works. Pumping machinery to create a flooded area on the west flank of the Jitra line was asked for but sanction was delayed so long by London that the plant was delivered only as the Japanese attack came in, and purchase of earth-moving machinery locally which was asked for early in 1941 was withheld by the War Office who decided to supply from the United Kingdom* and not a single item had reached Malaya when the war broke out.

Amongst the critics of the Government at home, and in particular of Churchill, none was more strident, and more abused, than Aneurin Bevan. Time has permitted a more objective view. These facts give point to an outburst by him at that time in the *Tribune* that "the continuance of War Office misrule remains the outstanding scandal of Churchill administration. The French Revolution had its Carnot; the last war produced Lloyd George; the Russian Revolution Trotsky; and we have Captain Margesson... that failure is costing us precious lives and will cost us more yet."† This virulent attack followed the fall of Singapore, and soon afterwards an able civil servant, Sir James Grigg, replaced Margesson as Secretary of State for War. He was by general consent an outstanding minister in that office.

It was only with the Americans in the war, and now with Sir Alan Brooke as Chief of Staff, that there were the strong and necessary counterpoises to a judgment that was sometimes erratic, and a sharing of the massive responsibilities which Churchill willingly took on his own broad shoulders.

Percival in his own post-war memoirs is mild enough in his references

---

* S. W. Kirby, *Singapore: The Chain of Disaster*, p.97.
† M. Foot, *Aneurin Bevan*, vol. i, p. 351-352.

to his lack of backing from the War Office. He says:

> It would have been very nice no doubt to have had defences (*in Singapore*) in addition to those up-country but finance prohibited that. As has already been stated, the expenditure on the defences in Malaya was always strictly controlled from home, and such money as was made available, apart from defences on the south coast and the fortress was, of course spent, and quite rightly so on defence works on the mainland. Even for these works there was never sufficient money available.†

Even though it appears that someone ruthless and driving, who was prepared to be unpleasant, such as Montgomery, was required to overcome these difficulties, it is not easy to understand Percival's own attitude as recorded by his Chief Engineer.

Shortly before his death in 1971, Brigadier Ivan Simson, who came to Malaya in August 1941 as Chief Engineer, Malaya Command, published his own account: *Singapore: Too Little and Too Late*. He had given the facts to the team writing the official history but they could not then bring themselves to believe all his astonishing revelations and incorporate them in the official record, although the chief author, General Kirby, did so later in his own book, published after his death in 1971: *Singapore: The Chain of Disaster.*

Brigadier Simson was called to the War Office in May 1941 and received verbal instructions from the Director of Fortifications and Works, Major-General W. Cave-Browne. These he states were in the following terms:

> To install the most modern type of defences throughout Malaya, including Singapore Island, and to bring all existing defences up-to-date specifically against possible beach landings and against tank and air attack. This was stressed as my most

---

† *War in Malaya*, p. 254.

important task...

He was told there was friction between the General Staff in Singapore and the Chief Engineer's Office. Simson asked for written instructions, and was informed that the CIGS (General Dill) was about to write to the GOC Malaya. He asked for a copy but this was not forthcoming.

No such letter has ever been traced, and there is some mystery. Dill was by this time getting towards the end of his tether. Winston Churchill was too much for him and in December 1941 he was replaced by General Sir Alan Brooke, who was of tougher tegument, and, to our great good fortune, could sustain and surmount such pressures.

Arriving in Malaya Simson first toured his command. He was "profoundly shocked" with what he saw. He asked Percival about the promised written instructions but he had not received them, and Simson sensed some restraint. Eventually he sought a further interview with Percival in mid-October, and put forward detailed proposals for defence measures on the mainland of Malaya and on the north shore of Singapore. Percival gave him the entire morning for discussion, but he decided against the actions proposed. He gave no reason.

Simson then wrote to Cave-Browne, but he had left his appointment in September 1941 and his letters have not been traced.

At the end of November, Percival sent Simson to report on the Jitra defences. He found little or none. The 11th Divisional Commander, Major-General Murray Lyon, was prepared for the order to advance into Siam under the "Matador" operation Malaya Command had devised. Simson reported that there was an anti-tank ditch under construction at Jitra but no defences across the main road.

He further discovered that War Office pamphlets on defence measures against tanks lay unopened in Singapore. Percival agreed he should condense them for issue as one pamphlet, and Simson got to work immediately with his staff. It was ready by 6th December with a covering letter intended for Percival's signature. After further discussion it went out under Simson's signature "for GOC" after the Japanese attack, and too late to reach many formations in time to be useful.

Simson, however, set off to deliver it personally to all formations he could manage, and to supplement it by personal contact. He met the Australian commander, Major-General Gordon Bennett, on 19th December and found some misconception that in Bennett's own words "he had little time for obstacles for tanks..."* Simson went on to III Corps HQ at Kuala Lumpur and met General Heath at his advanced HQ at Ipoh on 22nd December. En route he personally chose sites for anti-tank defences in the Slim River area as no orders had come from III Corps. Simson had a long discussion with the over-burdened corps commander. The upshot was a verbal message to Percival to have defences prepared down the peninsula for his tired and retreating troops. Simson prepared a draft which with some amendment was agreed by Heath, but despite Simson's efforts to persuade him, he refused to sign it. We have no record of the reason, but it may be surmised that relations with Percival were then strained and confidence shaken; and if Heath felt Percival suspected him of defeatism he would not have wished to give further substance to such suspicion, however unwarranted it was.

Simson returned to Singapore and reached Flagstaff House at 23.30 hours on 26th December, as Percival was about to retire for the night. In an interview and argument lasting two and a half hours Simson put his case for action, only to be met with a refusal either for defences up-country or on the landward coast of Singapore. Percival now gave his reasons: "Defences are bad for morale for both troops and civilians." He relented enough to permit Simson to put his points to Major-General Keith Simmons, Singapore Fortress Commander. He met with the same answer and the same reason.

Strangely enough, some 48 hours after this meeting, without reference to Simson, Percival arranged for the Public Works Department to be available to Generals Heath and Gordon Bennett for defence works. This by-passing of the Chief Engineer produced little.

---

* Gordon Bennett, *Why Singapore Fell.*

The official history concludes:

> To assist it in carrying out this task (a delaying action), the
> corps (III) required every artificial device which the ingenuity
> of military and civil engineers could devise: prepared positions
> where the enemy could be held and behind which its battered
> brigades could rest and reorganize, at frequent intervals in all
> the defiles, of which there were quite a number; and inundations
> where possible. The opportunity to provide these in the months
> before the war had not been taken, and it is surprising that,
> when time was all important, little was done after the true
> situation had become apparent on the 13 December.

Simson shared imprisonment with Percival and in one of those evening
walks round the barbed wire cage he relates that Percival admitted he
had been wrong not to order defences.

Percival accepted the Matador plan for an advance into Siam with
some misgivings. The hesitations at the last minute of Brooke-Popham,
and the delay in cancelling Matador and giving orders to 11th Division
for their new role when the plan was clearly impracticable will be
recorded, and Percival shares responsibility for this fatal delay. In his
own account, *War in Malaya*, he says this of Matador:

> There is no doubt that this change from an anticipated offensive
> to a defensive had a great psychological effect on the troops.
> Although the chances of being able to put Matador into operation
> had never, up to the last moment, really been very great, yet it is
> a fact that the offensive is always more attractive than the
> defensive and, when there is a possibility of both, people tend to
> concentrate on the former rather than on the latter. Perhaps we
> at Headquarters who were in a position to appreciate the political
> factors more clearly, did not communicate our views sufficiently
> to the forward troops, or perhaps they did not percolate through

to Corps Headquarters, or perhaps the degree of secrecy which it was necessary to preserve in this matter had its effect. I cannot say for certain who, if anybody was at fault, but the fact remains that the 11th Indian Division was much more confident of being able to operate Matador than were commanders farther back. So much so that on the seventh, Murray-Lyon, the divisional commander, had as a precautionary measure moved two of the battalions of his 15th Infantry Brigade a distance of some miles to Anak Bukit station to entrain.

Since the first degree of readiness for Matador had been ordered by Malaya Command, Murray Lyon's anticipatory moves are understandable. What is not is why there was such a gulf, as Percival admitted, between the appreciation of the position at HQ in Singapore and at Corps and Divisional HQ up country. Was it not the responsibility of Percival to ensure his views were clearly understood?

Given a well-nigh impossible task, Percival was no Chanzy. The drive, the ruthlessness, the personality that might have delayed and mitigated defeat were not there, and this is merely to say that a genius was needed, and he was not that.

There is no doubt that Percival bore the brunt of mounting disaster with calm and stubborn courage. His nerve never failed. He strove day by day and far into the night to cope with a succession of crises and calamities, and through those two months he had a burden which would have broken many men.

There is something poignant in the spectacle of Percival settling down to write his memoirs of these days after his return from the sufferings and indignities of imprisonment by the Japanese. His friend and mentor General Dill was dead. Honours had been heaped on his successful contempories, and it is with sympathy one reads that on the presentation at Buckingham Palace of a minor award made before his service in Malaya he received the solace of a private audience with King George VI. It has always been the practice and prerogative of our sovereigns since the time of Queen Victoria to assuage the wounded spirits of defeated and disappointed generals.

Percival's commander of III Corps was Lt.-General Sir Lewis Heath, fresh from his success as commander of the 5th Indian Division in March 1941 in Eritrea. There appears to have been complete harmony and trust between Heath and his superior in Eritrea as corps commander, Lt. General Platt, and with his fellow divisional commander, Major-General Beresford Pierse, and his tactical skill foresaw the need at Keren to seize Fort Dologorodoc and drive through the Dongolaas Gorge which achieved the victory at Keren.

He had held active commands in India, and was in every way suitable for the command of III Corps. Unfortunately, the same harmony and confidence did not exist between him and Percival, and relations deteriorated as differences over the conduct of the campaign increased down the peninsula. There is a last pathetic message from Heath to his old friend General Messervy written on 11th February 1942, when the fall of Singapore was imminent:

> There has been a most awful mess-up altogether here and the end cannot be far off. If only I had some of our old team with me, and if the show had been run properly from the top, I don't believe this terrible disaster would ever have taken place.*

Percival was a professional soldier, regarded by Dill as an exceptional staff officer, but it is probable he did not contemplate him in the role of an army commander if hostilities broke out. There was the project of appointing General Paget in his place, but, beguiled into believing there was time, and exhausted by other preoccupations, not the least of coping with Churchill, Dill was overcome by events.

There is a certain sad irony in the fact that Percival was his assistant when as CIGS he had to deal with the evacuation from Dunkirk, where Percival had contact with the cream of the British Army.

---

* Henry Maule, *Spearhead General*, p. 170.

How different was the position when he came to Malaya. There was a lack of professionalism especially amongst the various garrisons in the Colonies, all rather isolated and neglected. To illustrate this one quotation may suffice from the recollection of an able public servant, Humphrey Trevelyan, Resident in Mysore in 1940:

> The British Army was still not taking life very seriously. I visited a British battalion on exercise. The commander said to me, "You see that fellow, Major X; he really likes this sort of thing. I would much rather be at home catching butterflies." In the spring of 1940, just before the German attack on the Western front I listened to a lecture by a staff officer from headquarters. He said everything was going splendidly. Even I thought it wildly and irresponsibly optimistic..."*

A young officer, fresh from home, went to a lecture in Singapore by an expert on the Japanese who told them they were first-class troops, did not disdain using bicycles for transport, and were first-class at field engineering. On the return to the mess of this regular British battalion the general view he heard from the officers was that this was an exaggeration. The Japanese were "lesser breeds without the law", and could be treated with contempt.†

This is not to say there were not exceptions but such an attitude was only too prevalent, and it was such a heterogeneous collection of units, not an army, that the luckless Percival had all too short a time to mould into a fighting force; a process that took Alexander and Montgomery, Giffard and Slim, a year or more to do.

General Smyth, VC, who in Burma in 1942 also suffered personally from our unpreparedness and the under-estimation of the Japanese, has attempted an apologia for his former comrade and friend.‡ He does not,

---

* Macmillan, *The India We Left*, p. 96.
† Personal information.
‡ Gen. Sir John Smyth, *Percival and the Tragedy of Singapore*.

however, in his account delve deeply into the matters on which specific criticism has been made by the official historian, General S. Woodburn Kirby, in the official history: *War Against Japan*, vol. i, and in a later book published in 1971.* A judicious verdict on this is given by Michael Howard when reviewing both Smyth and Kirby's books in the *Sunday Times* of 27th June, 1971:

> Kirby's verdict seems altogether just: "a brilliant staff officer, quite untried as a commander, who had neither the drive nor the ruthlessness which was needed." He surrendered with dignity and stoically shared the hardships of his men as prisoners of war. On his return he was neither officially praised nor blamed, but allowed to live out the rest of his life in dignified retirement.
>
> That was not good enough for his friend Sir John Smyth, who considers that he should have received a hero's welcome and who is furious that General Kirby or anyone else should dare to criticise him at all. "One of the avowed objects" of the Official Histories, states Sir John, was "to produce some scapegoats on whom the blame for disaster could be pinned." One would like to know where, in those anodyne volumes, such an avowal is made. In fact Kirby makes very few criticisms of Percival in his official volume, and not many more in his posthumous work. Sir John's attempt to sway the verdict of history does him credit as a friend of the family, but as a work of rehabilitation it is neither particularly necessary nor particularly successful.
>
> Nobody has ever doubted that Percival was a competent professional soldier and an honourable man. But not even Sir John Smyth can show that he had the qualities of dynamic leadership which alone might have mitigated the effects of a catastrophe far beyond his powers to control.

---

* Kirby, *Singapore: The Chain of Disaster.*

Surely, however, the epitaph of Percival may well be that tested as few commanders were he behaved with stoicism, courage and dignity both during the campaign and during the bitter years of internment and after, and in this sad episode he will be remembered honourably for that.

# CHAPTER III

## Government And Civilians

An able young war correspondent, Ian Morrison, later killed in the Korean War, reached Australia and published a book in May 1942: *Malayan Postscript*, and in one of his concluding passages wrote:

> ...I felt strongly at the time, and I feel it strongly now, that those strata of the population of Great Britain who have been administering our colonial empire for the past twenty years had been found gravely wanting in the very qualities which had gained us an empire. And not only those who had been administrating our colonial empire, but those who had been residing in it and making profits out of it, and those who had been responsible for the formulating of its policies and the ensuring of its defence...

This broad indictment no doubt reflected the opinion of many at this time, and now that the imperial era has passed it is worth while examining it more closely.

There were, as Morrison points out, the government officials and, on the other hand, the large white population of traders, planters, tin miners, etc. There is the question of the relations between the official and unofficial members of the community, of what were the actions and attitude of Government before the war commenced, and what they did after it had broken out.

As regards the Government, we should want to know what military advice they received before the war started, and how they reacted to it. On this the evidence produced to date is somewhat obscure. With the weakness of our forces it is now obvious we would have had to give ground in northern Malaya whilst reinforcements arrived. Kirby states that the civil servants "failed to grasp" this fact.* Did the military so advise the civil authorities or did they shrink from this stark possibility? Only this can explain the failure of many contingency plans for evacuation of civilians, stores, etc., and the many problems associated with such withdrawal. It is said that after the war in 1948 Wavell made the significant admission to Shenton Thomas that the "original sin" for the lack of proper preparation must be placed on the military who, he was convinced, never really expected a Japanese invasion or prepared properly for it.†

Subsequent events certainly give countenance to this opinion. When Kota Bahru was attacked in the early hours of 8th December, at 04.30 hours the British Adviser (Major Kidd MC) warned all European women and children to leave by car for Kuala Krai. When in due course they arrived by train at Kuala Lipis in Pahang, they were firmly under the impression that their departure was only a matter of a few days whilst the Japanese were being dealt with, and that they would be able to return. It was similar in Kedah.

The civil government had, of course, formulated plans for denial and evacuation in case of necessity, but the emphasis was naturally on beating not retreating from the Japanese. They were reliant on the military for advice, and it will be seen that this advice indicated that there would not be an attack in the monsoon period but a breathing space would be likely until the spring of 1942. Men seconded from Japan, and others who had come from China and Japan, may have expressed misgivings about the underestimation of the Japanese but they were junior, uninfluential and unheard.

When at 01.15 hours on 8th December 1941 the Governor, Sir

---

* Op. cit.

† Noel Barber, *Sinister Twilight*, p.35.

Shenton Thomas, was awoken by a telephone call from General Percival announcing the Japanese landing at Kota Bahru his immediate response is reported to have been, "Well, I suppose you'll shove the little men off!"†

Someone had underestimated the "little men" and it is not surprising that the civil authorities were caught unprepared for the suddenness of the catastrophe at Jitra and the pace of the retreat which caused confusion, breakdown of communications, and failure to carry out denial schemes planned for circumstances not as cataclysmic as they turned out.

Speaking in the Singapore Legislative Council on Tuesday 16th December, whilst the 11th Indian Division was sorting itself out behind the temporary sanctuary of the Muda River, and contact was being made with the Japanese on the Grik Road to Kuala Kangsar, the Governor said:

> How the battle will go we cannot yet say. We hope that our men will be able to maintain themselves in the present positions but it must be obvious to everybody that the fate of Penang must depend largely on what happens in Kedah.
>
> I tell you this with the consent of the Commander-in-Chief and the G.O.C., Malaya, because we are sure the people of Malaya would wish to know the position as it is today.

Whilst he was speaking Penang was being hurriedly evacuated in much confusion, and on the very next day Percival gave Heath the permission he had so urgently sought to retire the remnants of the 11th Indian Division behind the Perak River.

As regards the civilians, it has been said that the rubber planters and tin miners were concerned only with the maximum production of rubber and tin in accordance with governmental direction; that the Europeans in general were convinced nothing could disturb their peace; that complacency dwelt in high and low places. The truth was more complex

---

† Barber, op. cit., p.28.

and less categorical.

When war was declared in Europe in September 1939, Europeans in Malaya, young and old, were keyed up for action. Casting their minds back, it was thought it would be the duty of the majority of young men of military age who could be spared to return to Britain, as in 1914, and join the Forces; and even after this lapse of time there still remained a residue of feeling amongst those who fought in the 1914–18 war against those of their contempories who had not. But the edict came of "business as usual": firms sent back their men on leave in the UK and commerce and government even recruited young men of military age and sent them out. The order was for maximum production of rubber and tin. Both commodities were vital to the home economy and Malaya was their prime source. There was a relaxation of tension, almost a feeling of anti-climax, as at home in the "phoney" war period until the fall of France in June 1940. With Great Britain now beleaguered, keen young officers in the garrison in Malaya sought to go home to the "real" war. All the planes and ships that could be made available were dispatched to Europe. The Eastern submarine fleet, whose crews had played football and cricket on the happy occasions of their visits to Singapore, Penang and Port Swettenham, was sent to the Mediterranean to fight the Italians – all alas! to be lost in those waters. It could be said that psychologically, and in some specific respects materially, Malaya was better prepared in 1939 than in 1941.

It is true that at the time of France's fall there was a flurry of activity. The Volunteers were embodied for training – an exercise more expensive than useful – but something had to be done. A jungle exercise of ten days in Jelubu under the Chief Game Warden, Mr Shebbeare, was promising but efforts to follow it up were unsuccessful. All sorts of ideas, such as this experiment in jungle training, pullulated, but with little practical result. In the relations between the military and civil authorities over the role and employment of the local Volunteers there can be seen examples of confusion, lack of adequate contact and co-operation, and a sad failure to put to the best use such assets as the country possessed, for which the Services must bear the chief responsibility.

The Volunteers comprised two commands, one in the Malay States and the other in the Straits Settlements. Originally each had two components: on the Malayan mainland, the Malay States Volunteer Rifles, the European element, and the Malay Volunteer Rifles, the local element, officered by Europeans, Malays, Chinese and Eurasians. The Europeans were generally encouraged to join the Volunteers, and for planters and miners there was the minor inducement of travelling expenses into the town on parade days, and for married men the payment of maternity expenses for their wives. In some cases there may have been a little coercion to join; there were the keen members, the reluctant bachelors and the expectant fathers. Each of the two forces had a regular army framework of Colonel-Commandant, Brigade Major, Staff Officer, and Adjutant and Permanent Staff Instructors. On one occasion in the placid days before the war a Guards Sergeant Major was giving a pep talk to the volunteers assembled on parade. He had begun his exordium, "In Volunteering there is some as is keen, and there are others..." when there sloped on parade in whites, with their *syces* (drivers) helping them on with their web equipment, two of the well-known habitués of the long bar of the Club. As the Sergeant Major caught sight of them he concluded his remarks, "... Here the buggers come."

In the late thirties a dedicated officer came out as Commandant of the Malay States Volunteers: Lt-Col. H. B. W. Savile, MC, of the Middlesex Regiment. He deemed the arrangement of two separate units unsound and wasteful. He formed the Federated Malay States Volunteer Force which amalgamated the two, and created battalions for the four States – Selangor, Negri Sembilan, Perak, and Pahang. In Johore there were the Johore Volunteer Engineers, mainly comprised of planters. The formation of battalions on the regular army model involved the recruitment of more of the local races to fill the ranks and complete the required complement of a battalion. In theory this was only sound if one could conceive the Volunteers ever being employed in a mobile or front-line role. In the event, as the Malay States were successively evacuated the local personnel had to be disbanded to return and look after their homes. The efforts of a fine officer, the last few years of whose life were spent on this reorganization, for he suffered severely from wounds received in the First World War, were tragically misplaced. It is easy to see now after the event and with the experience of hindsight that the Europeans would have been in the main better seconded for specialist and liaison duties utilizing their technical skills, and their knowledge of the people and their language, the countryside and its byways. All units of the Army would have found such men invaluable, as indeed they did when such action was taken very late in the day.

The original edict from London to the Governor that the production of rubber and tin to the maximum was first priority was occasioned by the desire of General Bond on the outbreak of the European war to institute compulsory military service for the Europeans, and mobilize the Volunteers for a period of training. It did not need a military expert to realise that such a force was of no military value in a mobile and front-line role, that it would have been sheer massacre to pit such men against the Japanese Imperial Army, but as at that time Bond had little else he had, *faute de mieux*, to allot them a role for which they were unfitted. As, however, the Japanese had not at that time reached the essential jumping-off positions in Indo-China for an invasion of Malaya, such illusions could be cherished without harm, but only for the time being, and ultimately such troops were designated for lines of communication.

In 1940 the civil authorities in Malaya were doubtless sceptical of the use of the Volunteers for such a front-line role, and it is not surprising that London informed the Governor that "the ultimate criterion for exemption from military service should be not what the General Officer Commanding considers practicable but what you consider essential to maintain the necessary production and efficient labour management."

It does not appear that the proper use of the Volunteers was examined, or, if so, that any action was taken to explore the best employment of local European manpower. Some indeed visualized their use for specialist duties and as liaison officers, and the necessary training for such duties would hardly have needed mobilization. Weapons training, knowledge of the languages, experience of the Malayan terrain; all such skills could have been acquired in part-time training whilst carrying on their normal civilian occupations. The various embodiments of two months or so in 1940–1941 were largely a waste of time, money and effort – a gesture – except for such units as the artillery and armoured car units. The Local Defence Volunteers, formed late in 1940, comprising the older and more senior men, the key men of commerce, etc., were available, as was the Home Guard in England, to assist the police; and if necessary the military.

There is also the question of labour. The military were apparently ignorant of the large amount of labour employed at the time on rubber planting, (i.e. not on production) although government Labour Officers were finding that it was competing with military needs; for example, the naval air station at Banting on the Selangor Coast was delayed by the demands of the estates surrounding it for labour for replanting work. It was a matter of discussion in some circles, and a letter on the anomaly appeared in the local *Malay Mail*, but there was no co-ordination, no meeting of minds, no close examination of the problem by military or civil, or, if there had been, it would have been perceived how helpful the planters and tin miners could have been in assisting the Army in essential defence works. As it was Percival fought in vain with the War Office for the means to supply the deficiency from India or Hong Kong.

A further example may be adduced to illustrate what could have been done. On the retreat to the Muar River in Johore, a planter in the area, Mr A. W. Porter, a character of exceptional drive and competence, was asked before evacuating his estates to relay a telephone line along the government road. By employing and paying the labour from the adjacent estates he completed the work in record time, and then departed to shoulder a rifle as a sapper in the Johore Volunteer Engineers, rather a misnomer as they were employed as infantrymen. All were planters living in Johore who knew the people, the language, the country, and would have been, if wisely deployed, of immeasurable value.

There was no one to give a lead, to focus these various skills and abilities, to canalize the ideas and urgings into fruitful enterprises, and thus to harness to the best advantage the civilian capabilities and impulses which existed under the superficial facade of the social life of Malaya in peacetime.

Such public opinion as existed in so far as it had an impact on defence preparations was from the European civilian. It found expression in the Press, then mainly European, through certain prominent and influential "unofficials" on the legislative councils, and in organisations such as the Ex-Servicemen's Association, the Chamber of Mines, and the United Planters' Association.

Towards the end of 1940 these latter bodies combined to express their anxieties and to press for the appointment of an officer of the fighting services to be in control of security and civil defence measures. The Acting Governor (Mr S. W. Jones) in passing on their views to London expressed resentment at these criticisms, but the Secretary of the Colonies (Lord Lloyd) in London countered with neither resentment nor disapproval, stating that the civil community should be "encouraged to make practical suggestions for improving defence measures."*

All this coincided with the appointment of Sir Robert Brooke-Popham as Commander-in-Chief, and these representations may well have had some influence on the appointment. These disputes are significant, however, as evidence of the dichotomy between official and unofficial amongst whom there had always been in the colonial empire an element of antipathy.

Mr Victor Purcell, one of the more volatile and striking characters recruited to the Malayan Civil Service after being badly wounded on the Western Front in World War I, was Protector of Chinese, Selangor and Pahang, and later Director-General of Information and Publicity. He records that "it was the problem of Government to keep the balance between the communities and to prevent Chinese underground activities against the Japanese in Malaya giving Japan an excuse for intervention

---

* Kirby, *War Against Japan*, vol. i, p. 159.

in local affairs", and with regard to the civilians he has to say that "The rubber and tin tycoons blamed communism entirely for the unrest in Malayan industry but the truth was that the Communist agitation was greatly assisted by their policy. The outbreak of war in 1939 was followed by a boom and a great increase in the cost of living but no move was made by the employers to increase wages."*

It was indeed unfortunate that serious strikes and disorders took place in Selangor in May 1941 which were quelled by Indian troops who dealt roughly with their compatriots in restoring order. There is no doubt that the rubber industry's tardiness in making adequate wage adjustments was viewed critically by many government officials, and an atmosphere of distrust and want of confidence was engendered between officials and unofficials by those events. Two senior officials were transferred from Selangor, the Resident and the head of the Labour Department, by the High Commissioner (somewhat deferential to business opinion), soon after the affair was over.

Nevertheless Mr Purcell's allusion to rubber and tin "tycoons" was really incorrect as regards the Europeans. The European heads of the commercial institutions had, for the most part, their headquarters in London, and were not the old pioneering *tuans besar*. They were the servants and subordinates of their masters, referring to them in London and obedient to their behests. They might give their opinions, and some might be occasionally bold and independent, but they tended to act, subconsciously perhaps, as they felt their superiors would wish.

By 1941 rubber replanting was in full swing, and it seems not to have been appreciated that it was using up labour badly needed by the defence services, and in fact making an immediate, though perhaps not significant reduction in the output of rubber, although commercially desirable. Income tax was introduced, and though companies made generous donations to the War Funds, the tax aroused intense opposition from the unofficials, partly on the reasoning that it would fall mainly on the European, but to the official the campaign seemed perverse and

---

* Victor Purcell, *Memoirs of a Malayan Official.*

unpatriotic, and certainly in retrospect it is difficult to justify.

Whilst there was this scope for misunderstanding and even mistrust between official and unofficial, there was amongst many an unease and conflict as to the measures being taken to defend Malaya from the then vague menace of Japan, as the representations to which we have referred *to* are evidence.

One of these leaders of unofficial opinion, for example, was Lt-Col. G. D. A. Fletcher, OBE, MC, a former member of the Straits Settlements Legislative Council, a Volunteer Colonel, and a director of one of the large rubber groups. In the Great War he had risen from private to acting-brigadier on the Western Front, and had for a time commanded his battalion of the Royal Scots. When he retired from Malaya after the Japanese war in 1948, the Kuala Lumpur *Malay Mail* described him as a "fighter who never held his punches when it has been in the interest of the public or his honour." He was an old-fashioned, stubborn and uncompromising patriot. He had been one of the prime movers in the criticism of October 1940 and had then formed the Local Defence Volunteer Battalion in Selangor. He thought "V" for Victory should be substituted by "F" for Fight. He was not alone in feeling disquiet at what was being done or failing to be done. Many of the facts that have been revealed since were of course not then known, but doubts there were, much as in the United Kingdom until the fall of Norway the doubts about the Chamberlain administration remained ineffective until disaster came. Lt-Col. James MC, DCM, another member of the commercial community, had obtained release from his firm to work full time as commander of the Selangor Volunteer Battalion. He was of like mind to Colonel Fletcher, and in after years as we walked in the evening within the perimeter of Tamuang Camp in Siam he told the writer how he had been at an exercise at Gurun when it was agreed to prepare defences in this naturally defensive position in Kedah and that nothing had been done about it.

When a letter appeared in the local *Malay Mail* in Kuala Lumpur, from a person who had returned recently from London, which drew attention to the contrast with the concentration at home on total war, some younger members of the editorial staff wished to write leaders expanding on the theme of the lack of preparation, but the editor forbade it, saying he was satisfied with what was being done. It is tragic to recall that this editor and his wife, much-respected and popular old residents of Malaya, approaching retirement, were both lost in the evacuation from Malaya just before the fall of Singapore.

To discover what one thought at the time is by now not easy, for "old men forget", but amongst my papers I found an obituary written on 17th November 1941, in the local paper, on an old friend and colleague who had just been killed in an air crash. I see that I described how "he took a leading part in the formation of the local unit of the Volunteer Air Force. Flying took up all his spare time and absorbed all his interest when his daily work was over. He was happy to find much useful and indeed valuable work to do, and it was his hope that eventually he might have an opportunity of participating in active operations against our enemies." So slender were the resources of the Royal Air Force that he, as a Volunteer, used to fly General Barstow, Commander of the 9th Division, over to his forces on the east coast. He was engaged in teaching an army officer to fly when he crashed.

These instances are adduced not with the intention of claiming that such efforts and attitudes were predominant. There was complacency; or, rather, ignorance; but the complacency was not as all-pervasive as is often maintained; the ignorance was.

It has been asserted in some quarters that planters were obstructive when it came to preparing defence works, and resisted the cutting out of their precious rubber trees for this purpose. There may have been cases of this, but, apart from the fact that there were legal powers of acquisition for military purposes, it is doubtful if there is any recorded instance of any of the large European Agency firms resisting such work. A leading planting adviser and expert was Mr R. O. Jenkins, MC, and he was asked to report confidentially on his visit to the Agency's Tanjong Pau estate on the effect on the estate's working of the defence works being undertaken at Jitra. He was a warrior of many hard-fought battles on the Western Front in 1914–1918 and knew what he was talking about when it came to defences, but to his surprise he found them so paltry that he remarked, "If these are the main defences of Malaya, thank God we have got a Navy!" It cannot be questioned that, given a lead, the planter, tin-miners and others were only too anxious to perform useful service, and that many felt that what was being done was merely playing with the problem.

The Governor of Singapore and High Commissioner of the Malay States, and titular Commander-in-Chief, was Sir Shenton Thomas, who after a career in Africa including governorships of Gold Coast and Nyasaland, came to Malaya in 1934. The busy seaport of Singapore and the complex federation of Malay States must have seemed to him a far cry from the quiet waters of Lake Nyasa, the large and lonely stretches of African bush, and the repose of Zomba, his capital when Governor of Nyasaland. He was affable and sociable and, after the austere Sir Cecil Clementi, was popular with the civilians, but he was not of any great intellectual calibre or force of character. He was due for retirement in 1940 when he was 61, and after eight months of leave, which to some seemed odd in time of war, he resumed his governorship in December 1940. About this time, Admiral Sir Percy Noble, who held the Far East naval command, arrived in London at the conclusion of his period of command in Singapore. He was aware of the dissatisfaction on the part of unofficial members of the Legislative Council at the way in which defence preparations were being conducted, and himself considered Shenton Thomas was an inadequate leader. He therefore approached Lord Lloyd, the Secretary of the Colonies, and whilst he recommended that Shenton Thomas should remain as Governor he pressed for the appointment of a Supreme Commander. It is one of the long chain of misadventures that Lord Lloyd fell ill the very next day, and died in February 1941, and in the hiatus, Admiral Noble proceeded to his new and onerous duties in the U-Boat war, and as far as Malaya was concerned nothing was done.

Percival discovered in Shenton Thomas a man easily swayed by the last person with whom he had been in contact, and at his meetings with him always ensured that a stenographic record of his discussions, signed by the Governor, was obtained.* Bowden, the Australian High Commissioner, dealing with him as a member of the War Council after the outbreak of war found him "more ready at producing reasons for not doing things than for doing them".†

Mr S. W. Jones, the Colonial Secretary, was an abler and more dominating character, and doubtless had great influence thereby with Shenton Thomas. Jones was one of the outstanding members of the service, of pre-First World War vintage. He had been a memorable Resident of the principal Malay State of Selangor, and impressed his personality on his service and on civilians. The tragedy was that he too was ready for retirement; tired, over-burdened, but above all, never really convinced of or reconciled to the possibility that the Japanese attack would come. If the Governor and he had had a clear lead from the military, things might have been different. There was an element of arrogance in him and, like many civil servants, his opinion of the military hierarchy and their competence and intelligence – rightly or wrongly – was not high. In the end he was the one to be dismissed, and he disappears like a stone cast in the waters. He never sought to justify or explain his actions.‡

When at Duff Cooper's insistence, Brigadier Simson was put in

---

* Kirby, *Singapore: The Chain of Disaster*, p. 194.

† *Australian Official History*, p. 204.

‡ A significant incident is related by Mr P. O. Wickens, then private secretary to the Colonial Secretary, for whom he had a high regard and respect. Receiving his call-up notice a week before the Japanese attack he informed Jones he had now to report to his volunteer battalion in Selangor. In a brief heart-to-heart talk Jones enquired in a manner as if it were incredible whether his private secretary thought the Japanese would attack. He did and said so but came away with the indelible impression that Jones never contemplated it could ever happen.                                    (Information to author).

charge of civil defence with, as his deputy, Mr Bisseker, an unofficial member of the Penang Legislative Council who had been very critical of Government, Jones is reported by Simson to have rudely rebuffed – "in very rude terms" – their initial request for help with the necessary office and staff.

On the question of evacuation, suddenly thrust upon them, the Governor and Duff Cooper were soon at odds. Shenton Thomas, mindful of his duty to all races impartially, wished to rescind General Heath's order for the evacuation of European women and children from Perak, which followed the muddled and disgraceful evacuation of Penang. Duff Cooper pointed out that for the first time in British history we would be leaving British women and children at the mercy of an enemy, and a particularly cruel Asian enemy at that; nor did he think that orders by the military issued so as not to hamper their operations should be countermanded. The War Council concurred in these obviously sound conclusions. It seems that Shenton Thomas could never resolve the perplexities of his duties to all races with the realities of the urgent need for drastic action to reduce the number of *bouches inutiles* from the country, and particularly from Singapore, which even if defence had been more effective would have probably rendered necessary an early capitulation on humanitarian grounds and exhaustion of water and food supplies.

There is in the archives of the Public Records Office now open for inspection a letter dated 26th January 1942, from the Indian Secretary of State, Mr Leopold Amery, to his old Tory friend and colleague, Lord Moyne, then Secretary for the Colonies, which reads:

> My dear Walter,
>     Shenton Thomas has not in the least grasped what the Cabinet had in view over a month ago, i.e. evacuation in bulk of useless mouths to nearest places. To discuss whether Australia or Ceylon take one Chinaman or a 1,000 is fiddling with the question. Surely, the only thing is by arrangement with the

---

* Ivan Simson, *Singapore: Too Little, Too Late*, p. 83.

Dutch to set up refugee camps at nearest places in Sumatra.

Brutal methods might have achieved this purpose, but in the event the result was a mad rush at the end with all the loss and recrimination involved. Many who ought to have been evacuated were not – many, to their honour, stayed who need not have done so.

That considerable energy and initiative were exhibited in regard to the removal of valuable equipment has received only recent testimony in an account* by Mr Chris Noble, post-war Surveyor-General in Malaysia, who was in 1941 Assistant Surveyor-General and in charge of map production for the Army. Mr Noble was on leave in Tasmania when the war broke out but immediately flew back to his post in Kuala Lumpur and until its evacuation was busy, night and day, on producing maps for the Army as they retreated down Malaya, and it was on civil, not military, initiative that copies of plans from the zinc plates were sent off to India in case of emergency.

When Kuala Lumpur had to be evacuated with some speed the Survey Department which had suffered casualties in the bombing set about exporting maps, destroying records likely to be of use to the enemy as transport was difficult to obtain from the Army. Machinery and zinc plates were loaded on rail but unfortunately were shunted off on the Tampin–Malacca line and lost to the enemy.

Noble and his colleagues set to work with borrowed machinery in Singapore to provide maps for the Army, and just before its fall he and some others were instructed to evacuate the precious records and equipment he had brought from Kuala Lumpur to Java. The detailed description by Mr Noble of how this was achieved, first to Java, and then to Australia, in the unimaginable chaos and confusion, is an epic one. A total of 8 tons of mapping material reached Australia intact, and as Mr Noble says, owing to the fact that reproductions from the copies sent to India would be imperfect, this material was invaluable for future military operations in reconquering Malaya. It is ironic to recall that

---

* *Journal of British Association of Malaysia*, March 1972.

despite a full report by Mr Noble to the Colonial Office, and much prodding, it was not until October 1944 that he was released from duty in the Australian Air Force and sent to London to help with plans for the recapture of Malaya. He found that none of his material could now be of use at this late stage, and so Operation "Zipper" to reoccupy Malaya was undertaken with the imperfect plans which had been prudently sent to India. Should the reoccupation have been contested, however, the lack of adequate maps would have been a severe handicap.

It is the more ironic in considering the criticisms of the civil Government in Malaya to find that Ian Morrison, whose indictment is noted at the beginning of this chapter, reports* that he visited the Survey Department in Kuala Lumpur after its evacuation:

> The office of the Governmental Survey Department was boarded up and barricaded. We wondered how much they had taken with them when they moved south... I threw a box through the large plate glass window, smashed the glass, and climbed in. (All of us were in a reckless, truculent mood). Not a thing had been removed. Motoring maps of Malaya, geological maps, forestry maps, maps of states, of districts, of villages, of islands off the coast, of rubber estates, maps of so large a scale that every tree was marked (sic), lay there, tier upon tier, not in their hundreds but in their thousands.

Reconcile this, if you can, with Mr Noble's detailed and factual account, and one sees immediately the difficulty of testimony uncorroborated, the gap between appearance and reality, and perhaps the effect of emotions on memory.

The atmosphere before the outbreak of the war, so often described by the ephemeral visitor as complacent, was then one of confusion and doubt, and complacency only in so far as the civil Government had received the military advice that an invasion in the December monsoon

---

* Ian Morrison, *Malayan Postscript*, p. 116.

was unlikely. For Kirby to state that the civil Government "failed to grasp that we would have to give ground in Northern Malaya until reinforcements arrived" overlooks the fact that the Governor was dependent on military advice, and there is evidence enough* that he was advised that no attack was likely in the monsoon period; moreover, in so far as he was taken into military confidence, which appears to have been little, the military underestimation of Japanese capabilities would not arouse in civilian minds any inkling or apprehensions of the military debâcle that was to follow.†

The civilians were engaged on their normal avocations and in the evenings and on weekends performed their duties and trained for the various Volunteer, Local and Passive Defence Forces. The dual duties were quite burdensome, and for some the outbreak came almost as a relief – for a short while.

The army garrison in Singapore lived in a peacetime atmosphere as young officers coming out from home discovered to their surprise. Rigorous jungle training by the Argylls, the Australians and the Gurkhas seems to have been an exception, and Lt.-Col. Stewart of the Argylls was described by one of Percival's staff officers in front of him as a "crank" without contradiction from Percival.** When Lt.-Col. Selby put his men of 9th Gurkha Rifles through hard training his Brigadier thought he was overdoing it, and when he undertook an outflanking movement through paths in the rubber in an exercise it was ruled to be "unreal".‡ Later the Japanese used just such manoeuvres.

"If the trumpet give an uncertain sound" – if the Malayan Command did not warn of the risks and dangers, only a few lone voices, it is understandable that the civil authorities did not repair the deficiency.

---

* H. P. Bryson, MCS, *"Review of Singapore: the Chain of Disaster"*, *Journal of British Association of Malaysia*, March 1972.
† Ibid.
** Simson, op. cit., p. 42.
‡ *The 9th Ghurka Rifles 1937-1947*, Lt.-Col. G. R. Stevens, p. 192.

To those who find a mystery in the complacency and unrealism of the time they key may be found in the massive counterpoise expected in the might of America which it was assumed would be the ultimate deterrent. Referring to the last pre-war forecast of the Joint Intelligence Committee in the UK in November 1941, the official history (*Grand Strategy*, vol. III part I) makes the point:

> Even at that date few people were really prepared to believe that Japan would risk an open conflict with the United States, or, to speak more exactly, that she would dare to commit her main forces to an operation in the south, while the US Pacific Fleet was still in being and able to act offensively against her. This supposition was, indeed, the basis of British policy in the Far East during this period: and it explains much that must otherwise appear complacent and over-confident in the attitude of the Cabinet and Chiefs of Staff. They knew that the forces they were sending to the Far East were inadequate; but they were unwilling to increase them to the detriment of other fronts, because they believed that our main defence (and the only deterrent that Japan would recognise) was to be found elsewhere – in American naval power.

Within the capability of the forces available, however, if properly and wisely deployed, was the possibility of delay in time for reinforcement. The military and the civil lacked one dominant directing head – vigorous and resourceful. An analogy could be drawn with the Malayan Emergency post-war, when General Sir Gerald Templer was given by Mr Oliver Lyttleton undivided control and undisputed authority.

Before Templer's appointment, much good groundwork had been done by General Briggs and Governor Sir Henry Gurney, in many respects, but it was the authority, dynamism, drive, personality and political percipience of Templer that rallied Malaya, and someone like that was needed in 1941.

Much has been written of the atmosphere of Singapore, a garrison town, and it may have seemed to some that the Army was living, to quote Tolstoy's description, in a state of "obligatory and unimpeachable idleness", but the social life of the East is peculiarly open to the public gaze in a city teeming with transient visitors – and newspaper correspondents. A journey around Malaya, to its town and villages and frontier with Siam, where Malayan volunteers such as Noon, the anthropologist, were engaged in patrols, may well have afforded a different impression.

There have been recorded, and will be further cited, instances of initiative, resourceful and courageous action, both military and civil, but it was dust in the balance of the grand scale of events, which ensured that they should be of no avail in the sudden onrush of a triumphant Japanese Army, Navy and Air Force; well planned, perfectly co-ordinated, ruthless and direct. Once committed to a desperate course of action no doubts or confusions impeded the blow.

The records of the Colonial and War Office may reveal some new aspects or incident, but this much can surely be said: that nothing the civil government or civilians could have done in the circumstances would have affected significantly the military defeat that ensued.

Winston Churchill, of course, never hesitated to test and even torment the Chiefs of Staff who gave him military advice, but in the pattern and diffusion of authority which existed in Malaya it would have needed a strong and exceptional personality at the head of the civilian government to question the advice he received from the military authorities.

It was a perverse quirk of fate that whilst in Singapore the civil government, according to the rules, accepted without question the military advice they were tendered, in London Winston Churchill's exercise of his own judgment in refusing the advice of the Army and Navy Chiefs of Staff on the military and naval reinforcement of the Far East had such baleful consequences.

# CHAPTER IV

## Brooke-Popham, Commander-in-Chief,

## Far East

Air Chief Marshal Sir Robert Brooke-Popham was 62 when, in November 1940, he was brought out of retirement and appointed to the Far East, a taxing task for any man and especially for one of his age in the tropical climate and perplexing picture of Singapore. He had a distinguished career in the Air Force until his retirement in 1937, and became subsequently Governor of Kenya.

His directive did not give him overall control; he was "Commander-in-Chief, Far East", in name, but he was a co-ordinator, for each of the Service Chiefs dealt directly with their ministries in London and with the civil authorities locally. It had no resemblance to the "Supremo" that Lord Mountbatten became eventually in the Far East. Kirby gives his opinion that "in retrospect, not only was the selection of Brooke-Popham unwise in itself, but the directive he was given was faulty."

He sent home his first appreciation on 7th December 1940. It is curious to note that he recommended therein reinforcing Hong Kong, which came within his sphere, by two further battalions, making six in all. Of the subsequent speedy loss of Hong Kong – in eighteen days, one-fifth of the time expected – Liddell-Hart has this to say:

> The early loss of this British outpost in the Far East was the clearest of all examples how strategy, and common sense, can

be sacrificed for the sake of fanciful prestige. Even the Japanese never committed such folly "for face" as did the British in this case. It was palpably the weak point in Britain's position, and inherently far more difficult to hold than Singapore.*

Winston Churchill's reaction to Brooke-Popham's recommendation was forthright; in a minute to General Ismay on 7.1.41 he wrote:

> This is all wrong. If Japan goes to war with us there is not the slightest chance of holding Hong Kong or relieving it. It is most unwise to increase the loss we shall suffer there. Instead of increasing the garrison it ought to be reduced to a symbolical scale... we must avoid frittering away our resources on untenable positions... I wish we had few troops there, but to move any would be noticeable and dangerous.

The Chiefs of Staff had already accepted in August 1940 that Hong Kong was indefensible and recommended withdrawal, but nothing was done. Their faith in Brooke-Popham's judgment seems not to have been shaken sufficiently for action, but they rejected his reasoning. Later, as Winston Churchill records, he allowed himself to be persuaded to add two Canadian battalions to the doomed garrison. One cannot but reflect on the frittering away of our resources on untenable positions and the valuable reinforcement in Malaya that 6 battalions and supporting arms would have provided.

In February 1941 Brooke-Popham visited Australia for discussions with the Australian Cabinet in preparation for an Anglo-Australian-Dutch conference, and the views he expressed here were equally surprising, especially to the Australians who, nearer the danger, had always a more realistic appreciation of the Japanese threat. Kirby says of these statements:

---

* Liddell Hart, *History of World War II*, p. 219

They were told that he expected Hong Kong would be able to hold out for some four months against a Japanese attack, although the Leased Territories on the mainland would have had to be abandoned shortly after the outbreak of hostilities; and that, in Malaya, Singapore Island would be held even if the Japanese succeeded in occupying Johore. He went on to express the view that the Japanese aircraft were not very efficient, and that the air force in Malaya would be able to inflict sufficient damage on them to prevent the RAF squadrons from being put out of action. He based the last statement on the belief that the American Brewster Buffalo fighters, with which the new fighter squadrons for Malaya were to be equipped, would prove to be more efficient than any Japanese fighter; a belief which later proved wrong...

The Australians clearly were not prepared to accept Brooke-Popham's palpably over-optimistic statements. They knew that the Chiefs of Staff considered Hong Kong more of a liability than an asset and could see that Singapore Island, with no prepared defences on the landward side, could not hold out for long once Johore was in enemy hands. The only effect of Sir Robert's statements was to undermine Australia's confidence in the ability of the British forces to hold the Far East.*

Brooke-Popham's faulty information on the Japanese aircraft could have been corrected, though late in the day, for on 26th July 1941 and on 29th September 1941, reports were received at Headquarters Air Command, Far East, emanating from the Air Attaché in Chungking, which accurately indicated the performance of the Japanese Zero fighter, but in the absence of an intelligence staff the information was merely filed and thus no action was taken on this vital information.

Prior to this at a meeting of the Chiefs of Staff on 25th April 1941, the Vice-Chief of the Naval Staff advocated the dispatch of Hurricane

---

* Kirby, *Singapore: The Chain of Disaster*, p. 73.

fighters to Malaya, only to be informed by the Vice-Chief of the Air Staff that the Buffalo fighters would be more than a match for the Japanese aircraft which were not of the latest type.

As one reads these melancholy facts, however, realisation comes how much the cards were already stacked against any successful defence by the attitude and actions of Whitehall, the starving of adequate and competent staff to Malaya.

Turning now to his immediate problems, Brooke-Popham endorsed the Matador plan which he had inherited, for a forestalling advance into Siam, and a subsidiary advance on the Patani Road to the "Ledge" position. The difficulties were immense: timely implementation dependent on Japanese moves; avoidance of premature action which might leave us as apparent aggressors without American involvement; paucity of our forces; so much so that subsequent military opinion is that it should never have been accepted.*

It has to be noted that by now the Chiefs of Staff had reached the stage of realising the need to replace Brooke-Popham with a younger man with up-to-date military experience, and since August 1941 the matter had been under consideration, but with the fatally slow pace by which Far Eastern affairs were bedevilled it was only by 19th November that they had received Winston Churchill's approval of the selection of Lt.-General Sir Henry Pownall, a man of vigour and experience having been Chief of Staff to General Lord Gort in France in 1940, (instead of General Paget who became Commander-in-Chief Home Forces in succession to Brooke who had replaced Dill as CIGS)

However, then there followed an argument as to whether he should have supreme control over all three services, as later with Eisenhower and Mountbatten, and it was not decided until 25th November 1941 that this should not be so, but that each service head would still report direct to London, and whilst jointly responsible with the Commander-in-Chief,

---

† Percival, *War in Malaya*, vol. i, p. 240.
* Op. cit.

Far Eastern Fleet, for strategy, he would not assume operational control. When war broke out thirteen days later it was felt better to leave Brooke-Popham in command, but Duff Cooper pressed for a change immediately. So Pownall started on his unpromising journey to take over command, arriving in Singapore on 23rd December and taking over on 27th December. Brooke-Popham, therefore, at a critical time, was aware he was being superseded. Pownall appears to have had little or no influence on events. On 5th January 1942 General Wavell was appointed Supreme Commander of the South-West Pacific, and Pownall became his Chief of Staff, a post for which he was eminently fitted.

Meanwhile we must consider how Brooke-Popham dealt with his problem as the dangers heightened and the crisis drew nearer, and an almost intolerable burden of decision faced this conscientious but tired and ageing airman, from whom it is impossible to withhold great sympathy in his dilemmas.

America was friendly but still not an actual ally. America felt that Singapore should have a higher place in British priorities but resisted suggestions for a joint fleet in Singapore. The history of British attempts to clarify and render explicit American policy on Japan is recorded fully in *Grand Strategy*, vol. ii, by J. M. A. Gwyer. American policy and actions were a dominant factor in the minds of the British, and this is the crux of the matter in judging Brooke-Popham's actions or inactions. Amidst all doubts and difficulties America would be the *deus ex machina*. The United States Navy would be our safeguard. Though there were Japanese precedents, no one envisaged the surprise attack on the fleet at Pearl Harbor.

It was not until 5th December 1941, three days before the Japanese attack, that understandings were received from President Roosevelt that America would support us, if necessary with force, on whatever action in Siam we felt it necessary to take, and accordingly on that day the Chiefs of Staff authorised Brooke-Popham to order Operation Matador as soon as he had reliable information, either that the Japanese were about to seize the Kra Isthmus or had already occupied some other part of Siam.*

When this telegram was received, Brooke-Popham's Chief of Staff, General Playfair, is reported to have said: "They've now made you responsible for declaring war," – a significant remark.† It still did not give Brooke-Popham the requisite authority to act if Malayan territory alone was first attacked.

Burdened with this responsibility, Brooke-Popham had also received a report that certain pro-Japanese members of the Siamese Cabinet were urging Japan to make her first attempt on Malayan territory – at Kota Bahru. If we reacted as they suspected by entering Siam we would be the aggressors and put ourselves in the wrong. Siam would then join Japan. The *Official History* records this story and its unfortunate effect on Brooke-Popham. The author surmises that it was deliberately planted by the Japanese to confuse, which it did. It is strange that it should have been treated with respect, for if Japan attacked Malaya, it would be bound to occupy Siam to secure its base; it was academic who crossed the frontier first.

Prior to receipt of London's authority, Brooke-Popham cabled London on 4th December seeking authority to order Matador in the event of an attack on Malaya without violation of Siamese territory. A reply to this giving him the requisite authority did not arrive until the morning of 8th December, after the Japanese invasion.

On Saturday 6th December 1941 our aircraft sighted the Japanese convoys, and Percival who was in Kuala Lumpur thought that Matador would be ordered. Awaiting a reply to his telegram of 4th December Brooke-Popham hesitated, however, despite the fact that at the ABDA conference of April 1941, under his chairmanship, it was recommended that any movement of the Japanese naval vessels south of latitude 67° north (which had taken place) should be considered an act of war. Action then might well have disrupted Japanese plans.

Sunday 7th December was a day of tension even as I recall in Kuala

---

* J. M. A. Gwyer, *Grand Strategy*, vol. ii, part 1, pp. 301–2
† Louis Allen, *Singapore, 1941–42.*

Lumpur, ignorant of events, with the volunteers mobilized and the town and clubs quiet and almost deserted. On that morning a Catalina had been sent out on reconnaissance and did not return; we know now it was shot down, the first overt act by the Japanese some time that afternoon. Later in the evening definite sightings were reported by Blenheims and Hudsons. On that same day Sir Josiah Crosby, our Minister in Siam, sent an urgent cable to Brooke-Popham urging him on no account to be the first to enter Siam.

Operation Matador was now clearly out of the question but Brooke-Popham merely postponed it, and Percival did not, as he should have done, forcefully represent this. Thus the front-line troops remained in a state of uneasy uncertainty.

In the early hours of Monday 8th January the Japanese landed at Kota Bahru in the east, close to the Siamese border, but the frontier troops were still kept in a state of uncertainty whilst Brooke-Popham ascertained by further reconnaissance that the Japanese had invaded Siam. The need for the 11th Indian Division to have a quick decision to cancel Matador and, more important, for Force "Krohcol" to advance into Siam at Kroh, does not appear to have been realised either by Brooke-Popham or Percival judging by events that morning. He received at 0800 hours that morning from London a reply to his telegram of 4th December authorising him to enter Siam, but it was not until after 0945 hours, after receipt of news of the air reconnaissance, that he gave Percival the authority he needed. Alas! Percival was away from his HQ reporting to the Legislative Council, and it was not until 11.30 that he received the news. There were further delays then before 11th Indian Division, despite repeated enquiries, received its orders. The reasons for this will be recorded later but for Krohcol it meant the Japanese reached the vital Ledge position just ahead of us and lost us the race.

Brooke-Popham felt he had the responsibility of war or peace, though we know now the Japanese were taking this out of his hands. The *Official History* in reference to London's telegram of 5th December states:

Thus at the eleventh hour the Chiefs of Staff gave Sir Robert (Brooke-Popham) the permission, for which he had been asking, to launch "Matador" without reference to London. They had however worded their instructions in such a way that the chances of it succeeding were greatly reduced, for it would be too late to take action by the time that he could be sure that a Japanese expedition was making for the Isthmus of Kra. This was to have serious consequences.*

Nevertheless on the facts recorded it is evident that a stronger will and clearer mind was needed in Singapore at that time, and that the disastrous beginning of the Malayan campaign might at least have been avoided.

The replacement of Brooke-Popham with a younger man with up-to-date experience had been under consideration in London since August 1941, but with the pace of things Malayan it was not until 1st November that Lieutenant-General Sir Henry Pownall was appointed. Pownall was then Vice-Chief of the General Staff in Whitehall where he had served before the war. He was Chief of Staff to Gort with the BEF in 1939–40. In the biography of Montgomery by Nigel Hamilton it is recorded that after Dunkirk he sent a mildly reproving letter to Monty, whose criticisms of the BEF had come to his ears. Let Nigel Hamilton take up the story:

> At the bottom of Pownall's warning letter Bernard had pencilled: 'Lt.-General Sir Henry Pownall, Chief of Staff BEF under Gort – he was completely useless' – a view seconded later by Field-Marshal Templer who was largely responsible for the successful defence of the BEF's western flank. . . under General Mason Macfarlane.†

---

* S. W. Kirby, *War Against Japan*, vol. I, p.175.
†Nigel Hamilton, *Monty*, vol. I p.395.
Brian Bond (ed.), *Chief of Staff - Diaries of Lt.-General Sir Henry Pownall*, pp. 53-4.

Pownall in his diaries describes the circumstances of his appointment piquantly. After relating that Dill was to be succeeded by Alan Brooke as CIGS, he writes:

> 19.11.41. The strange and unbelievable thing is that the PM wanted Bye to be CIGS! He has invited him to Chequers several times and has fallen in love with him. It was with difficulty that he was persuaded that Nye, at 45, wasn't really ripe for it. But he did not hold back entirely for last Saturday at Chequers he offered Nye VCIGS – my job. P. J. Grigg (Secretary for War) who was there immediately pointed out that there was someone in the job already. So they have got over that by sending me to Singapore, vice Paget, now for Home Forces. It is hardly a credible tale and really unworthy. But the PM is like that; he exercises his patronage in very peculiar directions with little regard for ordinary decencies . . . I don't want to go to Singapore one little bit.

Pownall left London on 9th December for the Far East. By then war with Japan had broken out, and the Chiefs of Staff were at first inclined to keep Brooke-Popham at his post, but Duff Cooper, who had already clashed with Brooke-Popham in council urged his immediate replacement.

Pownall finally arrived in Singapore on 24th December, and after taking over went north to visit Heath and III Corps. He spent 25th-26th December in the forward area in Perak. Here the battered 11th Indian Division was sorting itself out whilst the Japanese on the 26th crossed the river obstacle, the Perak River, unopposed (the river ran north and south and was difficult to defend).

From his diaries it seems that Pownall took a rather detached view of events and the state of 11th Division. Heath had sought reinforcement, and the *Official History* suggested that now was the time to bring over the 9th Division from the east, blocking the difficult mountain passes with state troops. Pownall seems to have been content to leave 11th

Division to work out its salvation unaided, which resulted in the catastrophe of Slim River in January. Even here he writes on Wavell in his diary (p.94): 'Perhaps he ordered the Malaya battle from north of Kuala a little to soon. I don't know. If he had not done so, maybe the troops would have been overwhelmed.'

When one reads of how Wavell travelled forward to visit the remnants of 12th and 28th Brigades, and saw it was a 'paper front', this seems an odd observation.

Pownall also shared Wavell's surprising and fatal underestimation of the prowess of the Japanese troops (see p.224).

Pownall's command was soon superseded by Wavell's appointment as Supreme Commander ABDA, and he became his Chief of Staff. Later in the war he was chosen by Alan Brooke as a 'wise old head' to be Chief of Staff to the young Supremo, South-East Asia, Admiral Mountbatten, where he did good work.

Pownall seems to have been a solid, unimaginative soldier, but his record and diary comments leave open to doubt whether his earlier appointment to replace Brooke-Popham would have made much difference to events.

As for Brooke-Popham, he had given distinguished service to his country in World War I and after as one of the pioneers of the Royal Air Force, and it was sad that his honourable career of public service should end in such humiliating circumstances.

# CHAPTER V

## Duff Cooper

A. J. P. Taylor (*English History 1914–1945*) has remarked of Duff Cooper's autobiography *Old Men Forget* that "it helps to explain why many men found Duff Cooper attractive and also why he was not a great success as a Minister."

Duff Cooper was a survivor of the "lost generation", one of that aristocratic and artistic circle so vividly and poignantly described in the World War I diaries of Lady Cynthia Asquith. Service in the Foreign Office spared him from the holocaust of the Somme and Passchendale, where so many of his friends were killed. He refers, as does Lady Cynthia, to the taunts which were levelled against those in reserved occupations, but displays a typically patrician indifference to vulgar opinion. Late in the war he joined the Grenadier Guards and in the concluding battles of August 1918 won the Distinguished Service Order on the Western Front.

Marriage to the gifted and beautiful Lady Diana Manners followed, and, leaving the Foreign Office, his progress in politics and literature soon began to match her fame. He was no longer just the husband of a famous beauty. He was described as one of the two ablest men who had been recruited to the Tory benches, the other being Edward Marjoriebanks who tragically took his young life.

Duff Cooper was a superb platform speaker, much in demand, and soon made his mark in the House of Commons as a progressive and liberal-minded Tory. Defeated in 1929, he wrote his first book,

*Talleyrand*, which became a best-seller. In 1931 he returned to the House, taking up Baldwin's cause somewhat belatedly and perhaps with no great enthusiasm; he smote Lords Beaverbrook and Rothermere hip and thigh in the celebrated St. George's Westminster by-election, against their own candidate, whom he opposed with wit and vigour, thus securing the regard of Stanley Baldwin who in a famous phrase had characterised these newspaper proprietors' conduct as "seeking power without responsibility; the prerogative of the harlot throughout the ages."

His progress was then rapid: Under-Secretary of State for War, Financial Secretary to the Treasury, and then Secretary for War in November 1935, in Baldwin's Cabinet. Here he was unable to do anything effective to penetrate the conservatism of the Army.

When Neville Chamberlain succeeded Baldwin, Duff Cooper did not expect office. They were hardly *simpatico* in any way. He relates how Chamberlain stayed to listen to him introducing the Army Estimates without a note as was his wont. Chamberlain was apparently impressed by his performance, and he was appointed in 1937 First Lord of the Admiralty, Hore-Belisha being sent to rejuvenate and reform the Army.

Duff Cooper was now 47, and it is interesting to observe from his diary which he recommenced in 1938 that his ambitions and vitality were on the wane. He wrote:

> Whether I shall do well at the Admiralty remains to be seen. I doubt whether I have any particular gift for administration and during recent weeks I have been suffering from a certain lack of self-confidence which is new to me and depressing. I ought not really to mind for I think I should be happier out of office. My political ambitions have dwindled. I have always wanted to be a PM. I want to be no longer. I have got near enough to see the position without the glamour. I see more plainly the endless, thankless work, the worry and the responsibility and the abuse.

He viewed with increasing reluctance and frustration the course of events and policy of Neville Chamberlain and his close colleagues. He fought with increasing impatience with the Treasury under Sir John Simon for rearmament, and finally the terms of Munich decided him. Harold Nicholson's diary for 1st October 1938 reads:

> I go back to London. The posters say "Cabinet Minister resigns." I assume it is Buck (Earl de la Warr). But not at all. It is Duff Cooper, and his resignation is accompanied by a nasty letter. That is fine of him. He has no money and gives up £5,000 a year plus a job he loves.

This was his finest hour, and secures his place in history. He had always retained his friendship with Winston Churchill, which was both social and political, but he gravitated to the Eden Group, which was more numerous. He was not offered a place when the war came. Chamberlain, Simon and Hore had a poor opinion of his administrative ability (and perhaps his social gifts) and his vehement character was antipathetic to them all, but when Winston Churchill came to power he remembered his old friend and made him Minister for Information, a post for which he was unsuited and which he came more and more to dislike. Harold Nicholson, his friend and Under-Secretary, tells a revealing anecdote of him:

> 8.7.41. I drive down to White's Club with Duff and beg him to treat the Public Relations Officers with all gentleness. They are a touchy lot... Duff glowers at them as if they were coolies in some Cingalese copper mine. He then tells them an angry story about how he had been brought up from Bognor on false pretences. He then scowls at them and says that this is all he has to say. He then stalks out of the room. We are left ashamed and wretched and do not know which way to look. I cannot make out what happens to Duff on such occasions. He seems to lose

all power over himself. I think it is a sort of shyness.*

In July, 1941, both he and Harold Nicholson were removed from their posts. Whilst Harold Nicholson was disconsolate, Duff Cooper sighed with relief. The fiery Brendan Bracken took his place, and made a great success of the Ministry. In the presence of both, Winston Churchill referred to the unsuitable appointment of Duff Cooper as "harnessing a thoroughbred to a dung cart."

It so happened that at this time a cable was received from Sir Archibald Clerk-Kerr, Ambassador in China, urging the need for co-ordination of civil activities in Singapore. Duff Cooper was clearly not a success as Minister of Information, and a solution presented itself. Winston Churchill (*The Second World War*, vol. III) in his post-war account portrays what was a convenient switch as a process of natural selection.

> I felt the need for repeating in the Far East the institution of a Minister of State, who, in the closest touch with the War Cabinet, would relieve the Commanders-in-Chief and local Governors of some of their burdens and help them to solve the grave political problems which gathered swiftly. In Mr Cooper, then Minister of Information, I had a friend and colleague who from his central point of view knew the whole scene. His firmness of character which led him to resign office as First Lord of the Admiralty after the Munich Agreement in 1938, his personal gifts of speech and writing, his military record as an officer in the Grenadier Guards during the 1914-18 war, combined to give him the highest qualifications.

He was appointed Chancellor of the Duchy of Lancaster with the mission "to examine the present arrangements for consultation and communication between the various authorities in that area, military,

---

* Harold Nicholson, *Diaries and Letters 1939–45.*

administrative, and political, and to report to the War Cabinet how these arrangements can be made more effective."

Although Duff Cooper received his terms of reference on 19th July 1941, it was typical of the tempo of affairs as far as Malaya was concerned that he did not arrive at Singapore, with his wife, until 9th September. As he has emphasised, his terms of reference were vague but they were not concerned with the "military situation". Such was his unpromising mission. He relates that he found in Singapore, as in America, through which he passed en route, an atmosphere of optimism, but his observations and the opinion of Sir George Sansom, working there for the Ministry of Economic Warfare, convinced him that war with Japan was in the near future a likelihood, and decided him to accelerate his report. It is surprising, therefore, to find that shortly after his arrival in Singapore, at a conference on 29th September with the Service and civil chiefs, the British ambassadors from China and Siam, and a representative from Australia, the conclusion was reached that a landing on the east coast in the approaching monsoon was unlikely, and this despite the demonstration of its possibility by Dobbie in 1937. They were apparently impressed by intelligence reports of the concentration of Japanese forces against Russia. Kirby finds it "unbelievable" that they should have come to this conclusion, "for it ran counter to all the available evidence."*

If Duff Cooper, as he asserts, was not concerned with the "military situation" his participation in this conference is as difficult to understand as the conclusions to which his presence gave authority. Since both the Governor and the Commander-in-Chief were present at the discussions and since his terms of reference included making more effective "consultation and communication" between the civil and military it is perhaps understandable that Winston Churchill was at first inclined to blame Duff Cooper when after the war had broken out and it was too late he found so much wrong in this regard. He had an alibi, however, in that he was not a member of the War Council

---

* Kirby, *Singapore: The Chain of Disaster*, p. 119.

until that time, and apparently did not have the opportunity of discovering any of the various deficiencies about which he now complained. He had not the wide-ranging curiosity and energy of his master who would not have been inhibited by these restricted terms of reference.

Be that as it may, Duff Cooper completed his report a month later, his recommendation being the appointment of a Commissioner-General for the Far East at Singapore with broad powers, and he tells us he had in mind for the post Mr Robert Menzies, recently Prime Minister of Australia, whose personality and subsequent record and eminence mark it as a percipient choice, which if there had been time might well have had significant results. The report, however, did not reach London until 24th November, and it was overtaken by events.

On the outbreak of the Japanese war, Duff Cooper was appointed resident Cabinet Minister for Far Eastern affairs and was authorised to form a War Council. Mr Bowden, the Australian High Commissioner, was also a member of the War Council, and his observation in these stressful times was that he was an "able but not dominant character", and that "he did not provide strong leadership."*

His position was one of great difficulty. He was not the Supreme Commander. He still had to argue and persuade, and his temperament was ill suited to the exercise of tact needed in the circumstances to deal with Brooke-Popham and the Governor. The differences over the policy of evacuation have been recorded. He forced the appointment of Brigadier Simson, Chief Engineer, to co-ordinate civil defence.

The Duff Coopers had descended on Singapore like some rare and exotic species, birds of a different paradise, and in this strange new atmosphere, it was unlikely with his background and nature that he would have the tact and patience required in such an emergency to manage a collection of harassed and overworked soldiers and officials. He was not the man to reanimate the sultry tropical scene.

The appointment of Wavell as Allied Commander rendered Duff-

---

* *Australian War History*, p. 204.

Cooper's position otiose, and he was recalled by Winston Churchill. Before he left on 13th January Wavell asked him to stay, mainly for reasons of morale, but he said he felt he was without power or significance, yet he had the uncomfortable feeling he was running away. Winston Churchill makes the cryptic remark that "he was unlucky not to be allowed to go down fighting."* He returned home and was later to render notable service in employment more suited to his character and qualities as representative in Africa with the Free French and later Ambassador to France.

In Malaya the announcement of the appointment of Duff Cooper, famous for his courageous resignation after Munich, was a welcome but another delusive reassurance, in particular to those anxious about our preparation for defence against possible Japanese aggression, but few were aware of or appreciated its limited scope. At all events it was indication that the home country had not forgotten Malaya amidst its own more immediate perils, and although his belated departure has been remarked upon, when he arrived his personality, charm, and his intelligence impressed those who came in contact with him.

Here was a prominent politician and ex-War Minister from the Cabinet but it was unlikely that anyone then knew or realised as Liddell-Hart has said (*Memoirs*, vol. 1, p. 379) that "he had delightful qualities but was not a dynamic man"; that he had been replaced at the War Office because of his failure to reform its conservatism, and remove its incompetents. With the Nazi mechanized masses roaming through Europe in triumph who would recall that in introducing the 1934 Army Estimates he had referred to the importance of cavalry in modern warfare, and in 1937 when announcing a very modest and inadequate mechanization of certain cavalry units he had felt it necessary to mitigate the shock to the old diehards by declaring: "It was like asking a great musical performer to throw away his violin and devote himself in future to a gramophone."

Malaya was in fact sent an artist and a gentleman when it needed a

---

* W. S. Churchill, *The Second World War*, p. 544.

bandit and a bounder like Beaverbrook* to shake the establishment, civil and military.

When it was too late, fretting and fuming in frustration, Duff Cooper proposed drastic changes in the civil administration, but in the Malayan scene he was like Disraeli's description of a forgotten prime minister of brief duration, Lord Goderich, a "transient and embarrassed phantom."

Between this aristocratic survivor of the pre-1914 *jeunesse dorée* and a collection of harassed and overworked, middle-aged and middle-class colonial civil servants such as Shenton Thomas, the Governor, and S. W. Jones, the Colonial Secretary, there was little in common. Though Alec Newbould, the member of the service allotted to Duff Cooper as private secretary, found him charming, Shenton Thomas, more and more after the formation of the War Council when the war broke out, found him hostile and critical. It seems almost to have become an obsession.

In a biography of Shenton Thomas (*Shenton of Singapore* by Colonel Brian Montgomery, brother of the Field Marshal), the friction and even strife between them is fully recorded.

Shenton Thomas was a dedicated colonial servant who conceived it his first duty to protect the subject peoples over whom he ruled in the King's name, but Duff Cooper (like Winston Churchill, especially in the case of India) was rather cavalier in this regard. Montgomery records how horrified was Shenton Thomas when in a broadcast after the fall of Penang Duff Cooper stated that the majority of the whole population had been evacuated when he meant the European population.

From then on relations deteriorated. Shenton Thomas's feelings in this regard are eloquently expressed in the comment he made when Singapore fell (page 239).

---

* A senior civil servant said that "We need a Beaverbrook here" a short time before the outbreak of the Japanese war. This was H. W. Phear MM, head of the FMS Customs Service, a veteran of World War I, a fine character and a good friend, in the Montgomery mould.

# CHAPTER VI

## Wavell

General Sir Archibald Wavell was appointed Supreme Commander of ABDA (American, British, Dutch and Australian Forces) in South-East Asia in a letter from Winston Churchill on 30th December 1941, an appointment of which the latter was later to write, "it was almost certain that he would have to bear a load of defeat in a scene of confusion." The appointment was made against the advice and despite the misgivings of the Chiefs of Staff and the rest of the War Cabinet, but as Winston Churchill was to write to Attlee from America on January 3rd 1942: "Here again it is necessary to defer to American views, observing we are no longer single, but married."

With his accustomed loyalty and resilience Wavell assumed the burden, writing to his friend, General Dill, that he had heard of holding the baby but this was quadruplets.*

In the bleak winter of 1940–41 Wavell's name had resounded throughout the free world with the defeats inflicted on Italy in the Western Desert, but the triumph was fleeting. Soon it was downhill all the way, for the foredoomed attempt to help Greece, the loss of Crete, and the failure of the "Battleaxe" offensive in the desert, all conducted amidst a bombardment of missives from Churchill, led to his replacement by General Auchinleck in July 1941 and his appointment as Commander-in-Chief in India.

Wavell on his own initiative paid a visit to Malaya in October 1941,

---

* J. Connell, *Wavell, Supreme Commander*, p. 71.

and recorded his impressions:

> My impressions were that the whole atmosphere here in Singapore was completely unwarlike, that they did not expect a Japanese attack, that they regarded the existing (North East) monsoon months as quite impracticable, and were very far from being keyed up to a war pitch. On the other hand I was impressed by the difficulties of the country and could not see how a Japanese force could make very quick progress down the peninsula towards Singapore.*

In a brief note to Auchinleck in Egypt on 8th November 1941 he wrote: "From the very little I saw and what I heard of the layout, I should think the Jap has a very poor chance of successfully attacking Malaya and I don't think myself that there is much prospect of his trying..." On 7th December 1941, on the eve of the attack, in a public speech he emphasized the strength of our defences, and the reinforcements forthcoming. This was for public consumption, but as with others concerned, the tremendous potential deterrent strength of America was consciously or subconsciously a background of reassurance. Attack would be suicidal in the end, but the Japanese were addicted to suicide, as a study of their history might have shown.

Wavell flew into Singapore to face his clamant responsibilities on the 7th January 1942. It was a moment of grave crisis. A breakthrough on a dark night with heavy rain at 3.30 that morning at Slim River had resulted in the break-up of the 11th Division.

It is a measure of Wavell's quality to note his actions and his own words on his first and immediate visit to the front line. In a foreword to an unadorned but moving account of the 2nd Battalion Argyll & Sutherland Highlanders by Brigadier Stewart, who commanded the battalion with distinction during the campaign, Wavell wrote:

---

* J Connell, *op. cit.*, p. 41.

I had a provisional time scale in my head when I arrived in Singapore, and at once flew to the front to check it. The Disaster of the Slim River had just taken place, but at Corps HQ, where I landed (Kuala Lumpur) they were not aware of its magnitude and still in the dark as to the real position. So we motored to HQ of the 11th Division where Brigadier Paris (acting Major-General) cheered me by quite an optimistic estimate of the time for which the Japanese could be held on the existing line. But I decided to motor on and see the brigades myself... In a small building by the roadside I found Brigadier Stewart (then Commander 12th Brigade) and another brigadier (Brigadier Selby of 28th Gurkha Brigade). They were obviously very tired and under great strain but undaunted. From them I got a clear but depressing picture of the situation. The two brigades between them numbered only a few hundred desperately tired men, and the front was a paper front...

The facts must have come as a shock to Wavell, and the more so that they were not known, as he indicates, to the Army, the Corps and the Divisional Commanders. His confidence in them must have been shaken, and this must have influenced his actions, but it did not lead him to make any changes. He returned to Singapore and summoning Percival to his presence without further discussion presented him with a plan for withdrawal to the Muar River Line in Johore. No doubt impressed with the vigour and aggressiveness of Major-General Gordon Bennett, commander of 8th Australian Division, whom he had met in Johore, and comparing him to the weary Heath with his tired and dispirited Staff of III Corps, his plan entrusted the defence of Western Malaya to "Westforce" – a Corps command under Bennett – but without the necessary staff. It will be seen later that this was largely contributory in frustrating his own hopes of a stand, and resulted in the fiasco on the Muar River Line.* It does not appear however, that his directive was implemented in conformity with his intentions nor with conspicuous intelligence.

Wavell's need to be here, there and everywhere was an insuperable handicap to concentration on the manifold problems of Malaya command, and his on-the-spot decision here led unfortunately to the squandering of its remaining military asset, apart from the Singapore garrison; that is the ardent and well-trained 8th Australian Division, and the loss with catastrophic casualties of the last line of defence on the mainland. It does most certainly seem in retrospect how right were Winston Churchill and the Chiefs of Staff in preferring that Wavell was able to concentrate his attentions on the immediate battlefront, instead of having to cope with the multifarious problems of his widespread new ABDA command.

Whilst in Singapore on this visit he had to consider a recommendation from Duff Cooper who to Wavell's regret was about to depart, that Sir Shenton Thomas be superseded by a military Governor, and that other changes be made including the replacement of the Colonial Secretary, Mr S. W. Jones, by Mr Hugh Fraser, who had been Federal Secretary, and who later was fated to die in captivity after barbarous treatment by the Japanese. In the event it was decided that only Mr Jones should be replaced, and although he sought to stay and do his duty as a civil defence worker he was not permitted to remain, and left Singapore for home and retirement – a sad end to an honourable career.

---

\* It may well be wondered why Wavell retained Percival in command in the light of his discoveries on visiting the front after Slim River. That his confidence in Percival was shaken is evident from his subsequent actions which have been described.

There is a contemporary comment by Sir Stafford Cripps, quoted in Cecil King's diary *With Malice Towards None*, (p. 176): "Wavell suffered from one terrible fault; inability to get rid of the incompetents. It had been in his power to remove Percival when it was quite obvious he was no good – but he just could not bring himself to do it." Though crudely expressed this is not an unfair comment. Cecil King's diaries like those of "Chips" Channon record much wartime rumour and tittle-tattle but though shallow the diaries are often shrewd and revealing.

Wavell continued to make flying visits to Singapore – on 20th and 30th January, and a last one on 10th February 1942 when the city was doomed. Each time he met a deteriorating situation, news of some fresh disaster and the slow pace of steps to prepare Singapore's defences as he had ordered. He needed all his phlegm, resilience and energy which seemed inexhaustible.

All this was accomplished amidst the awful distractions of his far-flung command stretching to Burma, China and Philippines, with visits to Burma where a threatening situation was developing, and all of which demanded urgent attention, but he found time to send to his old comrade, Admiral Cunningham in Cairo, a telegram of support and sympathy in his tribulations, without mentioning his own.

Wavell's ABDA responsibilities finally came to an end with the invasion of Java on 22nd February 1942, and Winston Churchill, with whom his relations had been and were thereafter chequered, responded felicitously to his valiant but unavailing efforts with a message:

> I hope you realise how highly I and all your friends here as well as the President and the Combined Staffs in Washington rate your admirable conduct of ABDA operations in the teeth of adverse fortune and overwhelming odds.

He still had responsibility for Burma on his hands on resuming the post of Commander-in-Chief, India, but at least he soon had Alexander and Slim to conduct a skilful retreat to the sanctuary of the Assam hills.

Wavell was made Field Marshal in the New Year's Honours, 1943, but the abortive Arakan offensive in that year had shaken the British high command's faith in his military judgment, and in June 1943 he was replaced by General Auchinleck, and became Viceroy of India where he struggled nobly with the manifold and mounting civil and political problems of Indian independence. Here, too, he was replaced in 1946, and history records the achievements of Earl Mountbatten of Burma.

Nevertheless this episode in his career constitutes one of the most noble and honourable of his public services, and let an Indian make his tribute to Wavell.

> When the last chapter of British connection with India has been written, and when a complete picture of the political situation during the closing days of the British era is presented, Wavell's policy will perhaps be fully vindicated. Meanwhile, let not the world forget the loftiness of his motives, the sincerity of his purpose and his patience under adverse circumstances, discouragement and disappointment.*

Military critics, amongst whom is an authority to be treated with respect (Major-General Sir Francis de Guingand†) have cast doubt on his judgment, in Greece, Crete, Malaya and Burma. Major-General Sir John Smyth, VC, who was in command of the ill-fated 17th Division, has some illuminating and not ungenerous comments on his policy of fighting far forward of the Sittang River with a raw and scratch force which resulted in the disaster of the Sittang Bridge. There is no doubt he made a cardinal error in underestimating the Japanese, and overestimated what untrained and unblooded troops and Staffs could achieve. The same criticism applies to the Arakan offensive in 1943, which although a year after the Malayan campaign was a comparable defeat in military terms.

This apart, the wonder is not that he made mistakes but that he never broke under the strain. "What's done we ofttimes may compute but know not what's prevented."

As a soldier Wavell had a reputation before the war which was one of the highest in his profession. His fate was to deal with the early disasters. His integrity, his silences and his misfortunes make him a sympathetic figure. Alanbrooke wrote that he was "a devoted admirer of Wavell, as a man, commander and strategist," and that he "gave immense services

* R. P. Masani, *Britain in India*, p. 270.
† *Generals at War – Wavell: a Critical Assessment.*

under conditions of appalling difficulty."* Montgomery was another admirer, and his famous corps commander, Lt.-General Sir Brian Horrocks has written: "I remember him so well when I was a young officer and he was my divisional commander. He had at that time one of the most brilliant brains of any man I have ever met behind that poker face of his. He was full of imagination and had more of it in his little finger than had any other military commander I have ever met. I learned a lot from him and was devoted to him."†

The concluding words of Macaulay's essay and epitaph on Warren Hastings may be applied fittingly to Field Marshal Earl Wavell, the last but one Viceroy of India as Hastings was one of the first – "his noble equanimity was tried by both extremes of fortune and never disturbed by either."

* * *

Since I wrote this assessment of Wavell I have read Michael Howard's review in the *Sunday Times* of Ronald Lewin's recent biography of Wavell: *The Chief: Field Marshal Lord Wavell* and the following passages therefrom provide a definitive judgment, in my view, on that famous soldier whom he likened to Robert E. Lee:

> ... As Commander in Chief in the Middle East Wavell was not up to the job...
>
> In the Far East Wavell had more justification for failure. No one could have coped with the storm that broke over that unprepared region. Wavell's unjust harassing of his subordinates in the Arakan, is understandable if not forgivable. But in his handling of his Chinese and American allies he showed a failure to comprehend the new dimensions of the war that disqualified him from the positions of supreme command to

---

* R. Woollcombe, Preface to *Wavell's Campaigns*, 1959.
† Letter to author.

which he still pathetically aspired... yet he was sensitive enough to understand the problems of India, and to refuse to act as the figurehead there that Churchill intended when he appointed him Viceroy. Nothing became him like this last, civilian phase of his long and unhappy career.

# CHAPTER VII

## The Naval Aspect

### 1. The Genesis of Force Z

The discussions and decisions which led to the dispatch of Force Z* may be said to have started with a minute by Winston Churchill on 25th August 1941 labelled "Action This Day" to Pound (First Sea Lord) and Alexander (First Lord of the Admiralty). He advocated the sending of a deterrent force to Singapore, to exercise a "vague" menace, citing the case of *Tirpitz* – a false analogy as was pointed out by the Admiralty for conditions in the Atlantic were entirely different from the Pacific. Churchill's reasons were no doubt partly political. He has been much criticised for this decision but it has to be borne in mind that this overburdened Titan carried the widest responsibilities, and for some time he had had to endure the proddings of the powerful figure, Mr Robert Menzies, Prime Minister of Australia, reminding him of our oft-repeated assurances that an adequate fleet would be sent east if Australia and New Zealand were menaced. He must have been conscience-stricken on the subject, and felt strongly the need to appease Australia. On 20th October the decision was at last made, and Churchill was it seems strengthened by the opinion of Mr Anthony Eden at the Foreign Office – unpropitious support when one recalls that Eden was a prime supporter of the disastrous expedition to Greece. The decision to send the ships was then made against the professional advice of Admiral Pound. It may

---

* Arthur Marder, *Old Friends, New Enemies*, ch. VIII.

be surmised that if the decision had been in the sphere of General Sir Alan Brooke, who became Chief of Army Staff at the end of 1941, no such decision would have been accepted. Lord Noel Annan, who was at the time a colonel in Intelligence at Whitehall, has written in a recent review (April 1993), referring to Churchill's bellicosity and impetuosity: "The same impetuosity made Churchill send two battleships to reinforce Singapore in 1941; both, without air cover, were sunk at once. Had Churchill had his way the list of British defeats would have been even longer.

"But he did not have his way. The man who saw to it that he did not, Alan Brooke, had succeeded Dill in October 1941."

The British naval historian, Roskill, and others felt that Pound, in poor health, should have been retired by this time.

It was the intention to send also an aircraft carrier, but the chosen ship, the *Indomitable*, ran aground in Jamaica, and there was only the old and slow and unsuitable *Hermes* in Trincomalee to replace it.

Marder writes: "... it would have been sensible to stop worrying about capital ships and to do everything they could in 1941 to build up a modern airforce in Malaya."

The Germans certainly knew how to do it; witness the escape of *Scharnhorst* and *Gneisenau* through the channel with the aid of shore-based aircraft soon after the fall of Singapore, adding to our miseries.

Of the *Indomitable*, Marder writes: "It is fascinating to speculate whether the presence of a carrier would have made a great difference or whether the disaster would have been even worse. My view is the more or less orthodox one – that the presence of the fast *Indomitable* (23,000 tons, 30.5 knots) and her 45 aircraft (12 Fulmars, 24 Albacores and 9 Sea Hurricanes) would not have made any decisive difference to the result on the 10th December, and she might indeed have been lost as well, though the Japanese would have had to pay a much heavier price for their success."

The decision was made and *Prince of Wales* and *Repulse* sailed from the UK to the Far East in October 1941.

## 2. The Preliminaries

The man appointed to command the Far Eastern Squadron comprising *Prince of Wales* and *Repulse* was Tom Phillips, Vice-Chief of the Naval Staff, an old friend and confidant of the First Sea Lord, Admiral Pound, with whom he had served many years.

He was a very able staff officer and had served throughout the war at Whitehall and was due a seagoing appointment. The choice of Pound was endorsed by Winston Churchill whose approval for all such high appointments was obligatory.

Phillips had fallen out with Churchill in the strong views he expressed against the ill-starred decision to go into Greece in 1941 and there had been no contact between them since.

It seems this was a controversial appointment and according to Gen. Sir Henry Pownall, soon to be sent to replace Brooke-Popham, it was typical of Winston Churchill.

Phillips was an abrasive personality and one of his fixations was that the danger for ships from air attack had been exaggerated. Marshal of the Royal Air Force J. C. Slessor in his *The Central Blue* records the clashes he had on this subject with Phillips when he, Slessor, was Director of Plans for the RAF. He gave up the struggle to convince him and records a macabre story of a farewell remark of Air Marshal Harris who was Vice-Chief of the Air Staff when Phillips departed from Whitehall: "Tom, when the first bomb hits, you will say as you go up to heaven 'That's one hell of a mine.'"

Phillips' appointment was viewed with disfavour in the Navy's high circles. Admiral Cunningham in characteristic blunt fashion wrote: "What on earth is Phillips going to the Far Eastern Squadron for? He hardly knows one end of a ship from the other. His only experience is 8 months as Rear Admiral Destroyers in the Home Fleet 1938/9 and he had the stupidest collision."

After the loss of the ships, Admiral Somerville wrote to Cunningham that the whole thing was "a thoroughly bad show. Why the hell don't they send out there someone who has been through the mill and knows his stuff."

One who did, and proved himself later as C-in-C Ceylon, was Admiral Layton in Singapore, unceremoniously supplanted – an old sea dog of considerable experience.

This was just another item in the catalogue of mistakes and misfortunes in Malaya.

On December 2nd 1941, *Prince of Wales* and *Repulse* sailed into Singapore naval base. Admiral Tom Phillips had preceded their arrival by air from Ceylon. The scene was much trumpeted in the local press and caused some enthusiasm. No mention was made, however, of *Repulse*, much to the indignation of its crew. This futile attempt to mislead the Japanese was, of course, a failure as many Japanese spies lived in Malaya.

By this date the troops in Malaya had recently been placed in a state of readiness. The Volunteers had been mobilized; that is to say, all those (mainly white) expatriates under 41 left their offices etc. and joined their military units, mostly engaged on lines of communication, garrisons of aerodromes and suchlike while the more senior men kept the offices going and also served in the Local Defence Volunteers. There was an air of expectancy. We were not, of course, aware of the many deficiencies which concerned Brooke-Popham and Percival. In fact we had seen the arrival of impressive reinforcements, mainly Australian and Indian, but did not realise in the case of the Indians that this impressive display hid the fact that the troops were only partly trained, formations in India having been milked of officers and NCOs to provide new battalions, and that the cream of the Indian Army had been sent to the Middle East.

When in due course the Brewster Buffalo aeroplanes arrived on Kuala Lumpur aerodrome, where I was stationed, it was a heartening sight, and when the first air raid took place we expected to see a successful battle. Instead, the inferior Buffaloes were shot down like flies by the faster Japanese Zeros and one saw the first casualties of the war for us in those gallant but inexperienced Buffalo pilots. Further

71

shocks were to follow later.

Sir Andrew Gilchrist in his book *Malaya 1941* has given us a penetrating analysis of the military and diplomatic moves prior to the outbreak of war against Japan. Sir Andrew was No.2 to our Minister in Bangkok, Sir Josiah Crosby, and had frequent contacts with Brooke-Popham and Shenton Thomas. He adduces a fascinating scenario under the chapter heading "The Missed Chance".

When Admiral Phillips arrived in Singapore all were aware that a crisis was building up. He was required by London to consult with Brooke-Popham. Let us suppose that instead of flying off to meet Admiral Hart in Manila, a mission that in the end served no useful purpose, he had remained in Singapore to give counsel and support to Brooke-Popham, and had ready his two battleships. As it was, *Prince of Wales* was put in dry dock to deal with its boilers, and *Repulse* was sent off to Australia.

When on 6th December the vital sightings of the Japanese fleet and transports had taken place, his ships could have been got ready at 12 hours' notice. He could have sailed that night under cover of darkness. It would have taken 36 hours to reach the Kota Bahru area.

Would he have been attacked by the Japanese in the daylight hours of Sunday 7th December? Gilchrist points out why this would have been unlikely: the planned attack on Pearl Harbor was the reason why not. Yamamoto* would not have wished to alert the sleepy Pearl Harbor by an attack on the British. Phillips did not fear the two Japanese capital ships in the South China Sea; his two battleships were more than enough. He did fear the submarines more, and then there was the threat from the air. However, on Sunday 7th December our air force would have been fully operational and ready to protect the ships from aerodromes at Kuantan and Kota Bahru. It was only after the landing in the early hours of Monday 8th that the Japanese raided our northern aerodromes and put so many planes out of commission. Experience of the 9th–10th

---

* Admiral Yamamoto: C-in-C Japanese Navy who planned attack on Pearl Harbor, etc.

December sortie indicated they might have escaped detection.

Thus Phillips would have been in a position to deal with the Japanese early on Monday 8th December.

It is further surmised by Gilchrist that Brooke-Popham with the strong support of Phillips may well have activated Matador in time.

We know that the Japanese had plans that if Singora and Patani had been defended, they would have landed further up on the Siam coast, and thus given the British forces valuable breathing space.

Whether or not this scenario was feasible, at least the alternative that was adopted was just a desperate gamble, and too late. The result could hardly have been worse.

When Admiral Phillips arrived back from Manila by air in the afternoon of that fateful Sunday 7th December 1941 he faced a load of problems and perplexities. He is summed up well in Andrew Gilchrist's *Malaya 1941*:

> Phillips was insufficiently alert to the pressing realities of the strategic situation in which he was involved. Until it was too late he prepared no active naval role for his ships against the well expected Japanese amphibious invasion, and thereby missed his only possible chance of speedy intervention and historic distinction. Thereafter he came to realise that in his character of British naval officer, he had come to the point when he simply had no option but to sacrifice his squadron and his life. As the end approached, it may be said of Phillips – with *Repulse* sinking before his eyes and *Prince of Wales* beneath his feet – "that no British Admiral died so bitter a death. Indeed he cannot but appear as a tragic figure."

Phillips' first duty would be to concert plans with Brooke-Popham, as indeed was stipulated by London, and he could hardly have been encouraged when he learnt that Brooke-Popham had suspended Matador but incredibly had not cancelled it, leaving the troops in a state of indecision and confusion. It is interesting to have Andrew Gilchrist's assessment of Brooke-Popham whom he knew well and with whom he had frequent contacts: "I found him for the most part brisk and competent, although always too interested in detail. When confronted with an awkward or insoluble problem (this is something I particularly noticed) he was inclined to express changeable and indeed on occasions incompatible views, one after the other, not by way of responding to argument but through some switch of memory or perception inside his own mind."

We know that Admiral Layton regarded Brooke-Popham as "quite useless... he ought to be retired."

Phillips no doubt felt that it was necessary for him to get a grip on matters and make decisions.

A series of meetings was held at the naval base. In 1982 Arthur Marder, the great naval historian, in his *Old Friends: New Enemies*, recorded for the first time the minutes of this or these vital meetings, recorded as starting about 2.30 on Monday 8th December, that is after the landings at Kota Bahru were known in Singapore.

In Brian Montgomery's *Shenton of Singapore*, we have this extract from the Governor's diary written at Government House:

> December 8, 1.15 am. Percival telephoned that the Japanese were shelling beaches at Kota Bahru. I telephoned Police to collect all Japanese for internment and also to put in force the scheme for seizing Japanese power boats in the harbour. Both done very successfully and without incident. At 4 am. Pulford (AOC) phoned approach of hostile aircraft. I asked how far and he said 25 miles. I had just time to phone Harbour Board (Rogers) and Jeans (head of ARPO) before they appeared...

This is important in relation to what was recorded at this or these meetings.

The provenance of this account which first appeared in Marder's book was a certain Commander McClelland who had been put into the meeting secretly by Admiral Layton.

Layton recorded after the war in a conversation with (now) Captain McClelland that he was convinced that the inevitable conclusion of Phillips' conference would be a decision to sail forth and engage the enemy, and that he stuck his neck out and sent a signal to the Admiralty recommending that the two capital ships be sent westwards out of harm's way. To this there was no reply.

Winston Churchill describes the deliberations of his War Council on 9th December (*The Second World War*, vol. III, page 547): "After much discussion as the hour was late it was decided to sleep on the matter."

He then describes how on awaking on 10th December and opening his boxes Admiral Pound gave him the shocking news of the loss of both ships and Admiral Phillips. He says: "In all the war I never received a more direct shock."

The effect on everyone in Malaya can be imagined.

To return to the early morning conference with Brooke-Popham; Marder includes in his book a passage from McClelland's letter in which he recalls Admiral Phillips' comments at that time:

> As regards attacks by aircraft, he (Phillips) dismissed high-level bombing as only likely to achieve any great result in the face of his anti-aircraft armaments if he was extremely unlucky. Dive bombing was likely to score damaging hits, but should not cripple either of his two capital ships: in any case he understood that the Japanese dive bombers only operated from carriers and he had already said that he did not at all expect to encounter one. As the torpedo was the weapon to which heavy ships were especially vulnerable, the principal danger came from the torpedo bomber, as had been amply illustrated in the case of the *Bismarck*. And to double the number of aircraft taking part in any simultaneous attack quadrupled their chances of scoring hits. (That is, they would swamp the defence, leaving many aircraft

unfired at.) But in the thick north-east monsoon weather prevalent the execution of simultaneous attacks was very difficult and the torpedo bomber itself was very vulnerable indeed to attack by fighters during its approach to the dropping position. Against this form of attack his protection by shore-based fighters thus became essential, as his arrival without *Indomitable* meant that he was completely devoid of any fighter protection whatsoever.

He wound up by saying that, if the factor governing the situation was the preservation of his ships so that they could be used with greater advantage later in the campaign, there was no doubt at all that he should retire to the westward and await reinforcements, and sat down. Greening\* said afterwards that there was a smile on the face of the Tiger. I knew that smile!

The Little Man had, for the victim, the unpleasant habit of deciding what was to be done before a conference and getting the victim, to state that it was essential to do it. In this instance, the victim was Brooke-Popham. As he (Phillips) very rarely smiled over work, all of which he treated very seriously, he can only have produced the rather puckish grin which told his intimates that he had set his trap for the unwary. Like many others before him, B.-P. fell straight into it.†

Marder continues:

A dead silence followed which nobody seemed inclined to break. Finally, the Governor gave his views. The heavily-built but fit Thomas, a Cambridge man, quiet, scholarly, dignified, even-tempered, and very good at his job, always said that he knew nothing about warfare, except of the tribal kind. But he certainly had a clear mind when the occasion arose to talk about

---

\* Commander R W Greening, RN Staff Officer
.† Captain McClelland's letter to Marder, 3rd March 1979.

it, as now. It had, he said, come as a complete surprise to him to learn that the arrival of the battleship was only a piece of bluff, and, further, that the Japanese might be about to call it. If they did, would not this change the circumstances completely? Ought they not immediately to ask the Government what they wished the Admiral to do, if war broke out? After all had been said and done, the Japanese must be as aware of the shortcomings of the British force as the Admiral himself, and would go flat out to exploit them. "The Brigadier† at once rushed to speech, blissfully unaware that the man who was causing the trouble to which he referred, was seated at the table." Speaking with reference to the Governor's question, to judge by the confusion over, and the delay in, ordering either Matador or "Krohcol" (a stop-gap in lieu of Matador whose object was to seize "the Ledge", certain strong positions in the mountains in Thailand about 35 miles above the Thai border, if the Japanese landed before Matador was executed), the War Office had no idea what to do, let alone how to do it. Brooke-Popham, "obviously shocked by the lèse-majesté and scared stiff that worse might follow", interrupted. He agreed that it was useless to ask for fresh orders, produced his "usual disparaging remarks about the Japanese", said he did not expect a seaborne attack during the north-east Monsoon, and still hoped that the occupation of Thailand was the Japanese objective. "His only two useful contributions to the discussion were statements that he had been amazed by the speed at which, according to intelligence reports, the Japanese air forces could both transfer aircraft from base to base and improvise new ones, and that people must remember that, 'Once he is in the fight, the only way to get a Jap out of it is to kill him.'" Pulford, who had been listening impatiently, spoke very briefly on the limitations of his aircraft and the lack of training of his fighter pilots in a fighter-protection role, stressing the difficulties they

---

† The Brigadier on the Staff of GHQ Malaya Command.

would run into out of sight of land. He wound up saying that his operations staff had discussed the Admiral's possible plans with Goodenough* and had recommended that he (Pulford) should agree with them within the limitations he had just named. He then nodded a brief "Goodnight" and left. Thomas spoke again, in the assumed capacity of an "umpire". As he saw it, given another week the Admiral would have sufficient destroyers to permit offensive operations as far as Japanese submarines were concerned; but the ships should not be employed on any offensive task unless fighter protection could be guaranteed. The AOC having left, perhaps the C-in-C, Far East, could give the necessary assurances? Brooke-Popham did not reply to this. "Possibly the realisation that his aircraft were still on the ground when they ought to have been attacking any transports approaching the anchorages, brought something home to him. But, according to Greening, he 'suddenly shook himself like a dog' and said, slowly and distinctly, 'Do you know, Admiral, that I am beginning to believe that if the Japanese intend to attack, your intervention is the only thing that can prevent the invasion succeeding.'" He turned to Terence Back** and gave him some order which took Back out of the room at the double, then explained to the conference that he had sent him to his office to get on the "green" line to Pulford's HQ to tell them to carry out armed reconnaissance in force from Singora to Patani and off Kota Bahru and to attack any transport anchored off or approaching the coast. Phillips made no reply to this sudden declaration, but the Governor, after rubbing his chin for a little time, said gently yet very clearly that he sincerely hoped that Brooke-Popham's original ideas (presumably on the inferiority of the Japanese and his conviction that war in the East could not happen) were correct, because, if they were not,

* Commander Goodenough, RN Staff Officer to Admiral Phillips.
** Captain Back, RN His naval liaison officer.

it looked as if they would be in a "regular pot-mess and no mistake". He then addressed the C-in-C directly, asking how long he thought it would take the Japanese to unload their force. This talk was going on when the "Air Raid Warning Red" (an attack was imminent) was announced (0400). It being too late to get to the shelters, those in the War Room lay down on the floor under the table. When the sirens sounded the "All Clear" at 0440, the conference broke up in a hurry.*

This account is curious in that it purports to relate to a meeting held in the early hours of 8th December, 02.30 or so onwards, after the landings at Kota Bahru were known. It is, therefore, odd to read Brooke-Popham's remarks which surely must have been made *before* they were aware of the landings. Shenton Thomas's remarks also in their tenor would seem to indicate he had not yet heard of the landings.

We venture to surmise that there were two meetings: one held, say, before midnight, and before the landings were known and at which Shenton Thomas was present; and another meeting, which appears to have lasted from about 2.30 am to 4 am, when the air attack on Singapore arrived. Timings must be approximate, but Brian Montgomery is puzzled how Shenton Thomas could have got back to Government House from the naval base in time to receive the telephone call (at 4 am) from Pulford about the air attack.

It would seem logical that the Governor should be at the earlier meeting *before* war had broken out but not at the later meeting after the war had begun, when it would have been purely a matter for the Service Chiefs.

Brian Montgomery calls it an enigma.

Those who knew Shenton Thomas regard his prescient remarks as very much in character.

The pronouncement from the civilian Governor appears to have been

---

* Arthur Marder, *Old Friends: New Enemies*, pp. 408–11.

ignored; Phillips, it seems, had made up his mind. He would in accordance with the great naval traditions set forth to engage the enemy next day.

But where was the enemy? By daybreak on 9th December all the troops had successfully landed at the various ports from Kota Bahru to those up the East Siam coast. The transports had landed their supplies and with astonishing speed retired empty back to safety. The Hudsons from Kota Bahru airfield had bombed three transports, one of which caught fire and later sank, but the landings had been a success. Such was the unpropitious prospect. He signalled his intentions to London who vouchsafed no reply before he sailed next evening.

The die was cast, however, and we now relate the circumstances in which the fleet went forth to its doom.


## 3. The Sortie

At 5.35 pm on Monday 8th December 1941 Phillips sortied from Singapore with his attendant destroyers, and taking a circuitous route north reached a position 6°N, parallel with Kota Bahru, when he was aware he had been sighted by three Japanese aircraft. At 8.15 pm, realising that surprise had been lost, and bereft of the air cover he had hoped for, he decided to return to Singapore. As he sailed south during the daylight hours of Tuesday 9th, 8th Brigade at Kota Bahru were in dire straits. The force named Krohcol, having received the order to enter Thailand too late, had failed to reach the Ledge position in time and were in trouble; on the Jitra front an advance guard sent forward to delay the Japanese were also in trouble. At 8 am on the 10th Phillips, having received a report of a landing at Kuantan, which turned out to be false, diverted his journey south to investigate. This was a fatal diversion, and at about 11 am the Japanese bombers attacked the two battleships.

By 12.30 *Repulse*, and by 1.20 pm *Prince of Wales,* had been sunk with the loss of 513 lives from *Repulse* and 327 from *Prince of Wales* which included Phillips and his captain, John Leach. Some 2000 had been picked up by attendant destroyers which had not been attacked by the Japanese.

There were many brave deeds. On *Repulse* a midshipman, A. C. R. Bron, a lad of 17, was in charge of a 15-inch transmitting station. At the order "Abandon ship" there was a natural rush for the ladder. Bron got there first, restored order, and was the last to leave. He did not survive.

Another midshipman, 18-year-old L. R. L. Davies (RAN), in charge of an oerlikon which he kept going until the last, also went down with the ship. Mr Page, a director gunner on *Repulse*, gave his lifebelt to a wounded man who was saved; he was not.

On *Prince of Wales*, the Executive Officer, Commander Lawford, was buried in Damage Control Headquarters attempting to correct a fault in the steering caused by a bomb. He carried on cheerfully, and went down with the ship.

The hapless, gallant Phillips had no intention of surviving the disaster, but with him went nearly 1000 men, innocent victims of a misconceived and misguided venture, accompanied by a catalogue of errors. They now lie, far from land, in the tropical waters of the South China Seas.

Phillips' seamanship came in for criticism. In his *Old Friends: New Enemies*, Marder writes (p. 439): "Aircraft were sighted just after 11 a.m. approaching from the starboard bow. Phillips now manoeuvred the Force by Blue Pendant (Blue 3), the ships turning 30° to starboard facing the enemy. The capital ships were now in starboard quarter line formation. At 11.13 as a wave of high-level bombers approached on the port bow, 10,000 feet altitude, fire was opened. Quickly realising that the Blue 3 signal was a mistake he countermanded it and ordered Blue 5, a turn together 50° to port."

Middlebrook and Mahoney (*Battleship: The Loss of the* Prince of Wales *and the* Repulse, pp. 174–5) describe the resultant confusion graphically:

> Both ships were swinging right in answer to BT3 (Blue Pendant 3) signal, and the Control Officers correcting to the left were

thus being counteracted. This turn caused all the guns on the starboard side of the ship to cease firing as the superstructure of the ship masked their line of fire... Phillips soon realised he had made a mistake and countermanded it... but a big ship cannot reverse course quickly, and *Prince of Wales* and *Repulse* continued to swing right, so much so their port side guns were able to come into action and fire only a few rounds. But then the turn to port started taking effect; the port side guns had to cease fire; no guns fired for a few moments and finally the starboard side guns came into action again. By now, however, the Japanese had completed their approach and were about to bomb... These cumbersome fleet manoeuvres by flag signal had robbed the gunnery officers of their opportunity to settle down to their long 'run' of firing that would have enabled corrections to be steadily applied and more effectively fire brought to bear. The unswerving approach of the compact formation of Japanese aircraft at a constant speed was really a gunner's dream. Admiral Phillips had made a fiasco of his first handling of ships in action.

One can imagine the feelings of the tried and proven Captain Leach at witnessing the inept performance of an Admiral in whom he could have had little confidence and between whom there was little rapport. When the Fleet Gunnery Officer felt it necessary to proceed from the flag deck to the bridge to warn the Admiral of the adverse effect of his order all Captain Leach could do was to say to the Admiral: "I agree with the FGO, sir."

Phillips did not signal Singapore when attacked and eventually Captain Tennant on *Repulse* did so. When RAF Brewster Buffalo fighters arrived, the ships were sinking and survivors were in the water, and those sufficiently alive to bear resentment yelled curses at them in unprintable language.

With Phillips died also Captain John Leach. His son, later Admiral of the Fleet Sir Henry Leach, who in 1982 distinguished himself by organising the Naval Task Force for the Falklands War, was at the time in Singapore. Dining with his father on board *Prince of Wales* in reply to his father's enquiry what he thought of the situation, he replied with the ignorance of a midshipman: "Let 'em come; let's have a go at them." His father turned very serious and said: "I don't think you have any idea of the enormity of the odds we are up against." Later, when he went with his father to the Base swimming pool, his father said: "I am going to do a couple of lengths now – you never know how it mightn't come in handy."

Young midshipman Henry Leach noticed that there was little rapport between his father and the Admiral. This is not surprising. In John Leach's memory must have lingered what happened in the aftermath of the sinking of *Bismarck*. Pound, no doubt supported by Phillips, and prompted by Churchill, wished to court-martial John Leach for not re-engaging *Bismarck* after the loss of the battle cruiser *Hood*. *Prince of Wales* was badly damaged, and with its new guns giving trouble, Leach wisely made smoke and broke off the action, meantime trailing *Bismarck*. Admiral Tovey approved his action and later recommended Leach for the Distinguished Service Order which he received. When Tovey heard of the preposterous proposal of a courtmartial he declared he would haul down his flag and act as prisoner's friend. No more was heard of it.

When one reads the long, voluminous record of all that went on during the years before the fall of Singapore, the unfortunate appointment, the misguided decisions, the untoward incidents, and the unhappy interaction of personalities involved, it would seem that some evil genius presided over the destiny of Malaya.

Leach was by common consent a first-class officer, much loved, who would have risen to high rank; and his loss was a severe blow to the Navy.

Did Phillips have any premonition of disaster? En route from the UK he had visited General Smuts by air, and whether or not he expressed misgivings to Phillips, Smuts cabled Churchill warning him of the possibility of disaster "if the Japanese were nippy."

The writer has a vivid personal recollection of a talk given in POW camp by a petty officer who survived the *Prince of Wales'* sinking. He related how he last saw Admiral Phillips sitting on his bridge immovable in a chair looking, as the petty officer put it, "a bit fed up".

Inadequate words indeed to describe such a personal tragedy.

# CHAPTER VIII

## The Japanese Onslaught

### The Preliminaries

A decisive date in the preliminaries to the Japanese onslaught was 25th July 1941, when by an executive order the President of the United States froze Japanese assets in America which brought all trade between the two countries to a standstill. All the prolonged and complicated negotiations with the Japanese Empire were now reaching a climax.

As the *Official British History* tells us:

> There had been some doubt in London about the wisdom of this move, since it seemed to offer Japan an abrupt choice between the complete reversal of her policy and an immediate advance in search of the raw materials which she was now denied. Nevertheless, we had followed suit. With still greater trepidation, since they had not yet received any firm promise of support from either ourselves or the United States, if they were attacked, the Netherlands East Indies had also come into line.*

At the Atlantic Meeting which ended on 12th August soon after this event, Winston Churchill hoped and thought he had an assurance from the President of a warning to the Japanese in unmistakable terms of the

---

* *Grand Strategy*, vol. III, part 1, p. 131.

NORTHERN MALAYA
Airfields
Roads
Railways
Boundary (State)
Mountains
Swamp
miles
25
50
N
S I A M
K E D A H
P E R A K
K E L A N T A N
TRENGGANU
PERLIS
PENANG
Padang Besar
Kodiang
Changlun
Jitra
Alor Star
Gurun
Sungei Patani
Butterworth
George Town
B Mertajam
Baling
Kroh
Betong
Grik
Patani
Kota Bharu
Machang
K Krai
Gong Kedah
K Trengganu
Taiping
K Kangsar
Port Weld
Trong

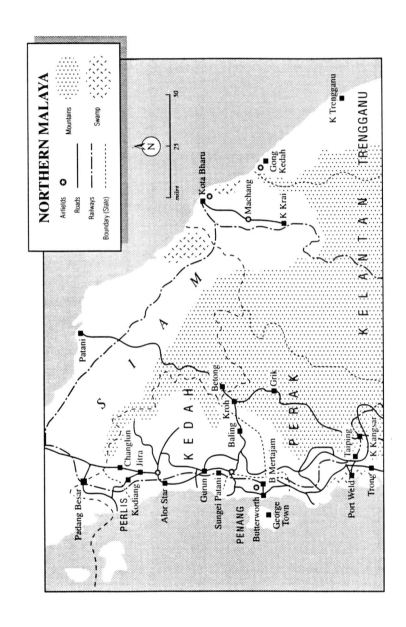

consequences of aggression, the salient paragraph being:

> Any further encroachment by the Japanese in South West Pacific
> would produce a situation in which the United States Government
> would be compelled to take counter measures even though these
> might lead to war between the United States and Japan.

but Roosevelt yielded to the advice of his Secretary of State, Mr Cordell
Hull, that these words were "dangerously strong", and an anodyne
statement replaced it, to the disappointment of the British.

Yet we now know that in any case the Japanese were now bent on a
course which did not shrink from war. Admiral Yamomoto, the dominant
figure in the military hierarchy after the Premier, General Tojo, was well
aware of American power, knew that it must ultimately prevail, but
realised that in the climate of sentiment and opinion, of national pride
and even suicide, he had no alternative but, fatefully, to go along with it.
The result was the plan to launch a surprise attack on Pearl Harbor and
cripple the United States fleet.

At an Imperial Conference on 6th September 1941 an attack on Siam
and Malaya was decided upon, and on 23rd September 1941, as a
preliminary move, the Japanese forces by an arrangement with the Vichy
French entered Saigon in Indo-China.

General Yamashita was placed in command of the 25th Army to
conquer Malaya, and set up his headquarters on Hainan Island. After an
argument with the army and navy planners it was decided with
Yamashita's concurrence that there would be no preliminary bombardment
of the points selected, to achieve surprise. Yamashita was offered five
divisions but said he could only maintain three, and could do the job with
that, his intelligence having informed him the opposition would be
mainly Indian troops and untrained. His diary records: "If Indian troops
are included in the British forces defending Malaya the job should be
easy."*

---

* A. Swinson, *The Four Samurai.*

The 25th Army was formed and disposed as follows:
*Initial Assault*
5th and 18th Divisions – Singora and Patani
Brigade Group of 18th Division – Kota Bahru
*Follow-up*
Imperial Guards Division.    The 56th Division was made available
                            but was never required.
All were well-trained, crack troops under able and experienced
commanders, the cream of the Japanese Army.

On the morning of 6th December 1941 the troop convoys and escorts
sailed from Saigon and Camranh Bay, and our meagre reconnaissance
aircraft tracked and traced them. It had been the recommendation of the
Allied (ABDA) Conference of April 1941 that movement of Japanese
vessels south of the latitude 6° north of the Equator would be regarded as
an act of war. The crucial moment of decision was arriving for Brooke-
Popham.

The troops awaiting to receive them in the north of Malaya were, as
the Japanese anticipated, mainly Indian, and, furthermore, they were
formations that had been heavily "milked" to provide the cadres for
further divisions in India, and had little training. At the points of invasion
these forces were as follows:
*Kota Bahru*: 8th Indian Brigade of 9th Division
            (Brig.-Gen. Key)   (Maj.-Gen. Barstow)
These were reinforced by one battalion from the 22nd Brigade at
Kuantan, also part of 9th Division which was only two brigades
strong.
*Patani:* Krohcol – one battalion of 3/16th Punjabis to be followed by
5/14th Punjabis from Penang. Their mission was to advance into
Siam to the strong Ledge position, and they were under the orders,
despite his protests on account of his responsibilities at Jitra, of
Major-General Murray Lyon commanding 11th Division.
*Singora – Jitra*: the 11th Division composed as follows:
6th Brigade – Brigadier-General Lay – with two Indian and one

British battalion.

15th Brigade – Brigadier-General Garrett similarly constituted, and in reserve was the 28th Gurkha Brigade under Brigadier-General Carpendale.

All formed part of the Third Indian Corps under Lt.-General Sir Lewis Heath. The sole reserve was 12th Brigade under Malaya Command.

At 10.10 hours on Sunday 7th December, Admiral Ozawa signalled Yamashita on transport *Ryojo*: "Landing operations may go ahead as scheduled on Sunday 7th December."

The British forces, in the light of air reconnaissance reports of the Japanese convoys, were put on first degree of readiness at 15.15 hours on Saturday 6th December. 11th Division was warned to be prepared at short notice to carry into operation the Matador plan for a forestalling advance into Siam, and the column at Kroh to be ready to advance to the Ledge. All through Sunday 7th December the troops were keyed up and waiting for the starter's pistol, but in the weather conditions which Dobbie's appreciation had foreshadowed it was difficult for our aircraft to keep track of the Japanese convoys.

It will be remembered that Brooke-Popham had received the authority of the Chiefs of Staff on 5th December to order Matador without reference to London if the Japanese violated any part of Siam or were advancing with the apparent intention of landing on the Kra Isthmus. The sighting of a Hudson aircraft at midday on Saturday 6th December 1941 had found the Japanese vessels south of the latitude 6° which had been agreed as constituting a *casus belli*. The Far East Combined Intelligence Bureau had also received warning of the actual points of attack, and information came from the North that Siamese frontier guards were erecting roadblocks. Swift action and decision was needed, but as we have related the perplexed and aged Brooke-Popham took counsel of his fears, and sought further endorsement from London, deeming insufficient the authority he had received on 5th December 1941 – an unhappy augury of future events. Indeed, on this Saturday 6th December, Percival was at III Corps Headquarters in Kuala Lumpur expecting the signal for action to come, and on returning to Singapore that night he was surprised to discover that no decision had been made. Heavy clouds provided cover for the Japanese, and there were no further sightings that day. A Catalina flying boat was sent out at dawn on Sunday 7th December and failed to return, and it was not until about 18.00 hours on this last Sunday of peace that a Hudson reconnaissance aircraft which was fired upon described Japanese vessels sailing in the direction of Singora and Patani.

It was clearly too late now for Matador and the alternative instruction for defending Jitra, and the immediate launching of Krohcol was now necessary. No such orders were given. Brooke-Popham instead gave orders at 20.30 hours that night that troops were to stand by still with the possibility of Matador and no orders went to the troops at Kroh. As Kirby says, "the blame for lack of action must be laid mainly on the Commander-in-Chief's shoulders, but Percival could and should have pressed him on 7th December 1941, for 11th Division to be released from Matador and for Krohcol to be allowed to start its move to gain the Ledge position."*

This was not the end of the delays in decision-making. The attack on Kota Bahru came in the early hours of December 8th, and Singapore knew by 01.00 hours, but it was not known from air reconnaissance that the Japanese had landed at Singora and Patani in Siam until 09.15 hours. Percival had gone to the Legislative Council to report, and so the vital decision to abandon Matador and send Krohcol on its mission was not conveyed to Percival until about 11.30. These orders did not reach Heath until 13.00 and at 13.30 11th Division received its orders.

An explanation for these fatal delays can be found in Louis Allen's *Singapore 1941-1942* and speaks for itself:

> This puts the gap of time at a crucial two hours between
> Percival and Heath on top of time wasted in deliberation over

---

* Kirby, *Singapore: The Chain of Disaster*, p. 128.

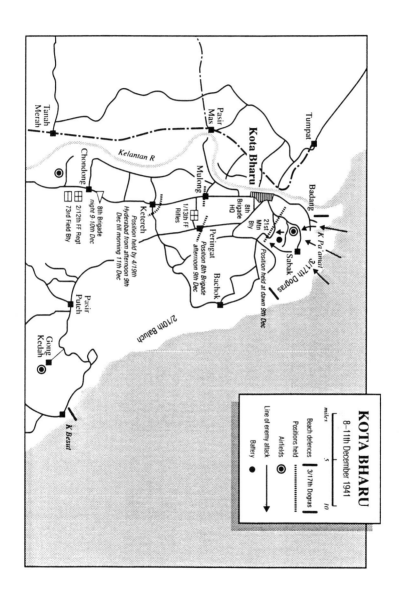

KOTA BHARU
8–11th December 1941

| | |
|---|---|
| Beach defences | 3/17th Dogras |
| Positions held | |
| Line of enemy attack | → |
| Airfields | ◉ |
| Battery | ● |

miles  5  10

Matador after sighting. In a letter to Professor J.R.M. (later Sir James) Butler (7th January, 1962) Percival says the gap occurred between III Corps and 11th Indian Division and gives the hair-raising explanation of inadequate lines:

"What happened between 3rd Corps and 11th Indian Division I do not know, but I would point out once again that there was only the one civil trunk telephone line, which we all had to use, and the Services only had limited privileges on it. It was not to be expected, therefore, that calls would go through very rapidly."*

We must now turn to the events in Kelantan.

*Kelantan – Kota Bahru*

At 23.55 hours on this Sunday night, 7th December, three transports containing the "Takani" detachment, a brigade group of the 18th Japanese Division, anchored off Kota Bahru. General Takani reported: "there was the dull light of an oval moon from over the sea to the east. A stiff breeze was blowing and I could hear it whistling in the radio aerials. The waves were now up to six feet."† These conditions were near danger point for landing and it took one hour before the first wave of troops was in the landing craft and headed for shore under Colonel Masu in four lines. According to a Japanese account it was about 02.00 hours when RAF planes from Kota Bahru and the gunners struck the convoy, and one ship which had General Takani on board was sunk. This caused the escort commander to seek abandonment of the landing but Takani was bolder and pressed on. He signalled Yamashita at Singora: "Succeeded in landing at 02.15 hours."†

The landings were on the Badang and Sabak beaches in front of Kota

---

* Louis Allen, *Singapore 1941–42*, pp.122–3.
† Arthur Swinson, *The Four Samurai*.

Bahru town and airfield, defended by the 3/17th Dogras who were very thin on the ground. South were the 2/10th Baluchs covering the area down to the Kuala Besut and Gong Kedah airfield. 1/13th Frontier Rifles and 2/12th Frontier Force Regiment were in reserve. The Dogras put up a stout defence in the circumstances, and one may ask why there was not one of the regular British battalions available from Singapore to stiffen the defence at this vital point. Attempts in the morning of 8th December for the two reserve battalions to counter-attack from both flanks failed. During the day the airfield at Kota Bahru was evacuated in circumstances over which the official history draws a discreet veil, and by evening further enemy transports were arriving. The withdrawal had started, and by the afternoon of the 9th December the troops were in the rear of Kota Bahru town. Brigadier Key conducted further withdrawals with skill and by 11th December the airfields at Gong Kedah and Machang had been evacuated in the face of increasing opposition. General Barstow now sought withdrawal from the exposed position to Kuala Krai down the rail line to Kuala Lipis in Pahang, and the first of the disagreements between Heath and Percival arose. Heath considered that it was the only sound step now the airfields were abandoned, the brigade out on a limb, and resources limited, but he could not obtain Percival's approval until the latter had consulted the Commander-in-Chief and the Governor. Heath decided to proceed to Singapore on the night of 11–12th December to press his point, and so it happened by this mischance was away from Kedah at a critical time.

As Kirby has maintained, the decision to defend the east coast with our meagre forces was a doubtful one, but as soon as Kota Bahru was lost, the 9th Indian Division was required on the west coast to support the hard-pressed 11th Indian Division. The few passes over the main range of mountains and the poor communications would have rendered defence and delaying action a relatively easy matter compared to the tasks these men now had to perform.

*Jitra*

Doubts have been expressed about the feasibility of Matador and the *Official History** considers it "fundamentally impracticable and should never have been accepted." Nevertheless if the order had been given to undertake Matador on the afternoon of Saturday 6th December, when the convoy was south of the latitude 6° North, then 11th Division — who were keyed up to this adventure — would probably have reached Singora by the evening of 7th December despite opposition from the frontier guards, and we know now that Japanese had alternative plans for such an eventuality which would have gained our defence valuable time.

As it was the Leicesters and 1/14th Punjabis had spent the morning at Anak Bukit Station south of Jitra ready to proceed north to Haadyi Junction near Singora. They waited until midday on Monday 8th December, and saw the Japanese planes which at 07.00 hours bombed and damaged severely Sungei Patani and Alor Star aerodromes. Then came the order to detrain and return and strengthen the inadequate defences at Jitra. It was a sad anti-climax and the lowering effect on morale was an inevitable consequence of the sudden and unexpected change of role from offensive to defensive.

A force of two companies of 1/8th Punjabis under Major Andrews with a section of 273 Anti-Tank Battery and two sections of sappers and miners were sent forward to Sadao some nine miles inside the Siam frontier. At 21.00 hours that evening in pouring rain – the monsoon season was now on – a Japanese mechanized force with headlights was encountered. The Japanese reaction was, however, swift and foreshadowed things to come. Three tanks were stopped by anti-tank rifles, but within a short time the effective Japanese mortars were in action, and they started a flank attack. Major Andrews considered it prudent to withdraw after demolishing three bridges. He re-crossed the frontier at about 01.30 hours next morning sustaining hardly any casualties. Two companies of 1/14th Punjabis took over the advance guard north of

---

* Vol. 1, p. 462.

Changlun.

On the railway to the west in the little state of Perlis a platoon of 2/16th Punjabis and a section of sappers and miners demolished the 200-ft girder bridge at Padang Besar on the border.

General Yamashita's diary records that it was at 23.00 hours that same Monday evening, 8th December, that he completed negotiations with the Siam Government to permit his troops to pass through unmolested by the Siamese.

It was now Tuesday, 9th December, and the *Prince of Wales* and *Repulse* were steaming up the east coast to their fate. At Kota Bahru the 8th Brigade of 9th Division was retreating, and the small column from Kroh had failed to reach the Ledge position and were in trouble. This column was within Murray-Lyon's command, despite his protests, and distracted his attention from his immediate and menaced front at Jitra where the 11th Division was trying desperately to repair and improve the rain-sodden defences.

Brigadier Garrett of 15th Brigade was ordered to delay the enemy north of Asun until dawn on Friday, 12th December in order to give 6 and 15th Brigades more time to prepare.

On Wednesday, 10th December, the remainder of the 1/14th Punjabis was concentrating at Changlun, a crossroads some seven miles from the Siam border where there was a bridge over the river Loko, whilst the two forward companies were fighting a withdrawal action to join up with them. Meantime 2/1st Gurkha Rifles (less one company) from the reserve 28th Brigade relieved the 1/14th Punjabis at Asun some five miles forward of Jitra in an area of swamp with a ready-mined bridge.

It was at about 09.00 the following morning, Thursday 11th December, that the Japanese attack on 1/14th Punjabis came in and throughout the morning there was heavy fighting. Brigadier Garrett was wounded in the neck by mortar fire and went back to receive medical attention, and Lt.-Col. Fitzpatrick commanding the 1/14th Punjabis broke contact and withdrew. At 15.00 hours Murray-Lyon came forward to confer with Fitzpatrick and with Garrett, who had returned after having his wound dressed. Garrett wished to withdraw behind the anti-tank obstacle at Asun, but Murray Lyon ordered him to maintain a position two miles in front of its protection at Nangka and hold it overnight. At about 16.30 hours in fierce tropical rainstorm whilst the Punjabis were moving to their new position, the first of those blitz tank attacks which the division came to know too well caught the Punjabis unprepared. They were overrun and with them the section of anti-tank guns limbered up and ready for withdrawal. At 18.00 hours the enemy reached the Gurkha position at Asun. In front was the vital bridge, prepared for demolition. Major Bate, commanding 28th Company Bombay Sappers and Miners, sprang forward to blow the bridge, but the rain had rendered the charge useless. He fell riddled with bullets. Havildar Manbahadur of 2/1st Gurkhas stepped into the breach and effected a brief respite by hitting and stopping two tanks with an anti-tank rifle. He rescued Major Bate but that gallant officer died in his arms. By 19.00 hours the position of the two forward Gurkha companies was critical. The tanks reached battalion headquarters and all communications broke down.

This disaster, ominous foretaste of things to come, left some 200 men of the Punjabis and 300 of the Gurkhas to find their way back to 11th Division. Brigadier Garrett and Colonels Fulton of the Gurkhas and Fitzpatrick of the Punjabis were cut off, but the two former found their way back; the latter was eventually taken prisoner.

On the left flank on the road to Perlis that branched off at Jitra, 6th Brigade had sent forward covering troops, and these were now ordered back to the Jitra position, but another catastrophe took place. Withdrawing after dark, the officer in charge of demolition of the road bridge over the stream at Manggoi, due perhaps to scare news from Asun, but for whatever reason, mistook the British column for Japanese and blew the bridge. The guns and transport of the retiring detachment of 2/16 and 1/8th Punjabis had to be left behind, and the troops got back on foot. Seven anti-tank guns and four mortar guns were abandoned.

Murray-Lyon on this day of woe knew that Krohcol was in difficulties, and now his division had suffered serious depletions. He placed Brigadier

Carpendale of 28th Brigade in command of 15th Brigade that night in place of Brigadier Garrett. He had already prudently that morning sent Lt.-Col. Selby of 2/9th Gurkhas back to Gurun to reconnoitre positions. The 2/2nd Gurkhas were brought up from reserve to join the depleted 15th Brigade and take positions on the River Bata astride the vital iron bridge.

The previous day *Prince of Wales* and *Repulse* had been sunk, and the news was soon known. The Japanese were quick to drop leaflets, some of exceptional crudity, particularly aimed at the morale of the Indian troops.

Such was the dismal prelude to the attack on the main defences at Jitra, but meanwhile we must see what has been the fate of Krohcol so belatedly launched on its adventure.

*Krohcol*

On Monday 8th December, upon receiving his orders to occupy the favourable Ledge position (certain strong positions in the mountains about 35 miles above the Thai border on the road to Patani), this column consisting of 3/16th Punjabis under Lt.-Colonel H. D. Moorhead reached at 14.00 hours the frontier beyond Kroh. As he opened the frontier gate the Subahdar was shot dead, and thenceforward the column was harassed by Siamese constabulary and roadblocks, despite the optimistic predictions of our Siamese Ambassador, Sir Josiah Crosby. Troops noticed that the Siamese left their boots at the foot of the trees from which they sniped. By dusk that evening as a consequence they were only 3 miles inside the border. They halted for the night and were continuously sniped. At dawn on Tuesday 9th December the column moved off, still under harassment which ceased at 03.30 hours. Some four miles from the Ledge they met the Japanese. The delay of twelve hours in starting and the opposition they met from the Siamese had lost them the race; although the belated orders were crucial, there has been criticism of the pace of the column's advance to the Ledge. Those that could explain this were killed in the campaign, in particular Lt.-Col. Moorhead.

In this first encounter battle, three companies essayed an outflanking move through the jungle. Captain Charlton, the Adjutant, forward with the companies, observed tanks ahead and hurried back to the bridge at Kampong Toh which was being strengthened for carriers. It was demolished instead and with anti-tank rifles the tanks were stopped. The disaster that next day overtook the 1/14th Punjabis and 2/2nd Gurkhas beyond Asun was averted.

Moorhead took up a position for the night behind the stream at Kampong Toh. "A" Company had fought with great heroism against infantry and tanks under Subahdar Sher Khan, and only eight men and an NCO returned. This very section was still a fighting formation at the end of the campaign.

Now the 5/14th Punjabis (Lt.-Colonel Stokes) from Penang had arrived in support with 10th Mountain Battery and one troop of 273rd Anti-Tank Battery from Jitra. They were disposed as rearguard nine miles north of Betong.

Thursday 11th December opened with heavy Japanese attacks at dawn. At 00.10 hours 2nd Lieutenant Mohamed Zarif Khan brought back "D" Company from the previous day's spirited action with the Japanese whose attacks intensified in the afternoon. Over at Jitra the disastrous breakthrough of tanks was taking place. Here the 3/16th held firm. Nevertheless, Moorhead now estimated, correctly as it transpired, that he was facing a brigade of Japanese and with increased pressure he sought at 20.00 hours, by telephone with Divisional HQ, permission to withdraw through 5/14th Punjabis. Murray-Lyon by then had a first-class crisis on his immediate front; he gave discretion to Moorhead to withdraw to Kroh which had to be held "to the last man and to the last round." One officer in that force recollected how often that order was given.

Moorhead decided to disengage at dawn next day, Friday 12th

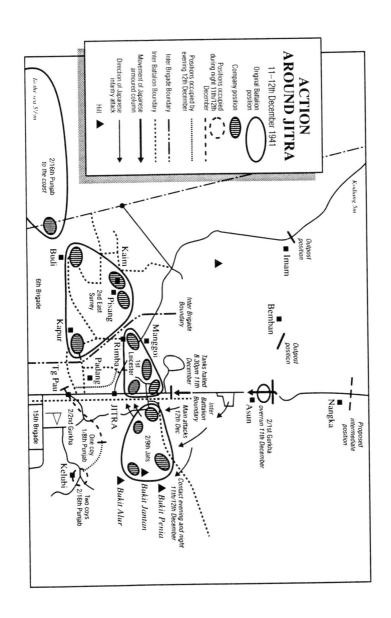

ACTION AROUND JITRA
11–12th December 1941

Original Battalion position

Company position

Positions occupied during night 11th/12th December

Positions occupied by evening 12th December

Inter Brigade Boundary

Inter Battalion Boundary

Movement of Japanese armoured column

Direction of Japanese infantry attack

Hill

December, the day of doom for Jitra. Heavy attacks commenced before dawn, and he gave orders for withdrawal for 09.00 hours. A fierce fight ensued in the withdrawal. "C" Company was surrounded and Lieutenant Casson in command and his second-in-command, 2nd Lieutenant Skyrnes, were killed in hand-to-hand fighting. Reduced to half its strength, the battalion disengaged during the afternoon and passed through the 5/14th position in front of Betong where the suspension bridge was blown. Moorhead was the last to leave with the carriers, rescuing a wounded lance-naik on his shoulders.

At midnight that day, Murray Lyon was relieved of his responsibility for Krohcol, and it came under III Corps direct, as he had repeatedly requested.

The 5/14th Punjabis withdrew next morning, Saturday 13th December, inside the frontier to Kroh after contact with the enemy.

The record of the 3/16th Punjabis, although like other battalions much milked, is noteworthy. Under the redoubtable and beloved commander, Moorhead, (later to be killed in Johore), it is one that deservedly received the praise bestowed on it by the historian of the Indian Army.*

On Sunday 14th December Brigadier Paris of 12th Brigade arrived to take over command of Krohcol, and reinforcements to protect the right flank of 11th Division now retreating to Gurun reached the front. The 5/2nd Punjabis guarded the bridge over the Muda at Bukit Pekaka east of Sungei Patani, and the 2nd Argyll and Sutherland Highlanders (Lt.-Col. I MacA Stewart) arrived at Baling on this day and Krohcol retired through them at 03.00 hours on Monday 15th December.

---

* Compton Mackenzie, *Eastern Epic*, p. 253.

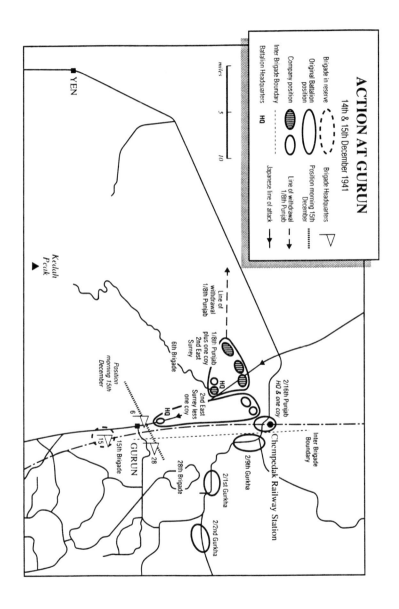

ACTION AT GURUN
14th & 15th December 1941

# CHAPTER IX

## The Kedah Front – The First Week

For the dispositions of 11th Division (6th and 15th Brigades with 28th Gurkha Brigade in reserve) we must look at the accompanying map. The weak spot in the position which was in many ways deficient was the right flank, defended by 2/9th Jats, which was some 2800 yards wide and 1000 yards in depth. The two forward companies were split by 1300 yards of paddy, and by a stream running north and south fringed with trees to a width of 50 yards on each bank affording a covered approach. The 1st Leicesters had about the same length of front covering the junction of two roads converging at Jitra, but it was easier to defend, and the Kamunting stream flowed east and west providing an obstacle to the attackers. The third battalion of this (15th) brigade, 1/14th Punjabis, had now been written off in front of Asun. 6th Brigade was responsible for the easier left flank covering some 10 miles of paddy and swamp that stretched to the railway and the sea. These dispersed dispositions, covering some 12 miles, instead of concentration in depth, are criticised by the *Official History*.* It should be recalled that efforts to flood the left flank of the Jitra line were frustrated by the War Office (page 14).

It was at about 20.00 hours on Thursday 11th December, after nightfall in the tropics, that the tanks which had broken through at Asun reached the main position in front of Jitra. Lieutenant Clarricoats of the Leicesters was sent forward with two men on receipt of reports to warn a forward patrol. He met the tanks and was last seen in hand-to-hand

---

* *The War Against Japan*, page 211–212.

fighting with the Japanese who had sprung from the leading tank. The tanks reached a demolition which failed to explode but 215th Anti-Tank Battery knocked out the tanks and blocked the road.

True to future form the Japanese were soon probing the Jat flank, and confused fighting took place as the night wore on, so much so that Brigadier Carpendale received reports, which it turned out were inaccurate, that Bukit Jantan and Bukit Alur in the right rear of the Jats had been occupied. We must remember that Murray-Lyon had at this time a crisis building up for Krohcol, but whether on this account he was unavailable or not, without reference to him, Carpendale called upon Brigadier Lay of 6th Brigade for help to bolster his right flank. Two companies of 2/16th and 1/8th Punjabis were then sent to extend the rear of the Sungei Bata held by 2/2nd Gurkhas with remnants of 2/1st Gurkhas from Asun, and were in position before dawn. Officers and troops were mostly inexperienced, and this was the first shock of war; as a result false and exaggerated reports to the Brigadier caused these moves to be made, which were not known to Murray-Lyon until the early morning of next day, Friday 12th December, and left him with no reserve. 2/9th Gurkhas (less 2 companies), the only reserve battalion now available, was brought up at noon astride the main road behind Tanjong Pau. As Murray-Lyon surveyed the situation that morning it was indeed critical, not only at Jitra but at the Patani Road. He had hoped to hold the Japanese north of Asun up to this day; now his line of communication at Kroh was threatened, the RAF had abandoned Alor Star airfield, and the morale of the troops was affected by the reverses and disasters of the last few days. He had already at 06.00 hours the previous day sent Lt.-Colonel Selby of 2/9th Gurkhas to reconnoitre the Gurun position some thirty miles back. He had no reserves and judged that his force, now facing the Japanese alone and extended, was in danger of destruction. He sought Heath's approval by telephone to withdrawal behind the Kedah river to Gurun. It was most unfortunate that Heath was on his way to Singapore for the purpose which we have noted (page 91) of pressing the need for withdrawal from Kelantan, and the request was passed to Percival in Singapore. Heath on arrival in Singapore urged Percival to give Murray-Lyon, who was on the spot and knew the tactical situation, the necessary permission; but Percival, deeming such an early withdrawal disastrous on morale, refused. In his own account* Percival states his action was "endorsed by the Far East War Council." Compton Mackenzie† does not resist the comment that "what value their approval or disapproval could have had in the tactical situation it is difficult, even impossible, to understand."

The opportunity for an orderly withdrawal had now passed, and the 11th Division was ordered to stand fast. It is now known that the Japanese 5th Division were planning for an attack with six battalions each side of the road at 03.00 hours next morning.

In the meantime, the Leicesters had repulsed attacks in the early hours of the morning, but the Japanese led with dash and daring penetrated east of the main road between the Leicesters and Jats in heavy rain about 06.00 hours, and overran an artillery observation post. Again Carpendale had recourse to 6th Brigade, and Lt.-Colonel Bates with his HQ and two remaining companies of 1/8th Punjabis prepared to restore the line. They were met with fire from the Jats to whose help they were coming. Lt.-Col. Bates went forward with his adjutant, Lieutenant Alabaster, to rally them and lead them into the attack. Both were killed and the attack failed in its purpose. The vital wedge between the Leicesters and Jats had been widened and a gap was being prised open. At midday "D" Company of the Jats fighting with great gallantry under Captain Holden and ordered to fight to the last was overrun, and he was killed. By 14.30 hours the Japanese had reached the 2/2nd Gurkhas on the line of the River Bata who held firm, and the Leicesters, assisted by a carrier platoon of the East Surreys checked a thrust that threatened to envelop the Leicester's right flank.

By now the Jat right flank was dangerously exposed, but it seems that Carpendale when Murray-Lyon visited him that afternoon was confident

---

* Percival, *War in Malaya*, page 133.

† *Eastern Epic*, page 256.

that the Japanese had been checked. He planned to withdraw the battered Jats from their exposed positions to fill the gap in the line from the Sungei Bata now partially covered by the Gurkhas and Punjabis. The Leicesters who had held firm under attack were to be concentrated west of the main road for counter attack next morning, assisted by the East Surreys, whom he envisaged should attack on the left or northern flank of the Leicesters. Murray-Lyon approved the plan except for the use of the East Surreys whom he needed badly for a reserve between Jitra and Alor Star.

Now misfortune came again, for Carpendale changed his mind, abandoned the approved plan, and instead ordered the Leicesters at 15.15 hours to retire to an oblique line, due south through Padang to link up with the Gurkhas on the Bata River and main road. Lt.-Col. Morrison of the Leicesters protested against the order: the new line had no depth, ran through sodden rice fields and there was no time to reconnoitre. The Leicesters felt secure in their prepared positions and had sustained only some thirty casualties. He was overruled, and the Leicesters took up their positions by 19.30 hours after dark in considerable confusion. The Jats retired to their new positions but one company on the right forward position received no orders for it was erroneously reported it had been overrun.

At 18.00 hours Murray-Lyon, ever staunch but hamstrung by orders, came up to see the situation at the front. He met scenes of confusion, even panic, around Tanjong Pau and at the Bata Bridge. At about this time Major Allsebrook was arriving with his 2/9th Gurkhas at Tanjong Pau to take up their reserve positions. He met a bedlam of lorries moving south, a gun in action on the road, heavy small-arms fire heard ahead, and a report of tanks over a bridge some 600 yards ahead. A body of men, probably survivors of Jats and 1/8th Punjabis, were rounded up to man a position but they fell back with two platoons of "C" Company of the Gurkhas.

Such was the near-chaotic situation that met the divisional general that evening, and so again at 19.30 hours Murray-Lyon sought Percival's approval to retire.

Approval this time came from Percival through III Corps accompanied by a message which stated:

> It is decided that your task is to fight for the security of North Kedah. It is estimated that you are only opposed by one Japanese division. Consider best solution may be to hold up the advance of the enemy tanks on good obstacles and dispose forces to obtain considerable depth on both roads and to obtain scope for your superior artillery. Reserves for employment in divisional area are being expedited.

These orders reached Murray-Lyon at 20.00 hours and he ordered a retirement at midnight to the south bank of the River Kedah whence he had sent Lt. Col. Selby who had returned from his task at Gurun to organise a defence and collect stragglers.

This permission came too late to avoid further severe losses. The withdrawal could take place only in appalling circumstances. Guns and transport got bogged down in the rain-sodden mire and had to be left. Two companies of Leicesters, one company of Jats, and a detachment of 2/1st Gurkhas did not receive the orders, and were still in position next morning. Some split up into small parties, some made their way west along the railway or to the coast and took boats to Sumatra. Lt.-Col. Morrison of the Leicesters evaded the enemy and got seven officers and 150 men across country to below Alor Star by dusk on the next day, 13th December.

The Gurkhas were the rearguard. After destroying the Bata bridge around 02.00 hours on 13th December, 2/2nd Gurkhas passed through 2/9th at 03.00 hours at their road block at Tanjong Pau. The Jats and Leicesters had not been seen. Major Allsebrook decided to delay the retirement of his 2/9th for another half hour. At 03.30 hours as he began to withdraw an attack came in east of the road. With his adjutant, Captain Graham-Hogg, and Captain Young, he led an attack to repulse it. The adjutant was mortally wounded, and Major Allsebrook wounded in the face whilst bandaging him in a monsoon drain, but the battalion managed to disengage in good order and reached Alor Star at 08.30 hours. Major Allsebrook subsequently received the DSO for his resolution in this rearguard action.

And so the retreat was on. It was to continue after a brief pause at Gurun with further losses, until 100 miles from Jitra on the Krian River, contact was broken and some respite afforded the weary, hungry and decimated battalions, a week after the attack began, on Wednesday 17th December.

The facts as set out may help to explain why an advance guard of only two battalions supported by a company of tanks had defeated a division. Out-generalled, out-manoeuvred, victims of faulty dispositions and long-range decisions, our forces new to battle were dispersed piecemeal, and individual acts of sacrifice and gallantry were of no avail. Kirby states that those responsible committed "every conceivable blunder".*

At Alor Star bridge Lt.-Colonel Selby was organising the defence of the Sungei Kedah crossings, and in his own vivid description:

> An ugly rush had started. Vehicles of all kinds were streaming through inextricably mixed in the columns of panic stricken men. Control of sorts was established, stragglers' posts were set up, but fear and panic were terribly infectious. Again and again men were gathered up and sorted out only to melt away as soon as the officers' backs were turned. It was not until the arrival of Captain Ridout with "A" Company 2/9th Gurkhas from Sungei Patani that some semblance of order could be restored. Our men were tired and hungry but they were cheerful; inspired by Ridout they bullied and cajoled the stragglers and put some spirit into them. A brigadier repeatedly moaned: "They've got tanks. They've got tanks." (It seems incredible that Army Intelligence did not expect the Japanese tanks that

---

* *Singapore: The Chain of Disaster*, p. 151.

caused such havoc in the first encounters beyond Jitra.)

It is a tribute to the small professional core of the division that they were able to pull it together and continue at all as a fighting force.

In these terrible circumstances what was left of 11th Division was got into position by about 09.00 hours on the morning of Saturday 13th December, after a bare week of war, on the Sungei Kedah south of Alor Star. Murray-Lyon, Colonel Steedman CRE and Lt.-Col. Selby were at this time gathered at the Alor Star bridge, ready mined with the last retreating troops coming through, when with daring audacity two Japanese motorcyclists appeared. The three officers dispatched one with their revolvers, and wounded the other who disappeared into the distance. Fearing a tank follow-up, Murray-Lyon now gave orders to blow the road and rail bridges, but the latter demolition was ineffective. A train was sent across to achieve the object but it passed over the damaged rails and sailed merrily on down the line to Taiping.

At 11.00 hours the enemy arrived and mortaring began. Colonel Steedman brought some anti-tank mines to be placed on the rail bridge. Captain Ridout, whom we have just mentioned, himself sprang forward to accomplish alone the perilous task amidst Japanese fire. He was hit and killed in this gallant but suicidal attempt. The loss of such men could be ill afforded. Short of stature, a Canadian beloved of his men, always at his best when things were at their worst, an outstanding officer was lost to the Gurkhas. His sacrifice was nobly supported by Subahdar Chambahadur and Lance-Naik Damarbahadur who with rifles and mortars then covered Captain Hart whilst he laid the mines on the floor of the bridge.

Night came again with pouring rain, and orders to fall back on the Gurun position. This, with the 4000-ft Kedah Peak dominating the road and rail and the country around, was potentially a strong one; but before the war though plans had been prepared little or nothing had been done to implement them, and very little had been possible since.

Here at 15.00 hours on Sunday 14th December, Heath was back to confer with Murray-Lyon at his headquarters some four miles south of Gurun and survey the sorry state of his main force. Murray-Lyon was blunt:

> 'What is our object, sir? Are we to hold the enemy north of Penang? Or protect the Kinta tinfields? Or what? It should be decided what we must hold and we should concentrate to defend it. I consider any withdrawal should be by long hops or by lorry. At present my men are quite unfit for a further series of dogfights.'*

Heath agreed with these views, and later that evening telephoned Percival in Singapore advocating a retirement to the Perak River to enable 11th Division to recover after standing on the Muda River line long enough to permit Penang to be evacuated. Although he would be aware from Heath's report of the state of the division no such permission was given; the order was that there would be no withdrawal further than the Muda River line without his sanction, and the immediate task was to hold Gurun.

The nub of the matter was Murray-Lyon's phrase: "we should concentrate". More explicitly this involved all our forces; and the failure, for whatever reason, to concentrate a fresh division, either the Australians from Mersing or the 9th Division from the east coast, in the light of the condition of 11th Division, led inevitably to an accelerated retreat to Singapore before reinforcements could arrive in time to be effective. This was a drastic and heroic solution which would have needed someone of exceptional insight and resolution to implement. It was too much to expect from a conventional and conscientious soldier with all the pressures and influences and authorities which surrounded him in Singapore. Nevertheless it can be said that in that one fateful week we lost Singapore in a brief two months' fighting.

---

* *History of 2/9th Gurkhas*, page 147.

*Gurun*

Whilst the commanders were conferring the troops were sorting themselves out and settling in around Gurun. Inaction prior to the war meant that they had now to prepare hurriedly their own defences. The Gurkha Brigade was the sole remaining cohesive fighting formation, and took up positions on the right flank covering a network of roads, and had a quiet day digging and wiring. On the trunk road and railway 6th Brigade were disposed – the 2/16th Punjabs around Chempedak railway station, the East Surreys between road and railway, and 1/8th Punjabis on the left flank at the foot of Kedah Peak. The 15th Brigade who had suffered most at Jitra and was now only some 600 men strong was in reserve.

After Jitra the Leicesters had been reduced as a fighting unit to negligible proportions. At Gurun this was to be the fate of the Surreys – the other of the two regular British battalions in the 11th Division. Though suffering from too long a boring tropical service, the two when combined after Gurun to form the British Battalion under the redoubtable Lt.-Col. Morrison of the Leicesters proved later at Kampar in Perak that, given a reasonable chance, they were a match for crack Japanese troops.

The 2nd Surreys arrived at Gurun fairly intact under the command of Major J. B. B. Dowling, MC, who at Jitra had taken over from Lt.-Col. E. W. Swinton, MC, injured in a motorcycle accident. During the campaign they lost a total of 13 officers, 3 warrant officers, and 169 men killed in action out of a total of 760. After Gurun they were reduced to ten officers and 260 other ranks. Many were left in the jungles and fields of Kedah; some got back, some were killed, and some were taken prisoner.

My memory goes back to an afternoon in the tense week that preceded the outbreak of the Japanese war when I saw emerge from the Selangor Club in Kuala Lumpur a batch of about a dozen young officers. I was told they were on their way north, recruits to join their regiments. How many of these seemingly carefree young men survived? It is a poignant recollection, for it is probable that most were swept away in these early disasters. It is the eternal tragedy of war – youth carried away before age withers them or the years condemn.

> When I remember all
> The friends so lik'd together
> I've seen around me fall
> Like leaves in wintry weather.*

The 2/16th Punjabis comprised only two companies. The Surreys lent one company to the other battalion in 6th Brigade – 1/8th Punjabis on their left across the main road. It was this that indirectly led to a particularly macabre event. Major Dowling, failing contact with the Punjabis and his other company, went with some of his officers that night to HQ of 6th Brigade to find out the position. There in a roadside bungalow these harassed officers conferred with the Brigade staff over their maps in the lamplight. Suddenly without warning a patrol of Japanese swarmed in. There were no survivors and no one to tell the tale of those desperate moments. But we anticipate; we must return to the troops as they settled in that morning and began hastily to fortify their positions in the all too brief breathing space.

Little time was given them to settle in, for at 14.00 hours on 14th December the Japanese were in contact again, and, to their surprise, in view of the demolition of bridges, with tanks. The 1/8th Punjabis on the main road, that battalion who had lost their colonel and senior officers two days before with heavy casualties, were understandably in no great shape, and began to retire under the pressure as the afternoon wore on, but Brigadier Lay himself led a counter-attack which prevented a disastrous breakthrough. The crossroads to the coast was now, however, in Japanese hands, and during the night at about 01.30 hours on the 15th December an attack came in down the road through the 1/8th

---

* "The Light of Other Days", Thomas Moore.

111

Punjabis and, as related, penetrated to the headquarters of the East Surreys and also 6th Brigade where the commanding officer of the East Surreys was killed with five of his officers and all the brigade staff. Brigadier Lay was absent from his HQ at the time conferring with Carpendale. At dawn a mixed force was hastily organised to support 6th Brigade. Confusion abounded. Our guns shelled the Punjabis and Surreys on account of inaccurate reports they had withdrawn. The Brigade Major of the Gurkhas, Major Bourne, was killed rallying a party of stragglers.

Whilst there was disarray on the left flank, on the right Lt.-Col. Selby of 2/9th Gurkhas had visited his adjoining unit, 2/16th Punjabis, and found them intact and standing firm. Major Vickers and a company of East Surreys had repulsed an attack with Japanese cyclists down the road but the heavy firing and the fog of war gave rise to alarm at the prospect of another breakthrough down the road and 1/8th Punjabis' new commander had withdrawn to the coast. Selby had heard the heavy firing but knew that the right flank was firm, so when a somewhat excited staff officer, a replacement for Major Bourne, arrived at 08.00 hours with the cry, "You must withdraw at once. The Brigade has been overrun and everyone is going back,"* Selby's reaction was sceptical and staunch, and on his own initiative he directed 2/1st Gurkhas, who were about to comply with the order to withdraw, to stand fast, in which its commanding officer (Lt.-Col. Fulton) fully concurred. Selby then sped on his way to 28th Brigade HQ to find two very apprehensive, indeed shaken, brigadiers, Lay and Carpendale, as well they might be. He reported that his flank was firm, and we now know that in fact elements of the East Surreys and Punjabis were still intact in their positions off the main road which was in enemy hands. Everything was being mustered to hold the main road, and west of Gurun village field and anti-tank guns were firing over open sights. Selby spoke against any precipitate retreat.

Murray-Lyon was soon on the spot and made a personal reconnaissance

---

* *History of the 2/9th Gurkhas*, page 149.

in a carrier, and reached 28 Brigade HQ about 09.00 hours where he had Selby's personal report and recommendation.

But for Selby's intervention there may have been a repetition of Jitra. There were now too few staunch veterans of such experience, and these events must be measured against the loss of senior officers in the catastrophes at Jitra and again at 6th Brigade and East Surrey HQ at Gurun.

In fact the position was much the same as at Jitra in the morning of the 12th. One flank had been penetrated whilst the other held firm. Selby recommended that his firm right flank buttressed by the Gurkhas should be used to strike the Japanese in their flank, and thus permit the retirement of the rest of the division. Murray-Lyon gave orders accordingly, and marked on the map the position at Sungei Lalang the division would hold. Selby was put in charge of all forces. Withdrawal was not to take place before 12.00 hours.

Selby ordered three companies of Gurkhas to occupy the railway line east of the main road facing west, thus forming a firm base behind which 6th Brigade could withdraw. He determined to hang on as long as he could, but at 13.30 hours as the volume of fire from his troops on the railway line indicated that further delay might endanger his mixed force, he gave orders for withdrawal to begin.

Throughout the afternoon the force moved south without molestation, but at dusk an all-too-frequently prematurely blown bridge necessitated a detour across the western main road, and here again the bridge had been blown. Selby gave orders to destroy all vehicles, which took two anxious hours, and the men then crossed the river by the light of his own station wagon, which was afterwards tipped into the river.

Selby had sent forward Major Winkfield of 2/1 Gurkhas to contact divisional HQ, which he reached at 23.50 hours. Murray-Lyon, anxious for the fate of Selby and his force, had proposed sending forward a support force, but Carpendale dissuaded him, saying: "I know Selby, sir. If anyone can make it, he can. If cut off he will fight his way out. If blocked on the roads he may come through the rubber and then bypass

113

your proposed bridgehead."*

Transport was sent forward when Winkfield reached the returning troops on a bicycle and arranged for the exhausted men (about 1000) to be ferried south.

Selby on arrival at Divisional HQ as the history of 9th Gurkhas records, "invoked the privilege of the battlefield to speak his mind on the Gurun action. The unauthorised withdrawals, panicky staff officers, the ahead-of-time demolitions, the general air of *sauve qui peut*, which did not please him."†

Murray-Lyon no doubt agreed, but he had other worries. His flanks at Kroh and Penang were threatened. Penang, defenceless and savagely attacked by air, was being evacuated. Whilst Selby was extricating the division Murray-Lyon gave orders at 13.00 hours, Monday 15th December, for the division to retire behind the River Muda south of Sungei Patani, a considerable obstacle, north of Penang. Here there would be rest and respite, for a while.

The Gurkhas and others were borne on through the night, and during the day of Tuesday 16th December the road south was an inviting target for the Japanese air force; sometimes blocked with triple-banked transport, sometimes crawling at two miles an hour. Fortunately they escaped air attack.

Heath came to visit his weary troops, took stock of the sorry position, and ordered withdrawal south of the Krian River obstacle below Penang (which was evacuated on that day) some 100 miles from their original positions at Jitra.

What were the results of a week's fighting? 11th Indian Division was in a parlous state. 15th Brigade mustered about 600 men. 6th Brigade had 10 officers and 260 men; 1/8th Punjabis had stragglers only; 2/16th Punjabis had lost 220 men; 28th Gurkha Brigade was in better shape; 2/2nd Gurkhas was intact except for 70 casualties; 2/1st Gurkhas had one complete company and remnants of others; 2/9th Gurkhas had 70

---

* *History of the 2/9th Gurkhas*, page 150.
† Ibid., page 151.

casualties. All four artillery units had lost guns, but only 80 Anti-Tank Regiment, which had been unable to extricate its two-pounders from forward positions at Jitra, was seriously depleted. The respite at Krian brought some dividends. On 17th December, 2/9th Gurkhas recovered 80 men of the carrier platoon which under Lts. Watson and Baxter had marched 50 miles with little or no food. Subahdar Chumbahadur, of whom we have heard, brought back 70 men of "A" Company. An entire company of 1/8th Punjabis got back from Gurun via the coast road. Forty men of 1/14th Punjabis made their way from the scene of their first clash at Changlun. "B" Company of 2/9th Jats under Subahdar Mohammed Hyat, cut off at Jitra, made their way through 80 miles of enemy-held territory. All honour to these men, British and Indian. They were a badly-needed boost to shaken morale.

On 17th December Brigadier Carpendale, who had been bombed in his headquarters at Parit Buntar, was evacuated to hospital. Colonel Selby was placed in command of 28th Brigade. As 2/9th Gurkha historian has written, "Colonel Selby, indomitable, sagacious and dynamic, had earned his promotion on the battlefield."*

We must look for a moment at the Kroh flank. Whilst the fight at Gurun was taking place, Kroh was abandoned, and this left open the Grik Road into the rear of III Corps at Kuala Kangsar. The possibility that the Japanese could use this road had been wrongly discounted by III Corps. The speed of the Japanese advance prevented planned demolitions, and whilst the heavy rain and poor surface prevented the Japanese tanks, the 42nd Infantry Regiment turned down this jungle road and vulnerable flank. A detachment of Argylls and armoured cars had been sent up the Grik road and contact was made on 16th December; meantime retiring through Baling and Kupang on the road south of the Muda the Argylls fought the first of their many spirited actions at Titi Karangan on Wednesday 17th December, to cover the withdrawal of 11th Division to the Krian River.

---

* *History of the 2/9th Gurkhas*, page 153.

On this day Krohcol was disbanded, and the Argylls and 5/2nd Punjabis were sent off to deal with the growing threat down the Grik Road, and the 3/16th and 5/14th Punjabis covered the east flank of 11th Division as it retired down the coast, for also on this day Percival gave Heath the permission he sought to retire behind the Perak River and travelled north to confer at Ipoh with him. The network of roads and extended front rendered a prolonged stand on the Krian River impossible with the forces available.

# CHAPTER X

## Krian to Slim River – The Next Three Weeks

The next phase of rearguard actions and retreats seemed to offer up hope that 11th Indian Division might be permitted to work out its own salvation until relief arrived, but two weeks later it culminated in the catastrophic breakthrough at Slim River on 7th January which shattered any such hopes, and scattered the exhausted division in disarray.

Whilst in Malaya these dire events were being enacted, elsewhere the widespread Japanese operations were proceeding according to or in advance of their plans. Hong Kong was now under close investment, the mainland evacuated, and the island to be invaded on the night of 18/19th December and to fall on Christmas Day. The Philippines were invaded. Guam had fallen and Wake Island was to follow, leaving Pearl Harbor as the nearest American Pacific base, and Midway as an advanced and perilous post, six months later to be the scene and centre of the decisive battle and turning point of the war. The Americans meanwhile could only hang on and try desperately to reinforce a lifeline to Australia, impotent to affect the issue in South-East Asia. On 15th December the Japanese occupied the vital airfield at Victoria Point in Burma, thereby cutting off the reinforcement route for fighter aircraft which now had to be sent a long way round by sea.

Winston Churchill on HMS *Duke of York* with his Chiefs of Staff, except General Sir Alan Brooke who remained in London "to mind the shop", were travelling across the Atlantic to confer with our new American allies, and Churchill was busy inditing vast cosmic memoranda for further action but with little relevance to the immediate fate and fortunes of the meagre Malayan garrison. General Sir John Dill was with him and might well have been reflecting on his own unheeded warnings that it would take three months to reinforce Malaya. This distinguished and high-souled officer, now worn and exhausted, was witnessing the realisation of his forebodings, and had handed the reins to the alert, tough and battle-tested Brooke, who at this critical time assumed the office which he was to occupy and adorn to the end of the war. Late in the day Brooke brought to the task, amongst other qualities, an ability to stand up to and apply a much needed corrective to some of the strategical ideas of his dominating and illustrious master.

Percival, in considering his strategy in the light of the first week's events, had now to fear seaborne landings on both east and west coasts. To ensure the safe arrival of reinforcements by sea the airfields of Ipoh, Kuala Lumpur and Port Swettenham in central Malaya must be kept from capture and use by enemy planes. He had to hold the Japanese, as he saw it, in Northern Malaya as long as possible. Heath, as we have said, sought fresh troops, in particular the Australians at Mersing, but Percival in view of the seaborne dangers on the east coast did not consider he could spare them. We have stated that on 17th December, before travelling north to Ipoh to visit his commanders, Percival authorised Heath to withdraw behind the Perak River, but after conferring with Heath and a personal reconnaissance he saw that, as the river runs north and south parallel with road and rail communications, it was a position difficult to defend. He now agreed to positions being selected down to Tanjong Malim on the Selangor border for maximum delay with these minimum forces.

The sole reinforcement of 11th Division – 12th Brigade comprising the 2nd Argyll and Sutherland Highlanders and 5/2nd Punjabis, a well-trained brigade which had been in Malaya for some time – had been sent, as we have seen, to hold the Japanese thrust down the Grik Road to the Perak River, whilst the Gurkha brigade was again ready for a fight and acted as a rearguard on the main trunk road and railway, behind which the rest of 11th Division crossed the Perak River. The Argylls bore the brunt of the Grik Road fighting, exhibiting what well-trained, well-led troops, given reasonable odds could do against the enemy, and on Monday 22nd December after successful encounters around the Chenderosh Lake with the Punjabis, they withdrew through the Gurkhas at Lawin during the night. The road and rail bridges over the Perak River were destroyed in the early hours of the morning by the Gurkhas, who were then sent south to safeguard the Blanja Bridge area in the mining flats south of Ipoh.

Despite these stout efforts, the state of the 11th Division was graphically described by the staff officer at this time when the Perak River was being crossed:

> It can't go on like this. The troops are absolutely dead-beat. The only rest they're getting is that of an uneasy coma as they squat in crowded lorries which jerk their way through the night. When they arrive they tumble out and have to get straight down to work. I've seen them. They're just stupid with sleep and have to be smacked before they can "connect" with the simplest order. They move like automatons, or cower down as a Jap aeroplane flies 200 feet above them. They're bound to crack soon.

It is certainly a pity that by now, and with such reports, a radical solution of bringing over the 9th Division from the east coast was not decided upon. It would have been possible to have had them in position for Slim with all the consequences that might have flowed from such a relief to 11th Division.

On 24th December Murray-Lyon was replaced in command of 11th Division by Brigadier Paris, and Lt.-Col. Stewart took over command of 12th Brigade. Lt.-Col. Moorhead of 3/16th Punjabis from Kroh took over the composite 6/15th Brigade. Murray-Lyon was the sole sacrifice offered for the failures of the first week. It may well seem that this was harsh. His experience and qualities of unruffled calm, always on the spot when the critical situation called, were all badly needed. His successor was to be replaced after Slim River.

The Japanese had advanced so fast they had by now become considerably strung out. Whilst the 11th Division was on the Krian, the Japanese advance troops with their van of soldiers on bicycles, purloined en route, were at Prai, and the remainder of the two divisions was widely extended back to Singora where the Guards division was in bivouac. From now on, however, Japanese air action from Siam and northern Malayan airfields which had hitherto been negligible grew in intensity, and the Argylls, Punjabis and Gurkhas, huddled together in billets in the village of Salak behind the Perak River through faulty staff work, were heavily bombed with many casualties.

General Yamashita had expected the British to make a stand on the Perak River Line, and its abandonment only gave a short pause to the Japanese advance. On Friday/Saturday, 26/27th December, 12th Brigade now joined by 4/19th Hyderabads from Kelantan under Stewart fought a sharp action at Chemor, and on the night of the 27th withdrew from the important town and tin mining centre of Ipoh. By now they had been in action almost continuously for twelve days, and General Paris was concerned about his old brigade, about whose condition an eye-witness has reported:

> The troops were very tired. Constant enemy air attacks prevented them from obtaining any sleep by day. By night they either had to move, obtaining such sleep as was possible in crowded lorries, or had to work on preparing yet another defensive position. The resultant physical strain of day and night fighting, of nightly moves or work, and the consequent lack of sleep was cumulative and finally reached the limit of endurance. Officers and men moved like automata and often could not grasp the

simplest order.*

On the other hand, the Japanese could always feed in fresh troops, and so often ours hoped for respite but it was denied to them.

South of Ipoh a strong position had been prepared by the reconstructed 6/15th Brigade at Kampar. On the east of the road the hills rose and dominated the landscape. Spread out in front and to the west were the mining flats, and from the point of view of the gunners observation was ideal.

12th Brigade was to have a further test before this line was reached, and amongst the flat open mining country south of Ipoh in the Gopeng-Dipang area, the Argylls' obsolete thin-skinned armoured cars went into action against Japanese tanks. The legendary Sergeant "Dinkie" Darroch DCM gallantly met his death leading such a forlorn hope, but it was due to such actions and the stout work of officers of men of the Scots and Punjabis battalions that no breakthrough occurred before the vital bridge in front of the Kampar position was blown. Thus in the evening of Monday 29th December this brigade, which had by now lost about 550 men and nearly all its armoured cars and carriers, passed through the 28th Gurkha Brigade, as with a valedictory jest, Stewart remarked to Selby: "I've come to hand over the business to you. It's a running concern." They passed through to Bidor for a brief rest.

Quite high hopes had been placed on the commanding Kampar position, and anyone today traversing the road that runs along the foot of Bujant Melaka (4070ft) and its foothills with the wide, almost coverless and swampy mining flats stretching to the west of the road can readily appreciate the natural advantages for its defence, but the fatal weakness, the Achilles' heel, from now on was the threat from the sea. Soon the much-tried 12th Brigade was called on again to meet this threat, and in the event the delay at Kampar was only a brief pause of a few days before the sad procession south began again. Meanwhile, however, we shall see what happened at Kampar.

---

* *Eastern Epic*, page 243.

*Kampar*

The composite 6/15th Brigade, after some time for recuperation, defended Kampar. The newly formed British Battalion composed of the East Surreys and Leicesters was now in the van, occupying three ridges on the slopes of Bujang Melaka – Thompson's, Green and Cemetery Ridge in front of Kampar village. The remainder of the 6/15th Brigade under Brigadier Moorhead, comprising 1/14th, 3/16th, and 2/16th Punjabis with a combined Jat/Punjabi battalion in reserve, defended Kampar village and the area around the railway which branched off west across the mining flats. The Gurkha brigade held the encircling road round the east of Bujang Melaka, supported by 155 Field Regiment RA (Lanarkshire Yeomanry), a fine unit which appeared so optimistic of a prolonged stand that its commander, Lt.-Colonel Murdoch, published in routine orders that in future no fowls were to be bought for the pot, but were to be kept for laying! There is evidence that, despite their appalling trials, the morale and spirits of the troops were still steady, though they were thin on the ground.

The 6/15th Brigade had had a week's respite to prepare positions. On 31st December the Japanese probed the Gurkha positions on the east flank, but this and subsequent attempts to penetrate were repulsed by these stalwart troops. On that day too, ominously, air reconnaissance reported small convoys of boats off Pangkor Island ready for a seaborne stroke, all of which caused Paris to make dispositions to protect his west flank. It was at 07.00 hours on 1st January 1942 that the main attack came in on the British battalion and continued throughout the day. Despite a stubborn defence, the Japanese had penetrated the northern edge of the foremost ridge, Thompsons, by nightfall, and during the next day, 2nd January, they had progressed as far as Green Ridge by midday, and threatened to overwhelm the right flank of the battalion. Brigadier Moorhead came up to Lt.-Colonel Morrison of the British battalion and ordered a counter attack by the Jat/Punjabi battalion under Colonel Tester. The Gujar and Sikh company led with great gallantry by

122

ACTION AT KAMPAR
30th December to 2nd January 1941
Battalion pattern
Company locality
Brigade Headquarters
Japanese line of advance and attack
Reconnaissance 31st December
Sungei Siput
Dipang
British Battalion
1/14th Punjab
3/16th Punjab
2/16th Punjab
KAMPAR
Jat/Punjab Battalion in Brigade reserve
Thompsons Ridge
Green Ridge
Cemetry Ridge
Outpost coy withdrawn night 30th/31st December
2/9th Gurkha
Withdrawn 30th December
Sungei Siput
G. Bujang Melaka
4070ft
2/2nd Gurkha withdrawn 1st January
withdrawn 1st January
Reconnaissance 31st December
Sahum
2/1st Gurkha replaced by 2/9th Gurkha 30th December

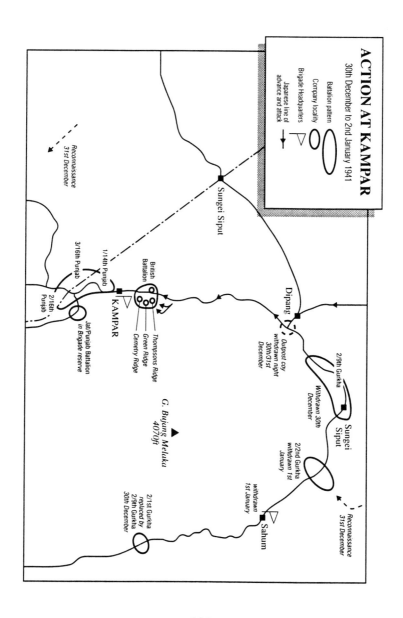

Captain Graham and Lieutenant Lamb, who were both killed, restored the position on Green Ridge with heavy casualties.

It is sad to record that the stout efforts of this brigade which had been much mauled at Jitra were of little avail. Brigadier Moorhead needed fresh troops to hold his position, and now the menace was materializing from Telok Anson on the flank. This decided General Paris to pull out of the Kampar position on the night of 2nd January, and it was the old faithfuls, 12th and 28th Brigades, which held positions at Tapah and Ayer Kuning on the Telok Anson branch road to enable 6/15th Brigade to disengage, which they did without much difficulty, such was the difference from Jitra and Gurun. There was no tank breakthrough and the tired troops retired in good heart after their valorous efforts. They moved via Sungkai and Slim to the rear at Tanjong Malim on the borders of Selangor, and the whole weary process of co-ordination of rearguards and demolition of bridges was repeated until the 12th Brigade on the night of 3/4th January found itself once again in the front line at Slim with 28th Gurkha Brigade in support.

It may well be asked at this juncture: could the Navy do nothing to prevent these sea flank "end-runs", as they came later to be termed by the Americans from baseball parlance? The roving and comprehending eye of the Prime Minister had not failed to seize on this, and on 9th January he enquired of Wavell, now ABDA Commander and later, dissatisfied with his reply, had recourse, with some asperity, to the First Sea Lord. The Japanese command of the air rendered our patrol craft vulnerable, and only the Dutch had submarines. Wavell reported to the Prime Minister on 10th January 1942: "Only three Dutch submarines are now operating in Malaya and arrangements have already been made of the first one returned from other operations to operate off the west coast between Penang and Selangor, commencing January 12th."

The failure to destroy the craft at Penang was a gift to the Japanese of which they took full advantage, but the possibility of the use of submarines, perhaps less vulnerable from the air, was introduced by

Wavell after his conference with the Navy, and it may be asked whether more might have been done with these craft. At all events, the coastal invasions were to continue with lamentable results, particularly in Johore, without hindrance from the slender forces of the Navy.

On 3rd January the first reinforcements, the 45th Indian Brigade, arrive safely in Singapore, but these troops were so raw and untrained they were not fit for battle.

It will convey some idea of what might have been, given adequate forces and equipment, if one reads the description of the performance of the British Battalion of which the East Surreys then formed a part, in the account of its conduct in the engagement at Kampar over the New Year, 1942, in the *History of the East Surrey Regiment* by David Scott Daniell:

> At Ipoh there was a three-day respite, during which drastic changes were made to knit together the battered units and formations of the (11th) Division. The 6th and 15th Infantry Brigades were amalgamated, and on 20th December the 2nd East Surrey and the 1st Leicesters were merged to form the "British Battalion". While the reorganization was going on, small parties of officers and men of both battalions who had got away from Gurun reported, and eventually the strength of the British Battalion was brought up to war establishment at 760 all ranks.
>
> The Commanding Officer and the Second-In-Command of the British Battalion, Lt.-Colonel C. E. Morrison, MC, and Major R. G. Harvey, were both from the Leicesters. The Surreys provided the Adjutant, Major C. O'N. Wallis, the Officer Quartermaster, Captain W. G. Gingell, MBE, MM. A & B Companies were Leicesters, and C & D Surreys, commanded respectively by Captain P. A. C. K. Bruckmann and Captain W. G. Vickers. From the start this integration of the Leicesters and

Surreys was a remarkable success, and the esprit de corps and fighting spirit of the British Battalion was of the highest order.

The new 6/15th Indian Infantry Brigade, commanded by Brigadier Moorhead, was now made up of the British Battalion, 1/14th Punjab and a combined battalion of Jats and Punjabis. The Brigade had abundant transport, but it was short of Bren guns and mortars. However, Vickers and Lewis guns were issued and deficiencies in clothing and boots were made up. But most important of all was the new morale of the British Battalion, Leicesters and Surreys were ready and willing to meet the enemy again.

The opportunity soon came. On 23rd December the 6/15th Brigade was ordered to take up positions at Kampar, some forty miles to the south, where it was intended to halt the Japanese advance. The Kampar position was a semi-circular perimeter of four miles covering the trunk road running south. It was a most promising defensive position for a full division but the 6/15th Brigade was all that was available to man it.

The British Battalion was deployed to hold the northern face of the perimeter, with the Punjabi battalions holding the west and southern flanks. The eastern flank was secured by a steep jungle-clad hill nine miles long and six wide, rising to a height of four thousand feet. The two Leicester companies of the British Battalion held three ridges on the east of the road: Thompson's, Green and Cemetery Ridges. "C" Company of the Surreys, under Captain Bruckmann, held a position eight hundred yards long on the west of the road, and "D", under Captain Vickers, was in reserve with the carrier platoon. C Company had a good field of fire of twelve hundred yards across open tin-mining country.

The British Battalion spent ten days in the Kampar positions, with a great deal of hard work at first, preparing defensive positions by clearing the ground, digging and wiring. Many reconnaissances were made into the hills to the east to discover the most likely approaches from the flank. The hills were steep and thick with jungle, but there were many paths by which the enemy could approach. Japanese aircraft flew over often, and it was only too clear that before long their ground forces would be upon them. One cause of anxiety was the many Chinese refugee camps in the neighbourhood, for the Japanese often disguised their scouts as Chinese.

Christmas Day came and Captain Gingell lived up to his reputation as the perfect quartermaster by producing a traditional Christmas dinner for the British Battalion, with turkey and an assortment of local poultry, and a free issue of beer. The memory of that dinner had to last the Battalion through the bitter years of captivity and privation. There were some casualties over Christmas from mortar fire, so close was the enemy, but their attack did not come in. On Boxing Day three officers, Captains Cater and Hoard and Lieutenant Bobe, rejoined the Battalion and were sent back to Kuala Lumpur to refit, where they were kept at Corps Headquarters. A few days later four officers and ninety other ranks reported for duty. Some had come from hospital whilst others had made their way back from Gurun through the Japanese lines.

The attack on the Kampar positions began at seven o'clock on the morning of New Year's Day 1942. It opened with the heavy shelling of Thompson's Ridge, after which a full-scale attack was launched against the front of the positions and Thompson's and Green Ridge from the jungle on the east flank. The British Battalion stood fast and drove back the screaming Japanese with steady fire; the only success gained by the enemy was a precarious footing on Green Ridge, from which they were repulsed but returned again. On this eastern flank there was only a thirty-yard strip of open ground between the jungle and the positions. Throughout the battle the enemy concentrated on attacking the ridges from the jungle.

By nine o'clock the enemy had regained some of Green Ridge and one of the Leicesters' platoons was hard-pressed from flank and rear. Colonel Morrison therefore ordered Captain Vickers to counter-attack with two platoons of "D" Company. Captain Vickers led the counter-attack with such spirit that he routed the enemy and restored the situation.

Throughout the 1st January the Japanese attack continued against the ridges on the east of the position. Pressure eased off during the afternoon, but a further attack was launched at five o'clock, in which Captain Thomas of the Leicesters was among the killed. Fighting stubbornly under extreme pressure the Leicester platoons valiantly stood their ground. At dusk the enemy attacks ceased and the British Battalion could take stock of its position.

Casualties had been comparatively light in the hard day's fighting, except in "A" Company, and the line was secure apart from the northern edge of Thompson's Ridge which remained in enemy hands. A Japanese report on the battle shows how it appeared to the other side, although the intelligence was at fault on the nationality of the troops opposing them:

For the first time in the West Coast campaign two complete Japanese divisions were employed simultaneously, but in spite of all they could do they were unable to dislodge the Australians from any but the most advanced positions. During the day three onslaughts were repulsed by the defending troops.

During the night there was a heavy artillery duel, and the enemy concentrated their shelling on Thompson's Ridge. At dawn their attack was renewed against the ridges, but the Leicester platoons resolutely held on, most inspiringly led on Thompson's Ridge by Lieutenant Newland. Eventually, however, the enemy got in between the positions and at least one platoon position had to be abandoned. A volunteer runner got through to battalion headquarters with a message from Lieutenant Newland, and once again Captain Vickers was ordered to counter-attack and clear the enemy from Thompsons Ridge.

Private Graves, who knew a route through the difficult country, volunteered to guide the counter-attacking party. He led them through the Japanese-infested area to a position from which the attack could be launched. Captain Vickers had a platoon and a section of "D" Company for the counter-attack, and the charge was made with the greatest dash and determination. Captain Vickers shot a Japanese officer at three yards' range and seized his company standard, while his men slew twelve of the enemy with the bayonet and routed the rest.

Half this gallant party were killed in the charge, and the enemy higher up the ridge immediately counter-attacked. Three immediate awards for gallantry were made; the Military Cross to Captain Vickers, the DCM to Sergeant Craggs, and the MM to Private Graves, who not only led the force through the enemy positions, but displayed dauntless courage throughout the day, bringing in wounded men under fire and refusing to be taken back when he himself was wounded.

The Kampar position had been stoutly held for two days, but in the evening of January 2nd news was brought that the enemy was massing troops for a heavier attack. Moreover, the Japanese had fared better in other parts of the line, and it was obvious that the Kampar position could not be held indefinitely. Accordingly orders were given to begin to thin out that night; then to abandon the forward positions and fall back through the 28th Brigade. This was done, though not without difficulty, for the Japanese were attacking heavily at the time. They actually got inside "C" Company's position in the darkness, but the company fought them off and withdrew according to plan.

The enemy was collecting in strength on the road at the wire, and Captain G. H. Green of the Leicesters took his Pioneers up to prevent any rush down the road, and to cover the removal of anti-tank guns. "A" and "D" Companies only got away after violent hand-to-hand fighting, and "B" Company which was acting as rear-guard, had to engage several pockets of Japanese before they could extricate themselves.

This battalion account does not mention the gallant charge of the party from the Jat Punjabi battalion which prevented its right flank being overwhelmed, and enabled it to disengage, in which that brave officer Captain Graham was killed.

For two days the British and Indian troops had withstood the onslaught of Japanese crack regiments, as formidable as any in the world, and the battle honours of the Surrey and Leicestershire Regiments rightly record the Battle of Kampar – perhaps the only encounter in the whole campaign that deserves to be dignified by that title, for the rest were skirmishes or debâcles.

At Waterloo the soldiers withstood a day of hard pounding, and the arrival of the Prussians decided the day for the Allies. On that hill at Kampar there were no reserves, and the turning of the sea flank was decisive anyway. It does not appear that the Japanese used their effective little tanks, but it seems that if they had the Surreys and others defending the road would have repelled them. The action at Kampar does indeed deserve an honourable mention, as a place where sound dispositions, a good defensive position, leadership and morale were the order of the day. It is sad to record that such elements so seldom prevailed in Malaya.

We have soon to describe the debâcle at Slim River where tired troops were overrun by tanks in the dark night, and faulty dispositions contributed to the disaster.

*The East Coast*

We must now consider the East Coast – that idyllic backwater of Malaya, where in the halcyon pre-war days the expatriate, to employ the modern jargon, could seek a glimpse of the old, the "real" Malaya, the unchanging East as it seemed. When work permitted he could take a passage in one of the little Straits Steamship boats with their Malay names, smelling of spice and diesel oil, and sail from Singapore up the quiet east coast to the little ports of Kuantan or Tumpat in Kelantan. He might travel by the jungle railway that branched off at Gemas through Kuala Lipis to Kota Bahru or he could wind his way in a car over the twisting road through the Semangko Pass to where the road ended at Temerloh on the Pahang River, or through the "Gap" near Fraser's Hill, the hill resort carved out by the Government mainly for European relaxation, through jungle-covered passes and down valleys "sleepy with the flow of streams" amidst hills the silence of which was broken only by the distant call of the wah-wah; he could cross by the ferry over the Pahang River at Jerantut and travel on by road to Kuantan to savour the silence and solitude of the golden beaches of Beserah or turn down to the old-world town of Pekan where the Sultan of Pahang resided. He might see in its quiet shady streets some minor raja strolling along stroking his cheroot and eyeing the "*orang puteh*" with what could be interpreted as a suspicious glance. Those Pahang Malays were very independent as could be learnt when chugging up the Pahang River to Temerloh on the Government launch *Teo Ann*, a slow meandering process as passengers were landed with stores at the *kampongs* en route.

With communications so sparse, defence and delay of an invading force over the main central range should have been relatively easy, but there were complications, or perhaps they are better described as distractions. The Air Force, at a time when this arm of the services and the others were ill-co-ordinated and even in open dispute, embarked on a programme of airfield construction without consideration of the Army's problem of defending them. First in 1936, at Kuantan, some nine miles from the coast west of the Kuantan River and ferry, an airfield replaced what was once a rubber estate. In Kelantan airfields were constructed at Kota Bahru near the beaches of Badang and Sabak, at Gong Kedah further south near Kuala Besut, and at Machang inland and south of Kota Bahru.

Kirby is convinced that with the exiguous forces available to Percival he was wrong to post the 9th Division at Kota Bahru and Kuantan, and that it should have been concentrated with 11th Division for defence of the West. He argues that as it was quite clear that the strength of the Air Force would not enable it to carry out its role of operating a short range strike aircraft from the forward fields, they were no longer of any value to the defence, and that it was a waste of valuable and much-needed troops to employ them in the hopeless task of defending the east coast airfields. He suggests that all that was required were troops such as the State battalions, employed on aerodrome defence, to cover the necessary demolition of airfields, destroying culverts and bridges, blocking the passes, which the nature of these little-developed States would permit. He contends that such a plan would have gained the Japanese very little more in time and effort and freed 9th Division to battle beside 11th Division as III Corps west of the range.* He further contends that when the position at Jitra was known, and Kota Bahru lost, then was the time to bring over 9th Division to provide just that relief and support the 11th Division needed.† This is a cogent and authoritative argument, and we shall see how in a vain attempt to deny Kuantan airfield to the Japanese the 22nd Brigade was to lose one-third of its strength.

The 8th Brigade at Kota Bahru had been overpowered as we have related. With one battalion, 3/17th Dogras, holding nine miles of beach in front of Kota Bahru on the Badang and Sabak beaches, there is little wonder. Another battalion, 2/10th Baluchs, had held a twenty-four-mile stretch as far as the river near Gong Kedah airfield. Two battalions, 1/13th Frontier Force Rifles and 2/12th Frontier Force Regiment, were in

---

* *Singapore: The Chain of Disaster*, page 114.
† Ibid., pp. 169–170.

reserve. The 4/19th Hyderabads had been dispatched from 12th Brigade to reinforce, but by 22nd December all these forces had been extricated from Kelantan and were in the Kuala Lipis/Jerantut area, and it must be remembered that it was to urge this necessary withdrawal that had led Heath, at a critical time for the forces in Kedah, to journey all the way to see Percival in Singapore; events which add force to Kirby's argument.

At Kuantan it was now the turn of Brigadier Painter's 22nd Brigade, to which the missing battalion, 2/12th Frontier Force Regiment, had returned after evacuation of Kelantan, to shoulder the onerous responsibility of meeting the menace not only of a sea landing but of avoiding being cut off by a Japanese thrust through the jungle and estate tracks in the State of Trengganu.

Whilst the 11th Division in the west was retreating and settling in at Kampar, this thrust from the north materialised, and on 30th December the brigade was under heavy pressure with a wide arc of territory to cover. Japanese aircraft now began to attack unhindered, yet the useless aerodrome imposed its dire influence on command counsels. General Heath was anxious that the brigade's strength should not be dissipated defending the airfield at Kuantan with slender forces which demanded deployment east of the Kuantan River with only a vulnerable ferry crossing. General Percival considered, however, that the first priority was denial of the airfield to the Japanese which he hoped could be achieved for over a week to 10th January, an extremely optimistic hope. There appears to have been a misunderstanding here between himself and Heath, for on 29th December the latter wrote to General Barstow:

> General Percival is in entire agreement with me that the preservation of the entity of 22nd Brigade is of greater importance than the imposition of two or three days' delay upon the enemy advance to Kuantan airfield... I therefore still adhere to the view that from the strategical aspect it is definitely wrong to risk the loss of a large number of vehicles and the mutilation of one-third of the force by attempting to fight the enemy east of

the river. I therefore wish to issue an instruction to the Commander 22nd Brigade to redispose his brigade in accordance with the view expressed above.*

The priorities were clear, and Barstow instructed Painter as follows:

The preservation of the future fighting efficiency of your brigade under existing circumstances is of greater importance than imposing a delay of a few more days in the denial of the airfield to the enemy.

Accordingly on the morning of 31st December, Painter proposed to withdraw to Maran along the road to Jerantut on the night of 31st December/1st January, and so informed Barstow who replied:

It is of the utmost importance that your brigade with its valuable material should not be jeopardised. Within the limitations the above imposes, you will ensure that every advantage is taken to hold the enemy and deal him such blows as opportunity offers. The question of denial of ground particularly applies to the Kuantan airfield. It is highly desirable that this should continue to be denied to the enemy. Reinforcements are shortly expected in Malaya, and their safe arrival might be hampered if enemy fighters had the use of the airfield.

This rather equivocal order exemplifies the horrible dilemma the wretched aerodrome imposed. The harassed Painter moved the 2/12th Frontier Force Rifles on this last day of the year to defend the airfield perimeter and ordered the Garhwalis west of the river during the night of 31st December/1st January, who then destroyed the ferry and moved, after crossing with great difficulty and loss, to the airfield. But now, on 1st January, Painter was told that for strategical reasons it was important

---

* Percival, *War in Malaya*, page 270.

to deny the use of the airfield for as long as possible, and particularly until 5th January. We can sympathise with the unfortunate Brigadier and his troops, and these changes and conflicting orders illustrate the nature of the task imposed on him and his brigade.

The situation in the West probably saved them from complete destruction, for the evacuation of Kampar released 22nd Brigade from their obligation, as it became necessary to concentrate 9th Division behind the Pahang River preparatory to withdrawal from Pahang and eventually joining up with 11th Division west of the main range. On 2nd January orders to retire to Jerantut were at last given.

Nevertheless the orders and counter-orders, delays and doubts, were to cause this unhappy brigade to suffer just those losses which Heath feared. The Japanese followed up as usual with vigour, and there was close fighting on the aerodrome as the retirement was taking place. Lt.-Col. Cumming of 2/12th Frontier Regiment was wounded in a hand-to-hand encounter, and was later awarded the V.C. for his conduct, during the evening of 3rd January as the final withdrawal from the ill-fated aerodrome was in process. Reduced to two-thirds of its strength the brigade retired down the long road to Jerantut some eighty miles away, and on the night of 6th–7th January, whilst the Slim River disaster was being enacted in the west, in pouring rain the Jerantut ferry took them over the Pahang River, and they moved to Bentong at the foot of the pass to the main range ready to cross in conformity with the retreat of 11th Division in the west.

At last there was a prospect of 9th and 11th Divisions operating together in close communication on the West under III Corps, but the disaster of Slim River doomed the 11th Division and they were never destined to fight together as a corps. 9th Division were next to join the Australians in the last stand on the Muar River Line on the mainland.

*ANZAC Day in peacetime Singapore, 25 April 1941. Australian and New Zealand troops on the parade ground before marching past the Cenotaph.*

*British Troops arriving in Malaya*

136

Close up of the C in C, Far East, Air Chief Marshal Sir Robert Brooke-Popham.

Lieutenant-General A.E. Percival, General Officer Commanding Malaya at the time of the Japanese attack.

*On his way to the N.E.I. General Wavell stops off in Singapore with Lt.-Gen. Pownall.*

*Lt.-Gen. L.V. Bond (front right) and behind Maj.-Gen. Gordon Bennett reviewing Australian troops.*

*The battleship HMS PRINCE OF WALES leaves Singapore on 8 December 1941 in search of a Japanese convoy. With no fighter protection the battleship and her companion HMS REPULSE were vulnerable to Japanese air attack.*

*HMS PRINCE OF WALES (upper) and REPULSE after being hit by Japanese torpedoes off Khartoum on 10.12.41. British destroyer in foreground.*

*European Women and children evacuate from Malaya.*

*Asiatic Despatch Riders are seen in rough Malayan country.*

*Indian gunners in action in a Malayan rubber plantation.*

*An artillery unit moving up to the front through typical Kedah paddy fields.*

*3 Buffalos take off over a Blenheim Bomber.*

*One of Singapore's Big Guns – blast has flattened an iron fence.*

*Royal Engineers prepare to blow up a bridge in Malaya during the British retreat to Singapore. In the background Chinese rickshaws, loaded with rice from abandoned government stocks, are crossing the bridge.*

*Japanese troops mopping up in Kuala Lumpur during the advance through Malaya.*

143

*A column of smoke from burning oil tanks rises above the deserted streets of Singapore.*

*A civilian casualty who was killed by a bomb splinter during a Japanese air attack on Singapore.*

*Lieutenant-General Percival and his party carrying the Union Jack on their way to surrender Singapore to the Japanese, 15 February 1942.*

*Japanese troops parading near Battery Rd., Singapore.*

# CHAPTER XI

## Slim River and Retreat to Johore

General Percival laid it down that III Corps held the Japanese until 15th January, north of Kuala Kubu, short of which the main road had a branch leading up over the main range through the Gap to Raub and Jerantut, though at the same time he appreciated that seaborne threats might accelerate the timing of retirement.

There is little doubt that by now relations between III Corps and GHQ Malaya were greatly strained, and brigade and battalion commanders must have felt a want of confidence in the high command. This is best illustrated by contrasting the message sent about this time by Percival to III Corps which expressed his view that "our young and inexperienced troops are now getting their second wind. While our policy for the moment is to keep our Forces in being as fighting formations, this does not mean that casualties must always be avoided. Provided greater losses are inflicted on the enemy, casualties can and should be expected within reasonable limits. Our Forces are now becoming more concentrated than hitherto, and therefore in a better position to hit back. I feel that the time has now come when we should accept casualties within reasonable limits if by doing so we can damage and impose great delay on the enemy...as time goes on greater risks may be accepted."* Contrast this with the reflections of Lt.-Colonel Deakin as he observed his men of 5/2nd Punjabis in 12th Brigade settling into their front line positions and awaiting the Japanese attack:

---

* *Eastern Epic*, page 321.

The battalion was dead tired; most of all the commanders, whose responsibilities prevented them from snatching even a little fitful sleep. The battalion had withdrawn 176 miles in three weeks and had had only three days' rest. It had suffered 250 casualties of which a high proportion had been killed. The spirit of the men was low and the battalion had lost 50 per cent of its fighting efficiency.

During 5th January I found a most lethargic lot of men who seemed to want to do nothing but sit in slit trenches. They said they could not sleep because of the continued enemy air attacks. In fact, they were thoroughly depressed. There was no movement on the road and the deadly ground silence emphasized by the blanketing effect of the jungle was getting on the men's nerves. It was broken again and again by the roar of engines overhead. The airman could not see the troops but knew they were there and continually attacked the road and railway areas in which the defences were sited. The jungle gave the men a blind feeling.*

This graphic and tragic account of the state of these men, Indian and British, many soon to die, is in stark contrast with the message from Singapore. It was Wavell, as we shall see, who by a personal visit to the front line discovered the truth, but only after the debâcle, and straightaway, without further discussion, ordered the long retirement to the last mainland defence in Johore.

General Paris in these circumstances wanted to give his troops as much rest as possible. This well-meant intention was to have unfortunate consequences for the Gurkha Brigade in support behind the 12th Brigade now stationed in depth, under Brigadier Stewart. There were three changes of plan extending the area covered by this brigade from Trolak to Kampong Slim, where the Gurkhas took over, and this all added to the strain. After the twisting and turning of the road from Tanjong Malim to

---

* *Official History*, pp 275-6.

Trolak village, the traveller on emerging from Trolak perceives a fine straight highway for many miles when a car can accelerate through the jungle and rubber estates which border the road, with here and there a manager's bungalow on some nearby hill now exposed to sight by the recent felling and replanting of rubber. It was at the 60th milestone between high cuttings that the 4/19th Hyderabads, the most inexperienced of the battalions in the brigade, took up their positions in the van. There were all the brigade's allotment of anti-tank obstacles, but behind and around went the loops of the "bullock cart" road of yore, since straightened by Government, and providing for the astute Japanese a bypass round the defences, of which in the event they made effective use. Next came the 5/2nd Punjabis a mile back, with the anti-tank mines (only 24 out of 1400 mines allotted to the division), and a troop of anti-tank guns, and the Argylls covered Trolak village to the 62nd mile. In the rear of Trolak the 5/14th Punjabis were next morning to take up a check position. The road was not cratered but left open for withdrawal of guns and vehicles from forward positions and the use of armoured cars. Only one troop of anti-tank guns was allotted, and the field regiment available, which in the close jungle country could not be used in its normal role, was nevertheless not deployed for anti-tank defence. Brigade Headquarters was west of the main road in the rubber estate, and, as it turned out, easily cut off from events on the main road.

At Kampong Slim were the Gurkhas, and Brigadier Selby wished to deploy his battalions with his artillery support, 155th Field Regiment, on the night of 6th/7th January, but Paris, considerate for the tired troops, ordered one more night's rest judging that no elaborate defences were needed. So the troops were left undisturbed in their harbours, and were not under orders to deploy before 12.00 hours on 7th January, ready to take over the front from 12th Brigade on that night. Selby urgently sought anti-tank rifles. The Gurkhas were uneasy, and Colonel Allsebrook of 2/9th recorded in his diary, "Everyone thinks we ought to be in our battle positions."* General Paris' timing and appreciation of the Japanese

---

* *History of the 2/9th Gurkha Rifles*, page 165.

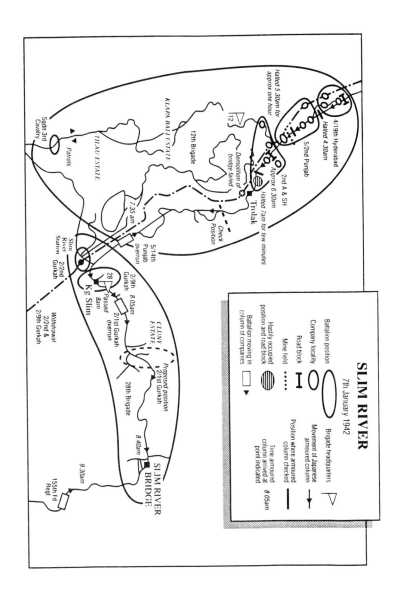

**SLIM RIVER**
7th January 1942

Battalion position — Brigade headquarters
Company locally — Movement of Japanese armoured column
Road block — Position where armoured column checked
Mine field — Time armoured column arrived at point indicated — 8.05am
Hastily occupied position and road block
Battalion moving in column of companies

movements had been skilful enough since the first contacts at Titi Karangan, but commanders, like their troops, are subject to fatigue, and so it was that the stage was set for a repetition of the breakthrough by tanks at Jitra, and the 28th Gurkha Brigade, which had been before a breakwater behind which the army could retire was, by an unhappy mischance, because of the divisional commander's concern for their welfare, caught out of position, and engulfed in the subsequent wave of destruction next morning.

The Hyderabads awaited with apprehension the fall of night, drenched by tropical rain or worn out by heat and pestered by mosquitoes. There had been ominous news from a Chinese of many vehicles at Sungkai five miles away, but the likelihood of tanks seems to have been discounted at Brigade Headquarters. At midnight the Argylls received 100 valuable reinforcements. An attack along the railway had been repulsed by the Hyderabads during the day, and they were due to withdraw from their outpost position early on 7th January.

At about 03.30 hours on the morning of 7th January, in bright moonlight, the tank attack came in, after preliminary probings, and with heavy shelling and lorried infantry the Hyderabads were overrun and the Japanese, using the old disused loop roads, reached the positions of the 5/2nd Punjabis about 04.30 hours. There they were only halted as a tank struck a mine in the rear of the Punjabis' position in front of milestone 62. Lt.-Col. Deakin describes the scene:

> The din which followed defies description. The tanks behind were nose to tail – the engines roaring, their crews yelling, their machine guns spitting tracer, and their mortars and cannon firing all out. The Platoon astride the road on the cutting hurled grenades on the tanks below them, and one tank had its tracks smashed by an anti-tank rifle. The two-pounders of the anti-tank battery fired two rounds, one of which scored a bull, and then hurriedly went out of action and retired unhurt to the Argylls' area. Many men of D and B companies were streaming

back through the jungle, though I could still hear some firing in
B company's area when there was a brief lull in the din. One
more tank wrecked itself on the mines. A few men tried their
hands with Molotovs, but the fuses were too damp. They
merely smouldered and burnt out...the chaotic conditions which
reigned on that day in the Brigade area besides being beyond
description leave no very clear picture in my mind of exactly
what did occur.*

All important communications broke down. Links between brigade
Headquarters and the forward battalions ceased at 05.00 hours, and the
Hyderabads area was shelled by the time the Japanese were through to
the Punjabis two miles forward. Brigadier Stewart, unaware of the
situation, no doubt felt confident his Argylls would hold the attack, but
by 07.00 hours the Japanese were through the Argylls and Trolak village
where the vital bridge demolition failed, permitting the tanks to sail on
and scatter the 5/14th Punjabis marching up to their check position one
mile behind Trolak, oblivious to the impending onrush. An infantry
encircling attack on the Argylls' right flank in Trolak Estate had been
met and repulsed, but now the Argylls were cut off and the sole escape
route was down the Klapa Bali Estate road to the railway at Kampong
Slim. Here remnants of the brigade fought and retreated, and here
Major Brown commanding the Hyderabads who had withdrawn was
killed in the mêlée. Lt.-Colonel Deakin escaped with some of his men
into the jungle and was later captured. Lt.-Colonel Robertson, newly
arrived from Duff Cooper's staff to command the Argylls, led a party
through the jungle, only to be ambushed and killed six weeks later in
Johore.

Meanwhile Brigadier Selby back at his HQ at Kampong Slim was
having a quick breakfast prior to visiting Stewart to discuss the withdrawal
when at 06.30 hours an officer of 12th Brigade came in to report that
"things seemed a bit serious up in front." Selby gave immediate orders

for his brigade to deploy to their positions. At 07.20 hours he reached Stewart who reported heavy fighting and some penetration but was confident of holding on. Selby on his way back met an excited officer who reported Selby's own death. He reached 2/2nd Gurkhas at Kampong Slim who had seen Japanese tanks pass through the village. Lt.-Colonel Holmes of 137th Field Regiment went off to ascertain the fate of his guns and was never seen again. An anti-tank gun sent forward was likewise overrun. Lt.-Colonel Stokes of 5/14th Punjabis, who had been wounded with his troops marching one mile short of Trolak, was taken prisoner and later died in Taiping gaol through lack of proper medical attention.

The trail of destruction had not ended. 2/2nd Gurkhas were west of the road and already deployed in its area. 2/9th Gurkhas were around Kampong Slim and had about 1 mile to march to complete deployment, but 2/1st Gurkhas had three miles to go back to reach their positions around Cluny Estate, and thus it was that at about 08.00 hours this battalion suffered a similar, even worse, fate than it had at Asun on 11th December. Major Winfield relates the story:

> We had marched about a mile when I sensed a feeling of unease behind me. I couldn't understand it. True, the battle sounded a bit close, but we were miles behind the front, and there was no air about. The men behind were looking back and hurrying... I sent back to tell them to keep their distance.
>
> The next thing I knew was a gun and machine-gun blazing in my ear; a bullet grazed my leg, and I dived into the ditch as a tank bore down upon me. It had passed through half my battalion without my realising that anything was amiss.
>
> The tanks, about a dozen of them, stopped for ten minutes firing into the rubber which flanked the road before they moved on. It was a terrifying experience. When it seemed clear that no more were coming, I crawled out to order the battalion to resume its march. It had vanished. There were a few casualties

on the road; that was all. After a further search which only discovered a few more men wounded, dead or dying in the rubber near the road, I pushed on to Cluny Estate, and found two batteries destroying their guns there. I waited for some time, hoping that the survivors of the battalion would make for the battalion position but no one materialised. So I pushed on towards Tanjong Malim. I found our transport lines a shambles on my way back. Eventually, after swimming Slim River in view of the presence of tanks on the bridge, I found 155th Field Regiment in action on the road.*

These personal stories vividly depict the awful concatenation of events on that tragic evening.

Lt.-Colonel Fulton commanding 2/1st Gurkhas was, like Colonel Stokes, badly wounded returning from a recce on a motor bicycle, and like him, died as a prisoner of war at Taiping, with little or no proper medical attention.

The two batteries of 137th Field Regiment on Cluny Estate, unsuspecting by the roadside, were next raked with fire, and the tanks sped on to Slim River Bridge which they reached at about 08.40 hours, brushed aside with heavy casualties the troop of 16th Light Anti-Aircraft Battery which gallantly but vainly tried by depressing their barrels to stop them, and now seemed set to break through to Tanjong Malim. Communication with Division had ceased at dawn, but warning had got through of a tank breakthrough at about 08.30 hours, and Lt.-Colonel Murdoch of 155th Field Regiment attached to the Gurkha Brigade harboured at Behrang six miles south of Slim River Bridge received orders to deploy for action. He went forward to open his advanced HQ, met the tanks and was killed. He was the seventh commanding officer to be cut off or killed that morning.

This fine regiment of gunners sprang into action, and in the twisting and turning jungle-dark road at 78th mile the Japanese tanks' career was

---

* *Eastern Epic*, page 327.

at last brought to a halt at about 09.30 hours. A leading gun was caught and put out of action but a warning got back; a shout from a lorry driver and an officer who managed to race back on a motor bicycle and give timely warning enabled the next gun at close range with five rounds to halt the tanks, the remainder returning to Slim River Bridge which was kept under fire by 155th Field Regiment. The Japanese tanks had advanced 18 miles, scattered two brigades, killed nearly all the British commanding officers, and left the remnants of the division in a precarious position now gathered around the railway station at Kampong Slim, eight or nine miles back.

Here at Kampong Slim Brigadier Selby was again engaged on a salvage operation. Collecting together remnants of 12th Brigade he decided to hold on at Kampong Slim until dusk and retire down the rail line to Tanjong Malim which was still held. At 10.40 hours Colonel Harrison, GSO1 of 11th Division, arrived on a bicycle after an adventurous journey since 07.45 hours having met the tanks in his car at milestone 73 on his way to ascertain the situation. He managed to escape, his orderly wounded and his car smashed. It was not until 08.30 hours that General Paris received definite information of a tank breakthrough and not until 10.00 hours he knew that the tanks had been halted and was fully aware of the morning's disasters. Troops were warned in the Tanjong Malim area, anti-tank guns posted, and 2/16th Punjabis were immediately ordered up from Rawang.

At Kampong Slim 2/2nd and 2/9th Gurkhas were the only remaining battalions fairly intact, and in position around the road and rail junction at Kampong Slim where the road branches off from the rail at almost right angles to the east. The tanks now ranging down the road were followed by lorried infantry and pressure of the latter increased during the afternoon. Stragglers from 12th Brigade came in, and sporadic actions with tanks and troops flared up again and again. With the Japanese closing in on the escape route it was time to move, and from dusk in great difficulty and with skirmishes and casualties the withdrawal

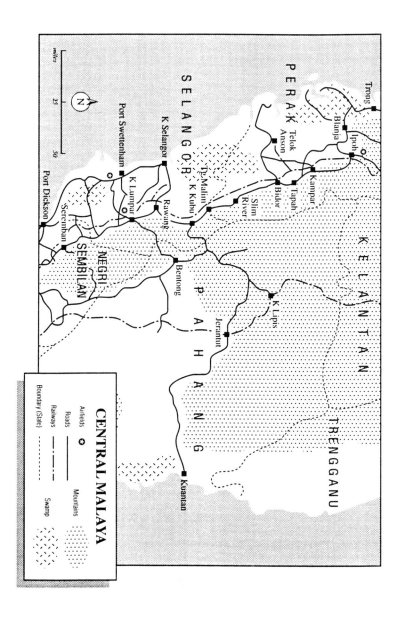

CENTRAL MALAYA

| | |
|---|---|
| Airfields | ⊕ |
| Roads | ——— |
| Railways | —·—·— |
| Boundary (State) | ········ |

Mountains

Swamp

took place down the rail line and through the jungle. As many vehicles as possible were destroyed but a large number of 12th and 28th Brigades' vehicles and carriers had to be left, and were to be seen months later around the railway station when the POWs went up by train to Siam – mute relics of a tragic episode.

In the early hours of the morning of 8th January the remainder of the two brigades found its way to Tanjong Malim. Some were drowned in the waters of the Slim River for Gurkhas in particular are normally non-swimmers. The muster roll of the two brigades that morning told this dismal tale:

> 4/19th Hyderabads – 3 officers and 100 men
> 5/2nd Punjabis  – 1 officer and 80 men
> 2nd Argylls   – 4 officers and 90 men
> 5/14th Punjabis – 6 officers and 129 men
> 2/2nd Gurkhas  – 400 all ranks
> 2/9th Gurkhas  – 350 all ranks
> 2/1st Gurkhas  – Nil.

Only two brigadiers and two battalion commanding officers returned, and all the vehicles and guns were lost. Once again Brigadier Selby, with the help of Brigadier Stewart, had to carry out a salvage operation.

An official explanation issued with General Wavell's approval stated that as the result of a month's continuous fighting the men had reached a stage of overwhelming fatigue and that there could be no doubt that their morale was in consequence lowered. Whilst this is true enough, it might be added that there were faulty dispositions, but that from the corps Commander down to the young sepoy sheltering in his slit trench on that dark and stormy night, most were in some measure mentally and physically worn out.

It was, however, Wavell, who now arrived in Malaya for the first time on taking up his ABDA appointment, who visited the front line and the two brigadiers that day, and without further ado ordered the retreat and relief of the skeleton 11th Indian Division, the abandonment of Kuala Lumpur, and the preparation of a new defence line some 120 miles back down the peninsula in Johore. The 11th Division had ceased to exist as a fighting formation for the time being, a repetition of Jitra a month before, and these facts must be borne in mind in judging what subsequently befall during the next and final month of the campaign.

*Retreat to Johore*

Now began the great retreat – there had been retreats from the north but now it was for 120 miles in one bound through the most populous and busy states of Selangor and Negri Sembilan, with their considerable road systems and beaches suitable for sea landings, as British planners found on their return in 1945, all rendering defence a difficult matter. Kuala Lumpur, the Federal capital, seat of Government and headquarters of III Corps with all its base installations, had now to be evacuated in circumstances of some haste. Some of those who had come down from the north had hoped it would be thus far and no farther. Fed with such few snippets of information as the censor vouchsafed, there was little realisation of the true state of affairs, certainly not of the disaster Wavell had discovered on arrival in Kuala Lumpur. There were few days available for removing all the military stores, and there was some chaos. All European officials and residents had to leave by Friday 10th January, and next morning, a Saturday, Ian Morrison surveyed the scene with the sharp eyes of a war correspondent:

> We went up to the Residency to see if the Resident was still
> there. It was a large spacious white house in park-like grounds
> filled with flowering trees surrounded at a distance by other
> official residences. The place was deserted. The flag was
> down. There seemed to be no one within miles. The big house
> was empty. It reminded me somehow of the *Marie Celeste*, that

ship which was found in the South Atlantic sailing under full
sail but without anyone on board and nothing to show what had
happened. In the Residency a half-finished whisky-and-soda
stood on the small table by the sofa in the drawing room.
Upstairs a woman's dress, half ironed, lay on the ironing table
in one of the bedrooms. Two dispatches addressed to the
Governor typed out but unsigned lay on the desk upstairs. In
the office on the ground floor the files were intact. The staff
appeared to have downed pens in the middle of whatever they
were doing and made off... the official portraits of the King and
Queen smiled down from the walls.*

Down through the countryside went the melancholy procession; first
the white civilians and civil defence workers, male and female; then
planters, after paying off and distributing rice to their bewildered
labourers; all leaving pleasant homes and clubs on the green *padangs*
beside the road, centres of social life, happiness and hospitality, all of
which the troops following found deserted and ransacked – and they at
times added their quota of spoliation. There were all the signs of a
society in dissolution; all the confusion and paraphernalia of an army in
retreat and population in disorder: looted shops and clubs and offices,
smoke rising from rubber stocks denied to the enemy, the wretched
Tamil and Chinese population streaming along the roads with such
pathetic possessions and perquisites, sometimes incongruous, as they
had been able to lay their hands on and could carry.

The Malays of the East Coast States, of Perlis, Kedah and Perak in
the West, had seen the "tuans" depart, and now it was the turn of those
in their wayside *kampongs* in Selangor and Negri Sembilan to witness
the same sombre spectacle. What must have been their thoughts after
years in which the oldest could remember only the placid protection of
British rule? The somnolence of nearly a century was now rudely
disturbed, and now, to the lowly *raiat*, here were the lords of creation in

* Ian Morrison, *Malayan Postscript*, page 115.

headlong flight before these Japanese warriors:

> The East bowed low before the blast
> In patient, deep disdain,
> She let the legions thunder past,
> and plunged in thought again.*

To those who had lived in and loved the country the realization of immediate and impending disaster was a shock, but events followed in such rapid succession that the effect was to produce insensitivity. It was almost too calamitous to be real; and personal survival, not personal possessions, was dominant.

On our return in 1945, a Malay would describe this as "*Lari punya jam*" – when the Tuans ran – not in sarcasm or derision but as a bald and bland statement of fact, for it seemed the Malay with his magnanimity and urbanity bore no grudge for our failure to protect him. There were doubtless exceptions, and some vicious, but recrimination against the old was silenced by the brutality of the new masters.

The disengagement and retirement from Selangor to Johore was not to be without further losses. Units of the 9th Division had now been brought over the mountain ranges from the east to assist 11th Division in the rearguard and the threats of sea landings which soon materialised at Kuala Selangor and nearer Klang.

So much has been written of air power that it is significant to note that whilst our forces were harassed by air attacks, the effect was more on morale than in casualties and material damage. In Wavell's view during this period, "had the Japanese used their air superiority effectively there would have been complete disaster."† British and Dutch bombers attacked the airfields at Ipoh, Sungei Patani, and Kuantan, but could do little appreciable damage with their meagre resources.

---

* Mathew Arnold, *Oberman Once More*, stanza 110.
† J. Connell, *Wavell, Supreme Commander.*

Selby's Gurkha Brigade continued the delaying action down the main road assisted by 2/16th Punjabis and 3/17th Dogras, whilst 6/15th Brigade, reinforced by the stout Sikhs of 5/11th Sikh Regiment from the 9th Division, covered the coast and the area from the Selangor to the Klang Rivers. Here the luckless 1/14th Punjabis, who had suffered so severely in the early days at Changlun outpost, were finally eliminated as a fighting force in a night attack at Kuala Selangor in which their new commander, Lt.-Colonel Anderson, was killed. At Serendah and Sungei Choh the forces on the main trunk road had some sharp actions and losses before shaking themselves free of the advancing Japanese.

Near Klang a mixed force under Brigadier Moir, in charge of lines of communications, including Volunteers, Local Defence Forces, and the Jat battalion decimated at Jitra, covered the coast roads around Klang, in the course of which the Jats were ambushed and reduced to negligible remnants.

In these skirmishes around Klang, the local Volunteers and Defence Forces were employed on their own home ground. The Local Defence Force comprised the older and senior Europeans, mainly for police duties, but ready to aid the military where necessary. A large number were First World War veterans. Except in Hong Kong, this may have been the only instance in which the British "Home Guard" was in the front line.

The Volunteers were the younger element, previously volunteers and now conscripted where necessary for military service. Battalions were filled up with recruited Malays who as their states were overrun had to be disbanded to look after their homes and families. It was a misuse of valuable European volunteer personnel to attempt to form them into fighting battalions, and as time went on, but far too late, men were taken for liaison and other duties with the various Indian and British and Australian battalions who welcomed their local knowledge.

Planters and Forest, Agricultural and District Officers knew the language, the tracks, the people. Instead of inexpertly shouldering a rifle, an explosives expert was sent off eventually to deal with unexploded bombs. Special units such as the Light Battery and Armoured Cars had a role and were in action early on in the campaign. On the evacuation of Kelantan the Resident, Major Kidd MC, a Gallipoli veteran, joined the Australians in Muar as Liaison Officer, having known the district well from his previous service there. He was on the verge of retirement, but he and Mr Neave, Resident Perak, were both cut off and killed when the Japanese overran 45th Brigade at Bakri.

Gradually the forces sorted themselves out and converged through the Tampin bottleneck to Johore, and the line of the Muar River.

It remained to be seen if the dispositions imposed by Wavell and the fresh forces in Johore could break the spell, but the omens were not propitious.

# CHAPTER XII

## *Johore*

We now reach the final phase of the fighting on the mainland of Malaya, the last "line" before the now palpably defenceless "Fortress" of Singapore, where if the Japanese advance, swifter than even they had envisaged, could be halted to enable reinforcements to arrive, there remained a hope, albeit slender, of stemming the tide in time to gather the forces being dispatched from far and wide. The losses of the 11th Division in Selangor during the retirement in men and material had not been light and Wavell knew it would be a close-run thing.

Now the Australians were to join battle, and it is tragic to contemplate the ardour, courage and high hopes with which the fresh 8th Australian Division entered the fray and the nemesis of defeat and imprisonment that awaited them. To the British troops Malaya was a faraway country of which they knew nothing, strange, hot and uncomfortable; for the Australians it was nearer home, and they sensed more directly the Japanese menace to their homeland.

Wavell, having gone to the front after the Slim debâcle and found out for himself the state of affairs, must have had his reservations about the Malaya Command. He also found Heath a tired man, for, like his troops, he had been burdened beyond human endurance. Returning to Singapore (on the evening of 8th January) with confidence shaken in Percival, who was unaware of the parlous state of 11th Division, he summoned him, and after keeping him waiting for some considerable time, without further discussion handed him the following plan for

162

JOHORE
Airfields
Roads
Railways
Boundary (State)
Mountains
Swamp
miles
10
20
30
N
Port Dickson
Malacca
M A L A C C A
Tampin
Gemas
Mt Ophir
Jementah
Muar
Jorak
Lenga
Bakri
Parit Sulong
Batu Pahat
Bt Pelandok
Segamat
P A H A N G
J O H O R E
Labis
Yong Peng
Senggarang
Ayer Hitam
Rengit
Benut
Paloh
Kluang
Kahang
Pontian Besar
Pontian Kechil
S Sayong Halt
Rengam
Layang
G Pulai
Sedenak
Kulai
Senai
Skudai
Tebrau
Johore Bahru
SINGAPORE
Kota Tinggi
Jemaluang
Mersing
Endau

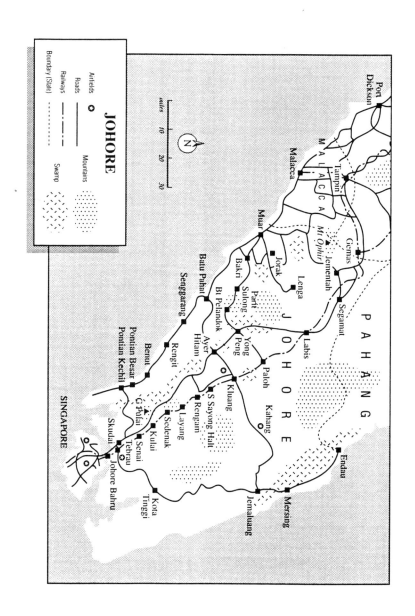

action:

(a)     III Indian Corps, after delaying the enemy north of Kuala Lumpur for as long as possible was to be withdrawn by rail and road into Johore, leaving only sufficient mobile rearguards to cover demolition schemes.

(b)     8th Australian Division (less one brigade group which was to remain in Mersing area) was to move immediately to the north-west frontier of Johore, and prepare to fight a defensive battle on the general line Segamat/Mount Ophir – mouth of Sungei Muar. The brigade group remaining in the Mersing area was to be moved to the same general line as soon as it could be relieved by troops from Singapore Island, but this could not be carried out until after the arrival of 53rd Infantry Brigade.

(c)     9th Indian Division made up from the freshest troops of III Indian Corps, and 45th Brigade from Malacca, were to be placed under command of 8th Australian Division and used in the southern portion of the position indicated.

(d)     III Indian Corps after withdrawal was to take over responsibility for the east and west coasts of Johore south of the line Mersing-Kluang – Batu Pahat, thus leaving General Bennett free to fight a battle in north-western Johore. The III Indian Corps was to reorganize 11th Indian Division, and organise a general reserve from reinforcements as they arrive.

The 53rd Infantry Brigade of 18th Division with field and anti-tank gun units and 51 crated Hurricanes was due and arrived in Singapore on 13th January.

Wavell recognised there were disadvantages in this plan which differed in two respects from that already prepared by Percival. It abandoned the idea of defending the Tampin bottleneck envisaged by Percival where the front would have been some 15 miles, compared to the 40 miles of the Muar front. The second difference was in the substitution of III Corps under Heath by West Force under Major-General Gordon Bennett of 8th Australian Division. Wavell had met Bennett and no doubt contrasted him, fresh and eager to show what he could do, with the tired and frustrated Heath.

The character and qualities of Major-General Gordon Bennett had much influence on subsequent events. He was a personality of drive and ambition. He had a distinguished record in the First World War, was awarded the CB, CMG and DSO, and at the end of the war was the youngest brigadier in the Australian Army. He returned to civilian life after the war but remained in the militia. He had great qualities of courage and leadership but was aggressive, tactless, and expressed himself freely. He had been critical of the Permanent Staff Corps, and as a militia man entered into press controversy over the appointment of commanders and training of the militia.

The Australian military command was mistrustful of his judgement and character, and there was a rivalry with that famous soldier, General (later Field-Marshal Sir Thomas) Blamey, and differences dating back a long way.

At all events he was not selected for the first overseas divisional commands, 6th, 7th and 9th Divisions which went to the Middle East under Blamey, and when the 8th Division was formed, Major-General V. A. H. Sturdee of the Permanent Staff Corps was given the post of GOC The death in an air crash of the Chief of the Australian General Staff (General Brudenell White) led, however, to Sturdee's appointment as Chief of General Staff, and Bennett took his place in command of 8th Division.

Kirby* is severe on him, and having read all the documents and consulted those in a position to know, his judgment will be difficult to controvert. Yet one feels an element of tragedy in his career. Bennett was a patriot who came to feel it was his destiny to lead the Australian armies against the Japanese. This was the mainspring of his action in making his controversial escape from Singapore, but it availed him nothing. His escape was deemed by the authorities in Australia "an error of judgment" which was confirmed after exhaustive enquiries after

---

* *Singapore: The Chain of Disaster*, pages 131–2.

the war. He was a man of action and ambition and, it seems, retained the regard of the men of his division despite this censure. Senior officers, however, who had to deal with him were less enthusiastic. His Chief Staff Officer (Brigadier Thyer) and Chief Signals Officer (Brigadier Kappe) in their post-war appreciations were critical of his operational handling of the division.* The facts have been recorded fully in both British and Australian *Official Histories*, and readers can judge for themselves, but his own recorded utterances and actions do explain the basis for the distrust felt by his professional peers in the Australian Army. He issued a stream of comment and suggestion, generally impracticable, to Sturdee in Australia, an able and level-headed officer who showed great judgment and prudence in the difficult period of Australia's weakness in 1941–2.

Bennett also recorded his lack of faith in the British commanders, and considered Heath had too much influence on Percival, and thus the continual retreat from the North. These rather wild and wilful charges were wide of the mark. 11th Division lost in battle a large number of its leaders, none lacking in courage or aggression, and was compelled, as we can see, to be kept in action too long. His own ideas of ceasing defensive methods and counter-attacking gave way to reality when his own fine division met the Japanese, though to be fair, the circumstances under which it did, with only one brigade, were not of his choosing. He was temperamentally not a good colleague, and his "hunches" were not always right. He seemed very ready to recriminate at inappropriate times. Despite his many considerable qualities and undoubted patriotism, it is understandable that the judgment of his army superiors was that he was by temperament and lack of professional expertise deemed unfitted for further active command and after a period as Commander of III Australian Corps in the backwater of Western Australia he retired before the war ended.

Bennett had reported to his superiors in Australia on 6th January that Heath's men were tired and in most units lacked determination, that the

---

* Frank Legg, *The Gordon Bennett Story*.

former "purely defensive attitude" should be replaced by "strong counter-attack methods", and to Lt.-Colonel Gallaghan who was to lead 2/30th Battalion in the first encounter with the Japanese he is reported to have said that "fixed defensive positions were dangerous and that fluid defence with as many men as possible for counter-attack was sounder."*

Bennett was, however, unfortunate in that he never was able to handle his division as an entity as he hoped and Wavell instructed. Percival stated that time was not available to make the transfer of 22nd Australian Brigade. Moreover, he had to operate what amounted to a corps front without the necessary staff and facilities. These were seriously inhibiting factors, and the latter necessitated Percival assuming the role of a corps commander in addition to his army command, a burden he took on with his usual conscientiousness but which was far too much and detrimental to successful control of events. He had to motor long distances between Singapore and the battle front and with little sleep, working 18 hours a day, he is described arriving at conferences in the forward area, "looking tired and worn and usually failed to take control. Bennett would then take the floor putting forward impracticable proposals until Heath would break in with a sensible suggestion based on sound military considerations, which Percival would accept and act upon."†

The 27th Australian Brigade took its position on the main trunk road in front of Gemas, the 9th Division (8th & 22nd Brigades) was in support and covered the road west from Segamat past Mount Ophir to Malacca, and the Loyal Regiment (less one company) was brought up to Segamat in the rear. On the coastal sector with its 25 miles of the tortuous, serpentine Muar River and the sea coast to defend, all that was allotted was the raw and untried 45th Indian Brigade, quite unfit for its formidable role. In view of past experience it is difficult to understand this decision, nor to doubt that Heath and III Corps would not have thus minimized the coastal threat. Moreover, Bennett compounded the error by ordering the

---

* L. Wigmore, *The Japanese Thrust.*
† Kirby, *Singapore: The Chain of Disaster*, page 205.

brigade to spread out over the 25-mile front. The 7/6th Rajputana Rifles with half its strength forward of the river held Muar and ten miles of the winding river; the 4/9th Jats held a further 15 miles upstream again with two companies forward of the river. The 5/18th Garwhalis based on Bakri covered Simpang Jeram and Parit Java and the coastal front. These dispositions are described by the *Official History* (*War Against Japan*, vol.1) as "Closely akin to those which contributed to the disaster at Jitra".

So we enter the last phase on the mainland under unpropitious auspices.

The 27th Australian Brigade prepared an ambush in the jungle country in front of Gemas at the Gemencheh bridge some three miles forward of the battalion, and on the night of 13th–14th January the last of the weary 11th Division passed through them on their way to rest and refit at reserve positions in southern Johore or in Singapore.

At about 16.00 hours on 14th January, Japanese on bicycles came down the road and the ambush was sprung successfully, but the telephone lines with the artillery, not properly concealed, were cut, and the guns did not come into action – the same sort of mischance that had so often bedevilled the 11th Division and which only experience can avoid. Nevertheless the spirited action of the Australians was a boost to morale, and the company after some skirmishes and few losses rejoined the battalion via the railway next morning.

At about 00.10 hours next day, 15th January, the Japanese came up against the main positions of 2/30th battalion. A participant in this battle, one of the crew of the two anti-tank guns which fought with valour and success in their first battle, testifies to the good morale of the Australians but relates that the battalion commander regarded the anti-tank guns as an encumbrance and sent back a third gun as not required.* During the day the battalion fought a determined action, counter-attacked and repulsed the Japanese, the two anti-tank guns destroying several tanks. Their casualties, killed and wounded, were about eighty men, but with the enemy being reinforced the battalion was withdrawn that evening

---

* K. Harris, *The Brave Japanese*.

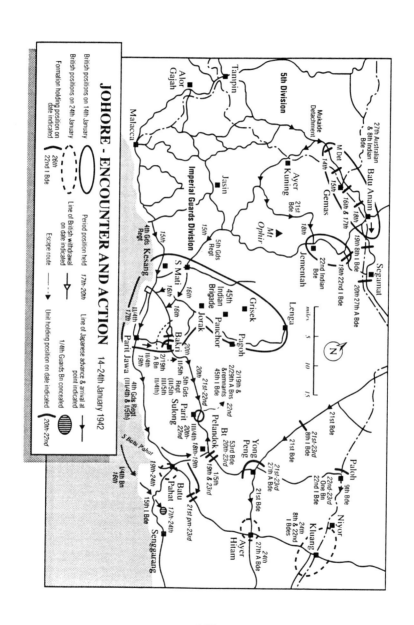

JOHORE - ENCOUNTER AND ACTION 14-24th January 1942

to the brigade position covering Batu Anam, and Gemas was relinquished. In the withdrawal some guns were bogged down and had to be left, including both anti-tank guns. The first brush with the Japanese had been encouraging, so much so that as the news percolated back to the rear there were stories that the Australians had pushed the Japanese back to Seremban! In the *Straits Times* of the next day, Gordon Bennett was quoted as saying that not only had they stopped the Japanese but had actually put them on the defensive.*

At the front the realities inspired a more sober approach, and on this day Major-General Barstow, who had experiences of the Japanese might and methods, recommended to Bennett preparing defence lines in the rear. Bennett, as we know, was suspicious of the determination of III Corps commanders and he refused.

Whilst attention was concentrated on the main road, ominous events were building up on the Muar River front, where the crack Japanese Guards Division of two Regiments (4th and 5th) were preparing to strike.

On the morning of 15th January, the forward companies across the river, the placing of which was ordered by Bennett, later termed a "tactical error" by Percival, were overrun and annihilated together with the forward observation officer of 65th Australian Battery at Muar. No word got back to the battalions or brigade. At 11.00 hours the artillery engaged the enemy who appeared on the wide waterfront at Muar where the ferry had been destroyed. Boats were seen in the afternoon off the mouth of the river, and there were some reports of landings between Muar and Batu Pahat. During the night of 15/16th January, whilst the Australians were taking the measure of the Japanese on the main trunk road, a battalion of 1/14th Guards left Malacca by boat to land some thirty miles behind the Muar River at Batu Pahat and lay up in a rubber estate some five miles from Batu Pahat. At the same time 5th Guards Regiment crossed the Muar on small boats they had collected, seized the craft moored on the south bank, and crossed the river some five miles

---

* *Australian Official History.*

upstream from Muar. There was a brush with a patrol of the Rajputanas, but these raw and bewildered troops withdrew without reporting, and at dawn, moving southwards, the enemy came across the rear company of Rajpatanas, unsuspecting with rifles piled, and routed them. The 5/18th Garwhalis in reserve were alerted by Brigadier Duncan to reinforce the town, and the commanding officer whilst conducting a reconnaissance was killed. They were forced back during the afternoon to Bakri with heavy loss. The Japanese pressed on to Muar town, overwhelming the remaining Rajputana company and killing the commanding officer and second-in-command. The 65th Australian Battery under Major Julius, a regular soldier highly respected by his men, firing over open sights sank and repulsed attempted landings in front of Muar, but with the shambles all around escaped with difficulty to Bakri. The 4/9th Jats further up the Lenga Road were still in position concentrated at Bukit Pasir near Jorak at the 12th Mile Muar/Lenga Road, but the rest of the brigade hardly existed and the Jats were isolated.*

Bennett received information of the crossing at his West Force headquarters at Labis. It seems he was in the habit of relying on liaison officers for his information. Visits to the scene in person were not his custom and so, not realising the full extent of the penetration or the state of 45th Brigade, he sent off his reserve battalion of 27th Australian Brigade, the 2/29th (less one company), and one troop of 2/14th Anti-Tank Guns, and informed its commander that the strength of the Japanese

---

* A former Malayan civil servant, Mr T P M Lewis, has recorded (*Journal of British Association of Malaysia,* November 1971) a full and graphic account of his experiences when with another Malayan civil servant he guided a party of the Australian 8th Division who were to patrol between the Main Road and Muar River Forces to give warning of infiltration by the Japanese.

This account illustrates how useful such local officers could have been if only timely use had been made of their knowledge and expertise. This party was however not assembled in Segamat until the afternoon of 16th January 1942, by which time the Japanese had already crossed the Muar River and were in the process of routing the 45th Indian Brigade.

was only about 200 men and that he should be able to restore the situation and return to Batu Anam within a few days.

Way back at Malaya Command the reports caused Percival, contrary to Wavell's instructions, to send up the newly arrived 53rd Brigade, which had landed only three days previously after eleven weeks in a troopship and was at this stage unfit for action. The release of 22nd Brigade from Mersing which Bennett naturally desired could not, in Percival's opinion, be carried out in the circumstances. The advance parties of the bewildered East Anglians reached Johore on 17th January and had their first taste of the hot and steamy landscape. Percival went up to Johore to confer with Bennett and Major-General Key (ex–8th Brigade), now in command of 11th Division, who had been alerted to strengthen the Batu Pahat – Yong Peng area, for by now reports of the landing at Batu Pahat had also been received. Inevitably the dispositions and situation resulted in the patching and splitting up of formations, compromises which contained the seeds of future trouble. Brigadier Duke of 53rd Brigade was ordered to send one battalion (52nd Cambridgeshires) to Batu Pahat to relieve the British battalion there; one battalion (6th Norfolks) was to occupy the important defile between Bukit Pelandok and Bukit Belsh on the road from Bakri to Yong Peng, the vital communication with 45th Brigade and its third battalion (5th Norfolks) was to be sent to Jamaluang to relieve the 2/19th Australians from 22nd Brigade who were ordered over to 45th Brigade at Bakri. 2/19th Battalion, who had considerable training and experience of Malaya, handed over to 5th Norfolks and looked with a somewhat sardonic Australian eye at the "pommies" with their masses of transport and baggage, and their obvious unreadiness for the ordeal in front of them.†

Though the vital communications at Yong Peng were now under threat, Percival was reluctant for reasons of morale to withdrawn from the Batu Anam – Segamat positions.

Later this day Bennett ordered Brigadier Duncan of 45th Brigade to counter-attack and reoccupy Muar, an order which was out of touch

---

† L. Wigmore, *Australian Official History*.

with the realities. Of the original 45th Brigade, 4/9th Jats were cut off at Bukit Pasir, and the 2/29th Australians were about to arrive at Bakri on the afternoon of the 17th January. They had been intended to relieve the 2/30th who had been fighting for several days in front of Batu Anam, and for whom Brigadier Maxwell was asking respite. Around Bakri were the remnants of the Rajputanas and Garwhalis, and whilst the Australians took over at Bakri, the Garwhalis were ordered to attack towards Parit Jawa on the coast. At 20.00 hours near this village they were ambushed and scattered by the Japanese Guards, and Brigadier Duncan accordingly cancelled the proposed counter-attack to re-take Muar, which in retrospect appears a quite fantastic prospect.

At 09.45 hours on 18th the control of the Muar front was transferred from Bennett to III Corps. Duncan now commanded a brigade, the sole effective fighting element of which was the 2/29th Australians, and one must pay a tribute to the stout-heartedness of these Australians and of the 2/19th battalion which followed, pitchforked into this imbroglio. They had now to face the crack Japanese Guards and sustain the morale of the now largely demoralized Indian troops bereft of all but a few officers.

The crisis centred around Bakri, which Duncan decided to hold with 2/29th Australians to enable the 4/9th Jats at Bukit Pasir to rejoin. The delay in effecting this proved fatal, and as subsequent events will show, enabled the Japanese to cut in behind Bakri and surround the force. The 6th Norfolks were quite unable to hold open the road through the defile to Yong Peng, and General Nishimura was out for annihilation. Whilst one regiment fought the Australians at Bakri, another went along the coast road unimpeded and cut in behind to seize the bridge at Parit Sulong and hold the road to the defile at Bukit Pelandok and Bukit Beloh.

At dawn next day on 18th January, the 2/29th were attacked by tanks in front of Bakri from Muar, and had some spectacular successes with their anti-tank guns, destroying eight of them. Eloquent testimony is given to this in some of the few front-line photographs of the campaign showing the felled rubber trees as obstacles, and crews coolly observing their handiwork. Lt.-Colonel Robertson of 2/29th was ambushed when going forward on a motorcycle and died of his wounds shortly afterwards. At 00.10 hours, the 2/19th battalion arrived after a 100-mile journey from Jemaluang – right into the cauldron. They were ordered to occupy positions around Bakri in support of 2/29th. The 4/19th Jats were to fall back from Bukit Pasir on Bakri but by dark on 18th January they had not arrived.

The 45th Brigade were in a critical position as day dawned on 19th January. 2/19th were heavily attacked from the south. At 00.10 hours Brigade Headquarters at Bakri was bombed from the air, the signal section was hit and some of the staff were killed. Major Julius, the commander of the 65th Battery was mortally wounded, and Brigadier Duncan stunned. Lt.-Colonel Anderson of 2/19th took over temporarily the command of the brigade.

The 2/29th were isolated on the road to Simpang Jeram, and Anderson wanted to withdraw them to Bakri, but as the Jats had not arrived he had to wait for them. At 14.00 hours the Jats reached 2/29th positions, but moving back to Bakri they were ambushed and suffered severe casualties, losing the commanding officer and adjutant, the rest finding their way back to 2/29th. During the afternoon counter-attacks repulsed Japanese thrusts, and with pressure on 2/19th from the south Anderson now ordered 2/29th back to Bakri village. It was too late. In the darkness and with strong opposition, this was the end for 2/29th; only seven officers and 190 other ranks were able to fight their way back through to Bakri and join the 2/19th, the remainder with the few Jats were cut off and lost, some struggling through swamp and jungle to inevitable capture.

Whilst all these events were taking place round Bakri, on the afternoon of 19th January Percival met Bennett, Key and Duke at Yong Peng, and it was decided to withdraw 45th Brigade by 20th January to a position west of Yong Peng, and wireless contact was made with 45th Brigade at 20.00 hours. Meantime, Anderson had on his own initiative already made the same decision to break out at dawn next day in order to avoid complete destruction. The order was 24 hours late, for at 13.30 hours on this same day, as the generals conferred, an advance guard composed of the Japanese 1/5th Guards Battalion coming up from the road from the coast forced the 6th Norfolks off Bukit Pelandok and Bukit Belah and controlled the road to Yong Peng (and south to Batu Pahat) and the next morning the isolated detachment forward at the Parit Sulong Bridge, out of touch and without rations or information, thinking rightly they were cut off, abandoned without orders their positions and made their way across country to Batu Pahat. A further Japanese battalion (111/4th) was cutting in behind the 1/5th to isolate the 45th Brigade at Parit Sulong and would doubtless have annihilated the two platoons.

The 19th–20th January was a day of fate for the doomed 45th Brigade as it set out to extricate itself under the indominatable leadership of Colonel Anderson. It would need firm and swift decisions and heroic efforts to reopen the wooded defile between Bukit Pelandok and Bukit Belah where the road from Yong Peng, after crossing an open causeway over the swamps, debouched on to the fork, one road leading on to Parit Sulong some three miles on, and the other a similar distance south down to Batu Pahat and the coast. Here the British Battalion on the 19th reinforced the 2nd Cambridgeshires of 15th Brigade, now with Brigadier Challen in command, and held the Batu Bahat town and area but with a viper in their bosom: the concealed 1st Battalion of the 4th Japanese Imperial Guards Regiment. The immediate need, however, was to clear the defile and open the road to Parit Sulong. By now battalions were thoroughly mixed up in other than their parent brigades. The command situation was equally unsatisfactory. Bennett in command of the main road area at Segamat was urging Key in command around Yong Peng to relieve his two Australian battalions. Piecemeal attempts followed to achieve this purpose, and in so far as it is possible to disentangle the confused picture, we set out the events of these fateful days.

During the afternoon of the 19th January a detached company of the 2nd Loyals arrived from Singapore – the rest of the battalions were at

Segamat with the 22nd Australian Brigade, and were ordered over to 53rd Brigade. The detached company was sent in immediately to attack Bukit Pelandok from the south. Strange to the ground, the company cut its way through the jungle and reached the crest of the ridge after dark where they remained throughout the night without food or water. At first light on 20th they moved towards the crest to find that Bukit Pelandok was being bombarded by our own artillery. The company withdrew to the road and rejoined their battalion which after a night move had arrived on the scene. This was a regular battalion which had formed part of the garrison of Singapore, and had little or no effective training in jungle warfare.

Whilst this abortive night attack was directed on Bukit Pelandok, on the other side of the road the 3/16th Punjabis were attacking Bukit Belah and the ridge to the north. The 3/16th battalion now down to half its strength was again commanded by Lt.-Colonel Moorhead who had reverted at his own request from brigadier to lead his faithful Punjabis once more as he had done from the initial encounters at the Ledge. The 6th Norfolk were ordered to attack Bukit Pelandok from the north by daybreak, assisted by fire from Bukit Belah after capture, presumably to coincide with the attack of the company of the Loyals from the south.

It so happened, however, that a company of Norfolks was still established on Bukit Belah from the previous day's battle with the 1/5th Guards battalion, but without wireless were unable to communicate their presence to the battalion headquarters. This was the Norfolks' first battle after many weeks cooped up in a transport.

Moorhead led his men to the attack at 04.00 hours on 20th January up the jungle slopes of Bukit Belah. They clashed with the Norfolks there in mutual ignorance and the attack stalled. Moorhead and his adjutant rallied them and both were killed in the confused fighting. So died this gallant and gifted officer who could ill be spared at this juncture. A havildar of this regiment expressed the grief of his men: "My heart is broken. There will never be a man as brave as he."*

---

* *Eastern Epic*, page 304.

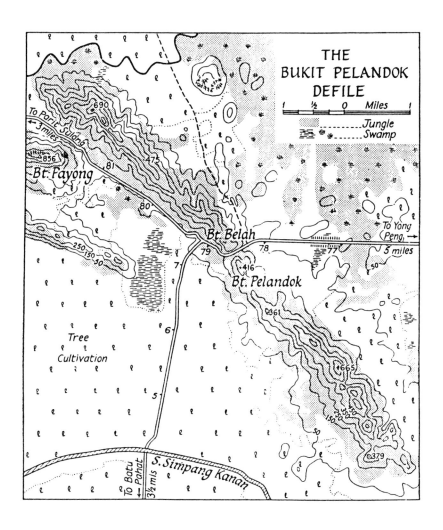

THE
BUKIT PELANDOK
DEFILE

1   ½   0   Miles   1

............ Jungle
............ Swamp

To Parit Sulong
← 3 miles

690

856

Bt. Fayong

81          473

80

250 150
50

7

Tree
Cultivation

6

5

Bt. Belah

79          78          77

416

Bt. Pelandok

361

To Yong
Peng →

5 miles

50

665

350
250
150
50

379

To Batu
Pahat ←   3½ mls

S. Simpang Kanan

177

As may be imagined these attempts against a determined and established Japanese Guards battalion flushed with success failed, and the remnants of the Norfolks and Punjabis retired to lick their wounds. Duke disposed his disparate brigade, of which only the Loyals were now capable of offence, in a defensive position between the causeway and the defile.

Aware of the situation, the 11th Divisional Commander, Key, responsible for the Yong Peng area, visited to confer with Bennett on the morning of 20th January. Anderson was now engaged in his desperate attempt to break out, and Brigadier Duncan was giving his life to preserve the rearguard. Bennett naturally urged Key to make an immediate further attempt, but Key feared that to do so with such forces as Duke now had might end in endangering the Yong Peng crossroads. The matter had to be referred to Percival, and Bennett was instructed to withdraw to Yong Peng area instead of Labis as previously decided upon; 27th Brigade to be in position there at dawn on 21st January.

Key returned from Bennett and ordered Duke to attack at dawn on 21st January, but Duke pointed out that he had only the Loyals capable of the task, and they had been continuously on the move for three days and nights. Key ordered that an attack should be made as early as feasible.

The disadvantages of the command arrangements which necessitated Percival doubling as Army and Corps Commander were having increasingly their dire effect in delay and lack of effective liaison.

Percival called a conference at Yong Peng with Heath, Bennett and Key for 12.30 hours on 21st January, and as West Force under Bennett would be now in position at Yong Peng and had wireless communication with 45th Brigade, he decided at 08.30 hours that Bennett take over command from Key of all troops in the Muar – Yong Peng area.

On his way to this conference Key visited 53rd Brigade at 10.30 hours and found that his orders had been mislaid and not transmitted to Duke who was away on reconnaissance!

Bennett and his Australians had wanted their 22nd Brigade from Mersing instead of the 53rd Brigade which was in accordance with

Wavell's orders. Percival states that the time factor prevented such a switch being made. Be that as it may, the official Australian war history is reasonably restrained in its account of these sad episodes: the 21st January was a "day of continued and exasperating delays by 53rd Brigade – arising it seemed at the time to Australian officers from failure to realise the urgency of the situation and no doubt largely from the brigade's lack of training and experience for the task it was set..."*

It may well be surmised that the remaining two battalions of the 22nd Brigade, well trained and experienced units fully up to strength, would under Brigadier Taylor have somehow got through to their comrades. But there were in effect only the Loyals, and changes in command and inefficient communications added frictions and delays.

Key was told by the brigade major that an attack could be organised about 14.00 hours. Key was aware that he was in the process of handing over the 53rd Brigade, and at this critical time all he could do was to issue the following instruction:

> At noon your brigade comes under the command of "West Force", but I am quite sure General Bennett will wish you to recapture the defile at the earliest possible moment. Make all arrangements for an attack at 14.00 hours and be prepared to send a carrier platoon through to Parit Sulong. I will ask "West Force" to confirm these orders.

Blandly the British *Official History*† records: "No action appears to have been taken within the brigade pending the arrival of the confirmatory order."

Only when Key's staff officer arrived at Duke's forward headquarters with the confirmatory order were the Loyals alerted. Bennett's staff officer, Colonel Thyer, records how he arrived at the far end of the causeway at 14.30 hours with Lt.-Colonel Elrington in command of the

---

* *Australian War History – Japanese Thrust*, pages 241–2.
† page 314.

Loyals and met Duke. He found the reconnaissance for the attack and the issue of the plan being made completely in the open in full view of the defile over 1,000 yards away. When it was suggested that this was an unsound and risky manner in which to conduct preparations for an attack...

> I was informed by the brigade commander that there were no troops on the hill feature. It was then suggested that if this was the case the forward battalion, the Punjabis, should be sent forward to occupy the hill immediately instead of waiting for a set piece attack by the Loyals. Failing this at least fighting patrols should be sent forward to probe the position and locate enemy localities.

Disturbed, Thyer returned to report to Bennett. The widely-dispersed Loyals had to be assembled and artillery support arranged. There were moves to obtain assistance from Westforce artillery, but this was found impracticable. An attack was provisionally fixed for 17.30 hours and, despite frequent proddings by Bennett for speed, it had to be postponed for 09.00 hours on 22nd January. When the morning came the exposed Loyals were subjected to heavy air bombing and machine-gunning. Surprise was lost, and the chances of the Loyal battalion overcoming opposition from what by now were probably two Japanese Guard battalions were judged correctly by Duke to be remote. The attack was abandoned.

It can hardly be judged that given the circumstances described there was any possibility that the British and Indian troops which at various times comprised the makeshift "53rd Brigade" could overcome two crack Japanese battalions and break through to their Australian and Indian comrades.

The sorry plight of 45th Brigade must now be related. At dawn on 20th January with Anderson in the van, and Duncan in the rear, the force set off to battle its way to Parit Sulong and beyond, some five composite companies of Australians and the remnants of the Indian troops, with the transport and wounded in the middle of the convoy. At about 08.00 hours on 20th the column met a roadblock, cleared only after some two hours of fighting and finally overcome by a bayonet charge led by Anderson himself. The delay, however, permitted the Japanese to catch up with the rearguard, and Brigadier Duncan was killed leading a counter-attack which resisted this threat to the rear of the column.

Since the Japanese landed across the Muar River it had been a Calvary for Brigadier Duncan, who had sailed with his raw brigade from India scarcely a month before, into the unknown. He must have known he was being given a task beyond the capabilities of his inexperienced young soldiers, but as a disciplined soldier he accepted it. He witnessed the successive disasters which now left him with a bare remnant of men and few officers, and now he was to give his life after five desperate days of defeat. When we contemplate the fate of his brigade it is worth recalling the comments of General Brooke on inspecting a machine-gun battalion which had been sent to France in 1940: he wrote that "it would be sheer massacre to commit it to action in its present state."* Was there really no alternative?

It was after the dusk, which in the tropics comes early, about 19.00 hours, that the forces under the dauntless Anderson covered the open ground, vulnerable to attack and encumbered with casualties, and reached an area of rubber some two miles from Parit Sulong and the vital bridge only to find it was occupied in strength by the Japanese, the small force of Norfolks posted there having withdrawn that morning.

Throughout the next day, 21st January, Anderson strove to overcome the opposition at Parit Sulong and get through to our troops at the defile at Bukit Pelandok some three to four miles away. There the dawn attempt of the Punjabis and Norfolks on 20th January had failed with the loss of the gallant Colonel Moorhead. Insufficient and inexperienced troops were available, and no relief came from the defile. All attempts

---

* Bryant, *Turn of the Tide*, pp. 58–59.

by Anderson and his men to get through failed against increased pressure from tanks and low-flying aircraft, casualties mounted, and the perimeter shrank. The condition of the Australians was parlous, and a survivor described it as a "pitiable inferno". When evening came Anderson tried under a flag of truce to evacuate his wounded through to Yong Peng but this was refused. On the morning of 22nd January two aircraft from Singapore flew over this beleaguered band of men and dropped medical supplies and food, and after the failure of a further attempt to break through Anderson anticipated an order that Bennett sent by wireless that morning, destroyed his guns and transport, left the wounded perforce in the hands of voluntary attendants, and ordered those who could to make their way through the swamp and jungle to Yong Peng. Some 500 Australians, including Anderson who was later awarded the VC for his courage and leadership, and 400 Indian troops, the remnants of 45th Brigade with a few junior officers, reached our lines. The Japanese in circumstances of shocking barbarity murdered the wounded, but miraculously one or two survived and retribution was visited on the Japanese commander after the war. During the week's fighting the Japanese lost a company of tanks and the equivalent of a battalion of troops.

Russell Braddon in *The Naked Island* and Kenneth Harrison in *The Brave Japanese*, both gunners serving in the AIF, give vivid and harrowing accounts of their experiences during this week. Both, too, give instances of some senior officers' distrust or misunderstanding of the anti-tank gun, and the latter relates the sad incident of the death of Lt.-Colonel Robertson of 2/29th Battalion in an ambush near Bakri, and of his last poignant words to his anti-tank officer: "I was terribly wrong. But for you and your guns not one of my boys would be alive now."

During the course of this forlorn battle by such a few troops the bulk of Westforce, 27th Australian Brigade and 9th Division were withdrawing with little difficulty to the line of Yong Peng to conform, and were established there by 23rd January to receive the remnants of the Muar survivors.

To sum up the ghastly story of that disastrous week: the Japanese Imperial Guards divisions met and massacred the untrained and utterly unprepared 45th Indian Brigade, and then proceeded to annihilate two fine Australian battalions fed into the pipeline of the Yong Peng-Bari road piecemeal, with no proper provision for protection and maintenance of communications to Yong Peng through the vital seven miles from Parit Sulong Bridge to the Bukit Pelandok and Bukit Belah hills which dominated the road. The gallant last fight of the Australians is shown in all its stark reality in a description of a diarist of 2/19th Battalion of the unavailing attempt on 20th January to break through the Japanese stranglehold and to fight their way through Parit Sulong to safety:

> Every man was fighting mad. Mortar shells were directed on to targets by infantrymen a few yards from the targets; gunners were fighting with rifles, bayonets and axes (range too short for 25-pounders except to Japanese rear areas to west). A gun crew pushed its 25-pounder round a cutting and blew out the first road blocks (vehicles) at 75 yards range. Carriers pushed within five yards of Japanese M.G.s and blew them out. Men went forward under heavy M.G. fire and chopped road blocks to pieces.*

Instead of a timely withdrawal of the force to a defensible line from Parit Sulong/Bukit Pelandok/Batu Pahat, two platoons of the 6th Norfolks, a battalion newly arrived and palpably bewildered and unequal to the task, operating on its own and without its sister battalions, was posted out of touch at Parit Sulong Bridge, the sole tenuous contact and security for withdrawal which would doubtless have been overpowered if it had not that morning of 20th January, albeit without orders, withdrawn.

During these days the command of the disparate forces on the Muar River front was switched backwards and forwards from Gordon Bennett

---

* *Japanese Thrust*, pages 239–240.

to Major General Key of 11th Division:

        15th January to 18th January  –  Gordon Bennett
        18th January to 21st January  –  Key
        21st January to 22nd January  –  Gordon Bennett

by which time there was no longer any force to command.

The defence of the defile entrusted to 6th Norfolks was quite inadequate, manifestly so one would have thought, and the reinforcements by 3/16th Punjabis, a depleted battalion of 11th Division, and the Loyals, without adequate artillery support, were belated and piecemeal. The sacrifice of the gallant Moorhead and his Punjabis on the night of 19/20th January sadly served no useful purpose.

Those misjudgments and failures of untrained and inexperienced troops were relieved by individual valour; and the record of Lt.-Colonel Anderson and his Australians in their first encounter with the Japanese on that bloody Bakri road surely illustrate that with sound command arrangements a very different story might have been told. As happened before Bakri and after, such forces as were available, exiguous as they were in the circumstances, were not marshalled to oppose the Japanese at the decisive point.

One may ask if this catastrophic result could have been avoided, and the official history* has this conclusion:

> The untried though well-trained and fresh 8th Australian Division was the best asset available to Malaya Command at this juncture. Earlier in the campaign Percival had rightly declined to take the risk of placing the defence of Mersing area in the hands of troops who were not acquainted with it, for at that time a successful enemy landing there would have been a major disaster. But once the enemy's main forces had reached the borders of Johore they became the greatest danger and risks might justifiably have been taken both at Mersing and Singapore.
> With the arrival of large reinforcements, the Australian

---

* Kirby, *War Against Japan*, vol. I.

brigade defending Mersing might with advantage have been relieved by units from Singapore garrison, all of which were trained in beach defence. Had this been done the whole of the Australian division could have been used at the decisive point. There would then have been a corps of three divisions to meet the main enemy threat, of which 9th Indian and 8th Australian divisions, totalling five brigades, could have been deployed, with 53rd Brigade on arrival, and the remnants of the battle-weary 11th Division held in reserve. No such regrouping took place. In consequence the battle was fought by a force of only eleven battalions which was insufficient to cover the approaches into Johore adequately, while 8th Australian division was used piecemeal on three separate fronts with only two-thirds of its strength fully engaged.

The allotment of the raw 45th Brigade to an impossible task, the command arrangements, the failure of communications, the transference of responsibility for command backwards and forwards, the intermixture of units – for all troops are better in their own formations – all adds up to the failure to hold the Muar River Line. The last frail hope of a stronghold evaporated, and now there remained to co-ordinate a retreat to the last ditch in Singapore, which was not to be achieved without further grievous losses.

This second stage began on 23rd January when Percival decided to hold a line covering Jemaluang – Kluang-Ayer Hitam, but to continue to hold Batu Pahat.

Over on the east, the Japanese had been working their way through difficult roadless country south, and on 14th January had their first encounter with patrols of 22nd Australian Brigade north of Endau, and on 16th and 17th both Mersing and Endau were bombed. With the events on the west, and withdrawal of 2/19th Battalion, Brigadier Taylor in command decided the time had come to concentrate at defensive positions at Mersing, which was done on 17th–18th January. On the 19th January, with the crisis building up in the west, "Eastforce" was formed, consisting of the brigade-less 2/19th Battalion, 6th Norfolks, the Jat/Punjab Battalion, the 3/17th Dogras, and Johore Volunteer Forces; and these would hold the Jemaluang/Kota Tinggi area. The follow-up was slow and it was not until 22nd January that contact was made on the line of the Sungei Mersing with 2/20th Australian Battalion. The long-awaited invasion of Endau took place on 26/27th January. This was what the Australians had prepared for so long, but now they were needed elsewhere, and two destroyers, one of which was lost, and the gallant old Vildebeestes squadrons, were all that could oppose the landing. The nine Vildebeestes were a sacrifice. They had been longest in Singapore and had reached a high state of training with torpedo bombing, but as the enemy ships were in too shallow water they had to be re-armed with bombs. Both commanding officers and half the aircraft were lost, many of the remainder were badly damaged and the crews wounded. Thus for little damage the best-trained pilots in Singapore were lost.

The withdrawal from Mersing and Jemaluang followed a successful action by the two battalions (2/18th and 2/20th) of Brigadier Taylor's 22nd Brigade. An ambush at midnight on 26/27th January at Nithsdale Estate badly mauled the Japanese 55th Infantry Regiment at the cost of some 92 Australian casualties, and the Japanese withdrew towards Mersing for reinforcement before further advance. Now we see the value of the defence ring recommended and started by Dobbie and discontinued by Bond. If defences covering Kota Tinggi, the approaches to Johore Bahru, Kulei and the west coast road to Skudai had been constructed when Brigadier Simson had asked at the end of December, not only would defence of this area been easier than of the north coast of Singapore but there might have been time for the 18th Division reinforcements to arrive and sort themselves out for battle. As it was, the withdrawal from Mersing and Jemaluang permitted the Japanese to bring in from the sea the supplies needed for the attack on Singapore Island. In the absence of these defences there remained only a co-ordinated withdrawal to Singapore Island and evacuation of the mainland.

The position on the morning of 24th January, with Eastforce in touch with the enemy on the Sungei Mersing, showed Westforce having broken contact around Yong Peng. The 9th Division of two brigades covered Kluang on the road to Jemaluang; the 27th Australian Brigade was at the Ayer Hitam crossroads on the main road. On the west coast 11th Division was committed with 15th Brigade at Batu Pahat under its new brigadier (Brigadier Challen), 28th Gurkha Brigade was back at Pontian Ketchil on the coast near Singapore; the battered 53rd Brigade had managed to disengage from Yong Peng during the night of 23/24th January, pass through the Australians at Ayer Hitam, and was on its way, via Pontian Kechil, to take up a position on the coast road half way between there and Batu Pahat. It was here on the west coast that the Imperial Guards were to disperse and destroy the 6/15th and 53rd brigades leaving only remnants to find their way back to our lines.

Batu Pahat was now the focus of attention. It was an extremely vulnerable position for Brigadier Challen, and General Nishimura saw a chance to surround the garrison by cutting the radiating roads from Ayer Hitam and Pontian Kechil. He already had the battalion, concealed in the rubber near Senggarang on the Pontian Kechil road, which had landed behind our lines on 16th January, where it appears to have lain doggo for a week waiting for its role. Contact with these troops was made, however, on 21st January, at Bukit Banang in the rear of Batu Pahat, and sensing the danger Challen asked Heath and Key who visited him at Batu Pahat that afternoon for permission to withdraw from the river line in front of Batu Pahat and cover the road junction east of the town to protect his communications along the roads to Ayer Hitam and Pontian Kechil. This was refused for Heath, now in command of all forces on the mainland, appeared to consider Batu Pahat could be made into a "Tobruk" – an ominous analogy – and disrupt the Japanese advance. The road to Ayer Hitam was cut by the Japanese soon after Heath and Kay returned from their visit.

The 5th Norfolks had now been returned from their attachment to

JOHORE – BATU PAHAT
24th to 31st January 1942
British position on 24th January
British brigade on the move
Formation holding position on date indicated
26th
8th I Bde
Escape or attempted escape route
Line of Japanese advance
1/4th Guards Bn concealed
miles
5
10
15
N
Paloh
5th Division
9th Inf Bde
Niyor
25th
Kluang
24th-25th
8th & 22nd I Bdes
26th
Rengam
9th Inf Bde
S Sayong Halt
8th I Bde
Westforce
Yong Peng
21st Inf Bde
25th
27th A Bde
Ayer Hitam
26th
26th am
25th pm -27th
27th A Bde
28th
27th
22nd
22nd I Bde
28th am
Layang Layang
8th I Bde
30th
31st
Sendenak
29th
21st Inf Bde
30th am
30th pm
Senai
Tebrau
Skudai
22nd I Bde
Surrendered 1st Feb
To Island night 30th-31st
JOHORE BAHRU
Johore Strait
G Pulai
Bt Pelandok
Guards Recce Regt
5th Guards Regt
24th
Imperial Guards Division
Batu Pahat
15th I Bde
19th-25th
23rd-25th
4th Guards Regt
Senggarang
15th I Bde
5th Guards Regt
11th Division
Rengit
Evacuated by sea 28th to 1st
27th-28th
53rd Bde
Benut
25th
Pontian Besar
Pontian Kechil
24th-29th
28th I Bde
30th

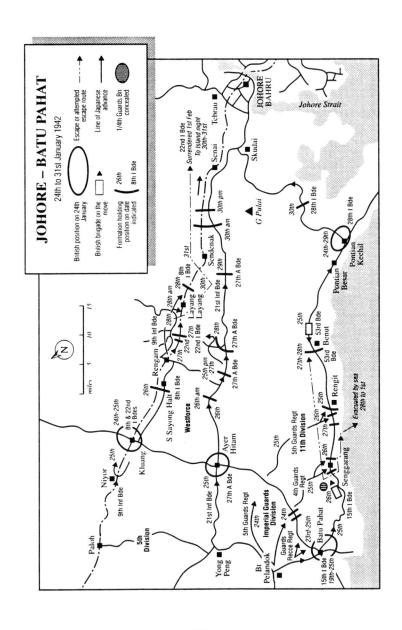

22nd Australian Brigade and on 22nd January were at Ayer Hitam preparing to hand over to 27th Australian Brigade. At 18.30 hours that evening they escorted a convoy through to Batu Pahat, but it was clear the Japanese were increasing their hold. The 5th Norfolks were not yet free to reinforce Batu Pahat, and by next day it was too late – the Ayer Hitam road was firmly cut at milestone 72 – and the 5th Norfolks were withdrawn to Ayer Hitam and the British Battalion to Batu Pahat by noon on 23rd January. The 5th Norfolks were then sent by bus down the main trunk road with the intention of reinforcing Batu Pahat via the coast road through Pontian Kechil.

Challen had under his brigade command the 2nd Cambridgeshires and the British Battalion at Batu Pahat, and pressure was increasing. He foresaw a repetition of the experience at Bakri, and made the sensible decision on his own initiative – wireless contact with 11th Division having been lost – to withdraw from Batu Pahat and take up a position in depth down the coast road to Senggarang. Unfortunately, communication was re-established and the withdrawal reported. Key had no alternative but to countermand the withdrawal, but represented the serious situation to Heath, who after discussion with Percival felt that the withdrawal would jeopardise the whole Johore line, and so on his orders by nightfall after light opposition the town was reoccupied. Nevertheless pressure increased during the night. The 5th Norfolks arrived, but without ammunition convoy, at 07.00 hours next morning, 24th January, and were directed to protect the right flank and communications. This battalion, new to battle, failed to reach its objective – the artillery, short of ammunition, could not give much help.

Once more on 24th January, Challen sought permission to withdraw from the GSO 1 who arrived from 11th Division but the original edict held. The following day, 25th January, the next in the chain of command, Key, took the matter in his hands and twice sought the required permission, emphasizing the increasing danger. Heath felt he had to await the conference with Percival at Westforce Headquarters due for that afternoon at 15.00 hours, and here at last a withdrawal to Rengit behind Senggarang was agreed, Westforce conforming on the main trunk road.

Like Greek tragedy, the inevitable followed; it was too late. The obsession with holding on to the "fortress" had its predictable result. Percival was later to doubt whether he was wise not to leave discretion to those on the spot.

Brigadier Challen lost no time in withdrawing. The orders came at 17.00 hours. He started to pack up and moved three and a half hours later, covered by the support now of the Navy, the gunboat *Dragonfly*. The rearguard was out at 04.00 hours next morning, and reached Senggarang early on 26th January. The coast road here is built along an embankment with swampy coastal clay land each side, and the Japanese had little difficulty in imposing an effective roadblock.*

We have told how the remains of the battered 53rd Brigade (now consisting of only 6th Norfolks and 3/16th Punjabs, each about two companies strong after their losses at the Defile) had been sent to hold open the coast road at Benut which they reached at dawn on 25th January. Challen's brigade was timed to reach Benut by 27th January.

Not only was the withdrawal too late, but 53rd Brigade was by now quite unfit for its role of holding open the coast road. Brigadier Duke sent detachments of 53rd Brigade forward to hold Rengit and Senggarang. The garrison for Rengit arrived safely, but at Senggarang a platoon of 6th Norfolks and a section of 336th Field Battery was ambushed and 15 men were killed, and there were now roadblocks between Senggarang and Rengit.

Contact was difficult for wireless communications were very poor, a state of affairs that plagued the Army throughout the campaign.

Key arrived during the morning at Duke's headquarters at Benut, halfway between Pontian Kechil and Senggarang and some 18 miles from the latter. On his orders a column was hastily organised to break through to Senggarang and open the road. The column under Major Banham of 135th Field Regiment consisted of 6th Norfolks and 3/16th Punjabis in carriers and lorries, a troop of Volunteer Armoured Cars,

---

* *War in Malaya*, page 239.

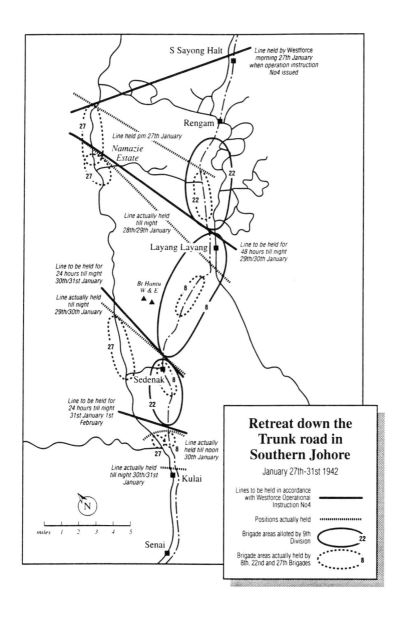

S Sayong Halt

Line held by Westforce
morning 27th January
when operation instruction
No4 issued

27

Rengam

Line held pm 27th January

*Namazie
Estate*

27

22

22

Line actually held
till night
28th/29th January

Layang Layang

Line to be held for
48 hours till night
29th/30th January

Line to be held for
24 hours till night
30th/31st January

*Bt Hantu
W & E*

8

Line actually held
till night
29th/30th January

8

27

Sedenak

8

Line to be held for
24 hours till night
31st January 1st
February

22

**Retreat down the
Trunk road in
Southern Johore**

January 27th-31st 1942

Line actually
held till noon
30th January

8

27

Lines to be held in accordance
with Westforce Operational
Instruction No4

Positions actually held

Line actually held
till night 30th/31st
January

Kulai

Brigade areas alloted by 9th
Division

22

N

Brigade areas actually held by
8th. 22nd and 27th Brigades

8

*miles* 1  2  3  4  5

Senai

191

and a section of guns, with a number of ambulances for evacuation of wounded. An attempt was made to run the gauntlet and barge through the roadblocks. It was quite hopeless. The troops in their thin-skinned vehicles were slaughtered, the armoured cars were stopped and ambushed, and most of the vehicles were ditched or destroyed. Major Banham himself got through on his carrier driven by an NCO of 3/16th Punjabis, in itself a remarkable feat, having negotiated under fire six roadblocks on his way, and reported to Challen, but nearly all the Norfolks' infantry in lorries were killed. The guns were saved after some heroic efforts. Two cars of the Volunteers were captured with their crews, and the crew of one car caught in the ambush got back through the swamp and rubber.*

The situation was not quite a repetition of Bakri though bad enough. It was so near and yet so far. Challen appeared to think he had to reach Benut some 18 miles away, but at Rengit the detachment of 6th Norfolks and 3/16th Punjabis were fighting it out. Survivors, including some Volunteer officers newly commissioned, pay tribute to the leadership and gallantry of Lieutenant Witherick of 6th Norfolks who was killed. All to no avail, for Challen, after receiving Major Banham's report and bearing in mind the condition of his force, in particular of the raw and by now much tried Norfolks and Cambridgeshires, decided it would be impossible to get through, destroyed his guns and vehicles, left the wounded with the padre and ambulance men, and directed his men

---

* Before this operation, the Volunteer Armoured Cars who had had experience up-country of running the gauntlet of Japanese ambushes, had represented that this in itself was a futile proceeding, and that when opposition was met it should be dealt with by the unprotected infantry in the thin-skinned vehicles debussing and attacking the ambush whilst the armoured cars gave covering fire. In the event, when the leading car bumped into the first opposition and stopped preparatory to following this course of action, the officer in command of the column ordered them on.
(Information from Mr W. T. Dunne who was in charge of the leading armoured car.)

across country. The wounded were not butchered as at Parit Sulong. Guided by a Malayan Police officer, Mr Wallace, some 1200 men reached Benut in an exhausted condition in the afternoon of 27th January. The remainder of the brigade moved west to the coast. Brigadier Challen was captured whilst reconnoitring, and then Lt.-Col. Morrison, who had given such sterling service since Jitra, took command of the troops. He concealed them some three miles from Rengit, and his brigade major (Major Lamon) reached Pontian Kechil in a sampan and reported their plight to Brigadier Selby of the Gurkhas. The Navy came to the rescue, and over three nights (28–31st January) the gunboats *Dragonfly* and *Scorpion* with other small craft ferried 2700 of the brigade to safety, an accomplishment which is some small solace in the awful story of failure and forlorn hopes.

Duke was ordered to hold Benut until dawn on 29th January, and the remnants of the garrison at Rengit came in during the 27–28th January, and what was left of 53rd Brigade now retired to Pontian Kechil where the Gurkhas and the rest of the 11th Division had fortified themselves for the final phase of withdrawal.

Whilst 6/15th Brigade and 53rd Brigade suffered their purgatory on the west, it was 22nd Brigade of 9th Division's turn to suffer a worse fate in the east of Johore.

Final plans for withdrawal on night of 31st January over the causeway were issued by Heath on 26th January. Eastforce, which had given the Japanese a bloody nose, withdrew without difficulty through Jemaluang on 28th January and reached Johore Bahru on 30th January.

11th Division now consisted of remnants of the Punjabis battalions, and mainly the Gurkhas under Brigadier Selby, who conducted an efficient and successful series of rearguards along the road to Skudai before crossing the causeway shortly after midnight of 31st January. By now most units had attached officers from the Malayan Volunteers, men who knew the country, the people, and the language, and they were welcomed with the reflection that this was an obvious measure which should have been taken early in the campaign.

On the main trunk road, however, whilst there was no great difficulty for the 27th Australian Brigade which now had the Gordons attached from Singapore garrison to replace the Loyals, the 9th Division covered the road and rail to the east and the former did not connect up with the main trunk road but petered out in the jungle country, thus creating a difficult problem of contact and communication. Whilst the phased withdrawal of the Australians and Gordons was taking place, the guns and transport of 9th Division had to be withdrawn down the remaining connecting road between the railway south of Rengam and Namazie Estate on the main trunk road. This left the two brigades of 9th Division bereft of their fire support and transport for wounded, and the only means of communication and supply was by rail.

The two brigades were to make their withdrawals by successive bounds, keeping contact and co-ordinating their movements.

Painter of 22nd Brigade was to deny a line astride the railway at milestone 437 till the night of 28–29th January, but he realised that a network of estate roads between Rengam and Layang Layang (see map) constituted a threat of being outflanked and cut off. He requested permission, therefore, to hold a position further back at Layang Layang, but as this would uncover the right flank of 27th Australian Brigade, about which Bennett was concerned, he was refused.

It was essential, therefore, that 8th Brigade behind 22nd Brigade should keep contact and assist its withdrawal, and Barstow himself personally selected a position for 8th Brigade at Layang Layang at 439.5 milestone on the railway. But now things went awry.

Firstly, at about midnight on 27th January, the railway bridge at milestone 439.5 over a stream was blown against orders, not only destroying vital telegraph communication but preventing rations and ammunition being sent forward in rail cars. Secondly, Brigadier Lay, whom we last met in charge of the unhappy 6th Brigade at Jitra and Gurun, failed to occupy the position selected by Barstow, moved further down the rail line and left a considerable gap between his brigade and 22nd. No attempt was made either to repair the telegraph line nor inform 22nd Brigade that the bridge had been blown.

During that night whilst Painter and his officers debated the position they heard the rumble of lorries as the Japanese cut between them through the estate roads on their flank and by the morning had isolated 22nd Brigade. Orders were orders and he adhered to them. When dawn came, however, and he saw the position, he did not hesitate to begin withdrawal at 10.15 hours on 28th January, moving down the west of the railway.

Barstow discovered this situation when early next morning, 28th January, he went forward to 8th Brigade, and annoyed and worried, he ordered Lay to send forward his leading battalion (2/10th Baluch) to occupy the ridge covering the bridge at milestone 439.5, and proceeded up the railway by rail car to 22nd Brigade with two staff officers. Alighting at the demolished bridge he was ambushed whilst walking along the embankment and was killed. So was lost General Barstow, an excellent officer, who, if the fates had been different, might well have been able to make his mark.

One has to relate that, despite all this, Brigadier Lay made no further efforts to move up the railway. Painter and his 22nd Brigade were cut off, and after a heartrending struggle through the jungle and knife-edge *lallang* country of south Johore, only a few men reached Singapore after the causeway was blown, and most of the brigade perished or were taken prisoner.

Amongst the brigade was the 5/11th Sikhs under Lt.-Colonel Parkin, which on 24th January at Myor above Rengam had engaged the Japanese in a bayonet charge. These achievements were but a flash in the pan, but good troops need good commanders, and Parkin was one. He was now entrapped with 22nd Brigade, and had argued for the brigade to escape before it was too late.

This last sad episode concludes the story of the fighting on the mainland.

The Argylls were brought up to hold the bridgehead beyond the causeway, but in the event all but the 22nd Brigade crossed without difficulty. The night of 31st January was quiet, and the moon was full. At 07.30 hours next morning, 1st February, the pipers played the Argylls across, and the causeway was blown.


*Note*


The author recalls an incident on the afternoon of 19th January. His armoured car was on patrol from Ayer Hitam to Yong Peng, and reached the latter as a conference was taking place in the *belukar* beside the road near the junction from Yong Peng to Bakri. I recognized Percival and Bennett from photographs, and by the road was Lt. R. A. Barnard, a volunteer liaison officer with Duke, Brigadier of 53rd Brigade. According to the *Official History* (page 309) General Key of 11th Division was also there. Whilst we waited a soldier came running down from the junction of roads and announced that a signal truck had passed and said that the Japanese had broken through. Barnard listened to him impassively and passed him to a staff officer who emerged from the *belukar*, perhaps on hearing the raised voice of the soldier. He bade the man depart and said it was nonsense; we had just sent up two platoons of Loyals (according to the record it was a detached company from Singapore – page 310, *Official History*). I recall being struck with the small scale of things – only two platoons! the seemingly casual conference in the *belukar*, and the general sultry, resigned atmosphere. At this moment, as the *Official History* relates, the decision was being taken, 24 hours too late, to withdraw the 45th Brigade. We were indeed remote from the realities of the desperate conflict then taking place not far away at Bakri.

# CHAPTER XIII

## Singapore

We have seen how within the space of under two months the British had been cleared out of the mainland of Malaya. Such a transformation was quite beyond any pre-war estimate or expectation. We saw Malaya, calm and some say complacent, until on 1st December the alerting of troops and mobilisation of the Volunteers and passive defence services warned the public that a crisis was near, exerting a feeling of vague apprehension but with no foreboding of future events. Somewhere up north there would be fighting, and patrols were skirting around in Siamese territory on clandestine operations. That much was realised. The first few days brought the shock of the loss of *Prince of Wales* and *Repulse* – only the arrival of the former had been announced and the effect of the double loss was all the greater. The loss of Kedah and Kelantan in the first week and the hurried and muddled evacuation of Penang followed on its heels, but the full force of the disaster was not known. A period of three weeks followed when the terrain, the Japanese logistic problems, and also the gallant efforts of the depleted 11th Indian Division delayed their advance. Then came the disaster at Slim, and the long retreat to Johore over a week to a new line. The Johore resistance was over in a fortnight. Little information but plenty of rumour found its way to the troops and the public. An exasperated war correspondent, Ian Morrison, was informed by a III Corps staff officer that there had been a "spot of bother" at Slim. We may pride ourselves on understatement but there are times when it is, perhaps, injudicious.

Wavell had arrived in Malaya at the time of the Slim disaster to undertake his vast and varied command. His tentative time-scale had been upset; the necessity of covering his wide responsibilities permitted only comparatively infrequent and brief visits to Malaya, where his immediate problems lay. He had now to consider whether to defend Singapore, which he had discovered on his second visit on 13th January had no defences ready on its north coast. This news reached Churchill on 19th January with "painful surprise". He had no more conceived there would be no landward defences "than a battleship would be launched without a bottom."\* Wavell had also to address himself to Duff Cooper's criticisms of the civil administration, as a result of which the Colonial Secretary, Mr S. W. Jones, was made the solitary scapegoat and was dismissed.

The news regarding the defences of Singapore, and Wavell's further warning in his cable: "I warn you that I doubt whether island can be held for long once Johore is lost," led Churchill on 21st January to put his thoughts to the Chiefs of Staff, raising the question of abandoning Singapore and concentrating on the defence of Burma. "We may by muddling things and hesitating to take an ugly decision lose both Singapore and Burma,"† were his prophetic words. His minute found its way to Australia whilst it was under consideration, and caused such an outcry from their Prime Minister, Mr Curtin, that it was decisive against what, as Churchill said, "a purely military decision would have been." It does not appear that the alternative was ever put by the Chiefs of Staff to Wavell, but doubtless weighed by similar political considerations he opted for Singapore's defence, and on 20th January gave Percival his thoughts on the problem. Deeming that the north-west coast would be the first and main point of the Japanese attack on the island he suggested placing the mainly fresh 18th Division there, using III Corps as a reserve. Percival differed, anticipating the attack would be on the north-east where he proposed to place 18th Division. Wavell deferred to his

---

\* *The Second World War*, vol. IV, p. 43.

† Ibid. pp. 50–51.

views. He could not have had much confidence but he hesitated to overrule him, as he had after Slim in the arrangements for the defence of Johore which had been so short-lived.

The island of Singapore has been likened in size and shape to the Isle of Wight. It is generally undulating with two hills – Bukit Timah and Bukit Mandai – of some 600 feet, and the Pasar Panjong ridge near the town and port and main population, then about one million, on the south. It stretches some 27 miles east to west and 13 miles north to south. The north-west and north-east coasts were indented by rivers and creeks and mangrove swamps. East of the causeway were cliffs and hills towards the naval base. It is well roaded and the main road and railway ran from the causeway into Singapore town, bisecting the island. There were airfields – at Tengah in the north-west, Sembawang and Seletar in the north-east, and Kallang in the south close to Singapore town.

Over a period of twenty years defences had been built in the south of the island with heavy guns to resist a seaward attack. These were the famous "guns facing the wrong way" which have been ever since the subject of so much comment and derision. As we know, there were no defences in the north. Two positions had been selected – one at Serangoon on the east, and one at Jurong on the west, in the event of a landing, which were intended as fall-back lines. Apart from some wiring they existed only in name, and later when the Jurong line was needed it was mainly a mark on officers' maps, with little prepared.

A general reconnaissance had been ordered on 23rd December, and after Wavell's visit on 13th January further reconnoitring was done, but despite his urgings, when the battle-weary Australians arrived back on the island they found they had to turn to and construct their own defences (in which they were assisted by the Johore Volunteer Engineers) and the same applied in the north-east for III Corps.

No convincing reason has been forthcoming why this was so, and Percival in his post-war memoirs (*War in Malaya*) is elusive on the subject. It was only when the Chief Engineer of Malaya Command, Brigadier Simson, published his own account in 1970 that the astonishing

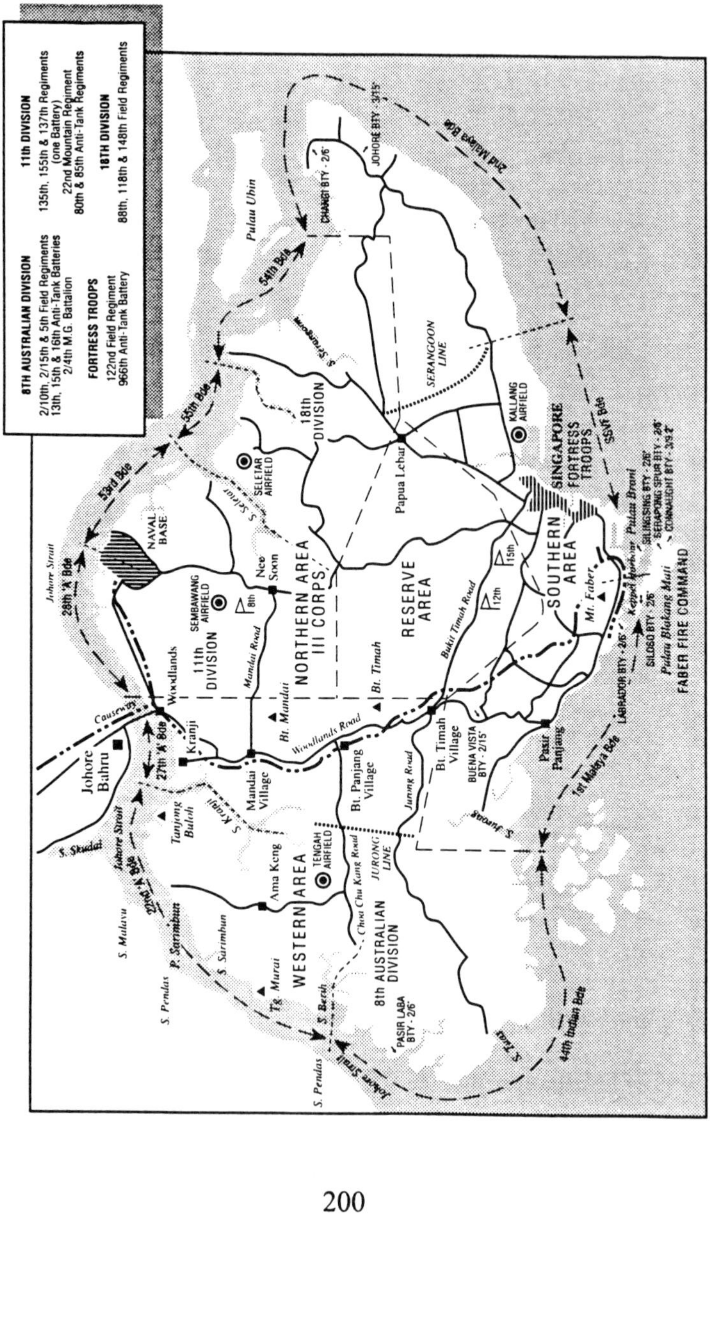
8TH AUSTRALIAN DIVISION
2/10th, 2/15th & 5th Field Regiments
13th, 15th & 16th Anti-Tank Batteries
2/4th M.G. Battalion
FORTRESS TROOPS
122nd Field Regiment
966th Anti-Tank Battery
11th DIVISION
135th, 155th & 137th Regiments
(one Battery)
22nd Mountain Regiment
80th & 85th Anti-Tank Regiments
18TH DIVISION
88th, 118th & 148th Field Regiments
Johore Bahru
S. Skudai
Johore Strait
Causeway
Woodlands
Kranji
Tanjong Buloh
S. Kranji
Mandai Village
Bt. Mandai
Mandai Road
Woodlands Road
Bt. Panjang Village
Bt. Timah
Bt. Timah Village
Bukit Timah Road
Jurong Road
BUENA VISTA BTY - 2/15'
Pasir Panjang
S. Jurong
Ama Keng
TENGAH AIRFIELD
Choa Chu Kang Road
JURONG LINE
WESTERN AREA
8th AUSTRALIAN DIVISION
PASIR LABA BTY - 2/6'
S. Malayu
P. Sarimbun
S. Sarimbun
S. Pendas
Murai
S. Berih
S. Tuas
44th Indian Bde
1st Malaya Bde
22nd 'A' Bde
27th 'A' Bde
28th 'A' Bde
53rd Bde
55th Bde
54th Bde
2nd Malaya Bde
SSVF Bde
NAVAL BASE
11th DIVISION
SEMBAWANG AIRFIELD
Nee Soon
8th
NORTHERN AREA
III CORPS
SELETAR AIRFIELD
S. Seletar
18th DIVISION
RESERVE AREA
Papua Lebar
12th
15th
S. Serangoon
SERANGOON LINE
KALLANG AIRFIELD
SINGAPORE
FORTRESS TROOPS
SOUTHERN AREA
Mt. Faber
Pulau Ubin
CHANGI BTY - 2/6'
JOHORE BTY - 3/15'
Pulau Brani
Keppel Harbour
SILINGSING BTY - 2/6'
SERAPONG SPUR BTY - 2/6'
CONNAUGHT BTY - 3/9.2'
SILOSO BTY - 2/6'
LABRADOR BTY - 2/6'
Pulau Blakang Mati
FABER FIRE COMMAND

information was vouchsafed that his urgings, finally as late as 26th December, to construct defences were refused by Percival on the grounds that it would be bad for morale – for both troops and civilians.* This referred not only to defences in Johore but landward defences on Singapore. It must be admitted that this astounding decision was confirmed by Major-General Keith Simmons, Fortress Commander, to whom he was referred. Wavell, who was apprised of the fact by Duff Cooper and Simson on his visit of 13th January, took Percival with him on a personal visit to the north coast of Singapore where it is recorded he was "very much shaken that nothing had been done" and "speaking with some asperity" asked Percival for an explanation "for his neglect".† He received the same answer as Simson, to which Wavell's predictable reaction was that the effect on the morale of the troops on finding there were no defences would be grave.

As 1st February dawned and the last of the mainland troops trundled over the causeway before it was blown, there were crowded onto this little island about one million inhabitants and some 80,000 troops of assorted nationalities, training and experience, the majority the large tail of a modern army. There were six general officers – Generals Percival, Heath, Bennett, Key and Keith Simmons, and the newly arrived Beckwith-Smith. The force from the mainland after its long retreat and defeats was an army no more, but with 18th Division, the bulk of which had arrived just before the closing of the causeway, it addressed itself to the new situation with a fatalistic phlegm. There was little confidence in authority, which expressed itself in jibes about "orders, counter-orders, and disorders", the strategic or tactical withdrawals of official bulletins were derided as "another balls-up by the High Command." But it was not really gloom, more philosophic resignation to fate, and just making the best of a bad job during the lull before the "brazen frenzy" broke again. By this time civilians on leave in Australia, of all ages, had returned to render such service as they could in the fighting and passive

---

* Simson, *Singapore: Too Little, Too Late*, p. 69.
† Noel Barber, *Sinister Twilight*, pp. 78–79.

defences services, and not a few returned to die.

Evacuation of *bouches inutiles* had been ordered by the Chiefs of Staff on 21st January, but the Governor, rightly mindful of his duty to all races, insisted on no discrimination. The evacuation of European wives and children would have been easy, but the other races presented difficulties. The result was frustration and transports returning empty until near the end when there was a dreadful last-minute evacuation mainly of white women, a large number of whom were killed when their ships were bombed and sunk. Shenton Thomas and his wife had no thought of going themselves, and remained to be interned by the Japanese. Many other women remained to render nursing and other services and readily accepted the risks and hardships involved.

In his dispositions for the defence of the island Percival had the alternatives of spreading his forces along the coastline to prevent landings or holding it thinly and retaining reserves for counter-attack at the point of landing. He chose the former, and apart from a small reserve of 12th (Command Reserve) and 6/15th Brigades (11th Division Reserve), each a little more than battalion strength, formations had to form their own reserves.

The "Northern Area" from Changi to the causeway was allotted to III Corps, consisting of 11th Indian Division reformed and 18th Division, the main body of which had arrived on 29th January. The "Western Area" from the causeway west to the mouth of the Sungei Jurong was given, under Percival's plan, to the Australian Division with the 44th Indian Brigade (even less prepared for battle than the now extinguished 45th Brigade) attached. The "Southern Area" from Sungei Jurong to Changi was the old Fortress Command under Major-General Keith Simmons. This included the original garrison of regular battalions – Loyals, Gordons and Manchesters, and the Malay Regiment, which apart from some detachment of Loyals and Gordons in Johore had been preserved intact, watching and waiting on Singapore Island as the dismal tale unfolded. This was their destiny on Singapore Island, to come into action when to all intents and purposes the battle was over.

For what was to be the decisive front, the 27th Australian Brigade covered two miles of front at the causeway and the woodland Kranji area with 2/26th and 2/30th Battalions, and the 2/29th so battered at Bakri was in reserve with mainly untrained reinforcements. The 22nd Australian Brigade, the stronger of the two, had eight miles to protect from the Sungei Kranji to the Sungei Berih. The only fresh battalion was the 2/4th Machine-Gunners. The 2/18th and 2/20th Battalions which acquitted themselves well at Mersing and were not seriously depleted stood in the principal sectors from the causeway, and 2/19th which had lost so heavily at Bakri and consisted of largely untrained reinforcements had the far sector next to the 44th Brigade, which covered an area unlikely to be invaded from the sea. Bennett and his brigadiers knew this front was far beyond the division's capabilities, and senior officers expressed their concern. Percival could not help, and Bennett formed a Special Reserve Battalion out of reinforcements. The allocation of artillery to the western area was less than to the eastern area. Attempts were made to prepare the Jurong line.

Those arrangements ignored the Chiefs of Staff's clear advice to Wavell on 20th January for "mobile reserves to deliver rapid counter-attacks". Kirby makes this comment:*

> It would have been sounder to have made one division responsible for the north coast from Sungei Seletar to the Sungei Kranji, with a brigade in reserve at Mandai prepared to counter-attack north or east, one division responsible for the coast from Sungei Kranji to the S.† Berih with one brigade holding the Jurong switch line or alternatively ready to counter-attack, and to have kept one division in command reserve in Bukit Timah area. The S.S.V.F. Brigade and one Malayan Brigade could have watched the southern coast from Sungei Berih to Kallang as long as the concentration of enemy shipping at the Anambas, a

---

* Kirby, *Singapore: The Chain of Disaster*, page 223.
† Sungei

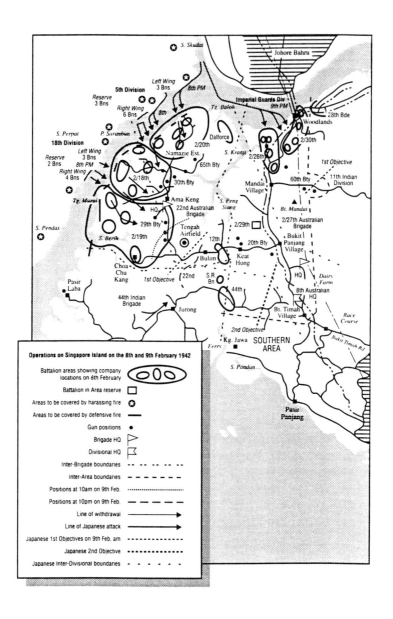

Operations on Singapore Island on the 8th and 9th February 1942

| | |
|---|---|
| Battalion areas showing company locations on 8th February | |
| Battalion in Area reserve | |
| Areas to be covered by harassing fire | |
| Areas to be covered by defensive fire | |
| Gun positions | |
| Brigade HQ | |
| Divisional HQ | |
| Inter-Brigade boundaries | |
| Inter-Area boundaries | |
| Positions at 10am on 9th Feb. | |
| Positions at 10pm on 9th Feb. | |
| Line of withdrawal | |
| Line of Japanese attack | |
| Japanese 1st Objectives on 9th Feb. am | |
| Japanese 2nd Objective | |
| Japanese Inter-Divisional boundaries | |

base off Endau established by the Japanese, constituted a possible threat and could then have come into reserve as soon as the Japanese had shown their hand. The remaining Malaya Brigade could have held the Serangoon switch line. Such dispositions would have made it possible for the Japanese to have been met with a reasonable force in both areas liable to attack, would have provided the best defence for the vital central area of the island, and would have given Percival a reserve immediately ready for action once the Japanese point of attack was known.

The Chief Engineer, expecting an attack in the Western Area had placed there barrels of petrol, underwater obstacles, car headlamps, etc., which Malaya Command had removed to the Northern Area, only to be countermanded and ordered to the Western Area too late. In the early hours of the attack on 9th February, a Gurkhas officer at Senoko Inlet near the naval base reported his position was on fire. Blazing oil was flowing down the creeks and threatening his company posts. Furthermore, at Kranji on the night of 9th February the Australian officer charged with the duty of demolishing the oil storage tanks had his truck of ammunition destroyed by shell fire. He eventually opened the valves and let the oil run into the Kranji where it caught fire, and with the incoming tide surging up the creeks, caused the Japanese invaders considerable loss. All these purely fortuitous events are ironic evidence of what might have been done if Brigadier Simson's initiative had been properly backed and used.

The naval base was by now evacuated and some denial undertaken in circumstances of considerable confusion and lack of co-ordination. As the Gurkhas entered the naval base to take up their positions, an acting Subahdar-Major said to his colonel: "Surely the Navy has not gone too?"*

Water supply from two reservoirs was a problem as the feed from Gunong Pulai in Johore was now cut off. Brigadier Simson seems to

---

* *The History of 9th Gurkhas*, page 180.

have exerted superhuman efforts to fulfil his many tasks, and made such emergency measures as time and conditions permitted, but if resistance had been prolonged the water supply would have been crucial.

The Japanese closed in on Johore for the attack. Yamashita's plan was for 5th Division to land on the Western Area held by 22nd Brigade, and the Imperial Guards Division the Kranji area of 27th Brigade. Diversions were planned and the island of Pulau Ubin off Changi was occupied by the Guards on 7th–8th February.

In Johore Bahru Yamashita had his advanced headquarters in a tower, a prominent landmark seen from Singapore. Its destruction would have helped morale on the island and might have caught the Japanese High Command but for some unexplained reason it seems the Malaya Command refused permission to the artillery to destroy it.

Japanese gunfire begun soon. Daily there were air-raids and by 5th February the bombing and shelling was general and heavy. On 5th–6th February shelling concentrated on the north-west area, and shells landed on Tengah airfield. Such brief opposition as our few fighters could produce then came from Kallang. Our guns did not reply, as Percival optimistically (and to the surprise of the Australians) planned for a three-month seige and wished to conserve ammunition. 'We had 266 guns, compared to the Japanese 168, which were scattered all over the island.'

The Intelligence Branch at Malaya Command had been reorganized and placed under a first grade staff officer who arrived in Singapore on 3rd January. By the 6th February they were convinced the assault was coming in on the north-west of the island, and at their instance Bennett was ordered to send over patrols. The *Official War Histories*, British

---

* *Australian War History*, page 327.

Note: Ironically, the Australian artillery received on the evening of 9th February an order from Malaya Command cancelling its previous limitation on non-operational expenditure of ammunition which had so heavily handicapped defensive artillery action whilst the Japanese were building up strength for the assault.

and Australian, record the bare facts, but Kirby states that considerable pressure had to be exerted on Bennett, and so it was not until the night of 7–8th February that patrols went over, returned and reported at dawn large concentrations of the enemy opposite 22nd Brigade front. When Percival visited Bennett's HQ at noon on the 8th February he did not know of these reports, which reached Malaya Command at 15.30 hours by which time the Japanese artillery bombardment had begun. Harassing fire on the reported Japanese concentration areas was put down. Malaya Command and, it seems, Western Force also, that is Percival and Bennett, appear to have thought that this was merely a process of softening up, and did not expect a landing, and consequently no orders were given to the artillery to bring fire down on the likely forming-up places of the Japanese on the Johore shore. The Japanese bombardment had cut communication lines, and the wireless sets of 22nd Brigade had been under overhaul; they were only returned on 8th February and no effective use was made of them. Beach lights were only to be exposed on unit commanders' orders but now there were no means of conveying such orders.

2/19th Battalion had a new commanding officer just before the battle as Lt.-Col. Anderson of Bakri fame had to go into hospital, and his successor Major Robertson of 2/29th had insufficient time to take over and reconnoitre his company positions.

Such are the melancholy facts. It is enough to explain the hopelessness of the chances of the Australians putting up an effective resistance. Mishaps and misjudgements did not even afford them the minimum support for their task, and so when the darkness fell on the bleak area of swamp and stunted rubber around Tengah airfield on 8th February 1942, after a day of ceaseless bombing and shelling, the Australian troops, whatever the hesitations of the high command, knew the crunch was now coming. The anticipated assault came in at about 22.30 hours on the whole front of the brigade, more strongly on the 2/18th and 2/20th. The Japanese mounted a force of sixteen battalions with four in reserve over a front of four miles. It has been estimated that a total of

13,000 Japanese troops landed during the night and another 10,000 after dawn. Such were the devastating odds; they provide a corrective to the subsequent statements of numbers, in secret session of the House of Commons by the Prime Minister, that 100,000 British and Colonial troops had surrendered to 30,000 Japanese.

The official Australian *War History* (*Japanese Thrust*) gives a most detailed account of the action down to company and platoon level. The Japanese swarmed ashore, infiltrated between extended defended localities. SOS flares were sent up for artillery support, which was belated and inadequate. One order got back by liaison officer, "Bring down fire everywhere!" Men were cut off, ran out of ammunition; the Japanese, some with compasses strapped to their wrists, pressed on relentlessly. There is a graphic and succinct note by an Australian officer in their *Official History*:

> The Jap barges carried mortars and much ammunition. The mortars were at a fixed elevation and were fired rapidly as the barges moved across, so that when they first began to move the bombs were falling short of the shore yet the elevation was not changed. The bombs falling in the water gave moderate screen of spray and smoke, then as the barrage moved on, the mortar barrage advanced across our positions. This barrage looked worse than it was and casualties were few. In many cases, however, men withdrew before this creeping barrage or else were destroyed by it. Thus when the Japanese beached they met stern opposition in some places and were repulsed but in other cases there were substantial gaps in our line, into which they penetrated very rapidly.
>
> The thinness of our line, the lack of artillery support, the forlorn hope to which the troops, some quite raw, were committed, had the result which it needed little enough imagination to anticipate.*

---

\* *Australian War History*, op.cit., page 317.

Back at Brigade Headquarters the noise of battle abounded, and it was around midnight that Taylor reported to Bennett, who concerned at the sounds of firing had roused himself and contacted Taylor from his headquarters, that he estimated six battalions were opposing his three, and urged the need for reserves. There was at hand only the 2/29th, decimated at Bakri and full of untrained reinforcements recently arrived. They were put in motion for a task that might have daunted veterans, and later in the night a company of 2/14th Machine Gun Battalion, and the newly-raised Special Reserve Battalion of raw reinforcements were added. It was not until 08.30 hours on 9th February that Percival placed the weak 12th India Brigade under Bennett's command and sent it to the Choa Chu Kang road.

In the meantime on the 22nd Brigade front, in the early hours of the morning of 9th February, between 01.00 and 03.00 hours, the battalion commanders gave orders for companies to make their way back to battalion perimeters. In the circumstances the withdrawal disorganized the whole brigade. Many were unable to comply, parties got scattered and separated far and wide, and only a nucleus of 2/18th and 2/20th gathered as dawn broke around Ama Keng village. 2/20, the battalion on the right, lost over 500 men killed and wounded, including their commanding officer Lt.-Colonel Assheton who was killed, and some survivors escaped over the swamps towards 27th Brigade area, a dismaying sight for their comrades. 2/19th at the mouth of the Sungei Berih were in similar affliction.

By dawn as the inadequate reinforcements were arriving around Tengah airfield, the brigade was withdrawing as best it could down the road and across the airfield.

Brigadier Taylor moved his headquarters from behind Ama Keng village at 06.00 hours and re-formed it at Bulim village on the Choa Chu Kang road, and here Taylor received from a liaison officer an order from Bennett to counter-attack with 2/29th Battalion "to recapture the general line Ama Keng/Sungei Berih." Bennett was talking into the void for there were just not the means for complying with this distant order and

209

Taylor had soon to cancel any such plans. The Australian *Official History* questions whether it would not have been better for Bennett to visit Taylor personally and find out the position for himself. Bennett's use of liaison officers instead of personal visits has been commented upon. If he had been on the spot he would perhaps have realised that something more than the scratch forces now being assembled were needed if the Japanese were to be stopped, let alone flung back. In addition, as has been mentioned, Percival at 08.30 hours had sent up the command reserve (12th Brigade) comprising only the strength of a battalion – the Argylls and Hyderabads – about 840 men all told. So once again these old stalwarts were brought up for their last impossible duty.

It is not easy to understand why now, in this crisis, it was only these beggarly formations – 12th Brigade; the reformed and under-strength 6/15th Brigade; the untrained 44th Brigade – that were the units contemplated for counter-attack, for which they were manifestly unfit. There was in this extremity the 18th Division, and now was the time to concentrate it at Bukit Timah with all speed. It is one of the tragedies of this affair that 18th Division was never able to show its mettle as a division under its commander, Major-General M B Beckwith-Smith, D.S.O., M.C., a Guardsman, who had commanded with distinction a brigade in France in May 1940 and for a time 1st Division at Dunkirk. Here, by all accounts, was just the man, and here was a division that with a little imagination should have been given its chance to do what it could to stop the rot. There was nothing wrong with 22nd Brigade but it had been thrown away on an impossible assignment, and in its wake came 12th, 6/15th and 44th Brigades, with all the hastily formed Australian reserves, that endeavoured to hold the so-called Jurong line. Bennett as commander of the Western Area had no grip on the battle. Brigade and battalion commanders perforce took their own decisions in the absence of co-ordination from above.

Poor overburdened Percival journeyed to Bennett that afternoon of 9th February and must have got cold comfort. He must have been a tired man, mentally and physically, by now, and in his own wry, uncomplaining way has referred to the long hours of work he had now had to endure for two months. Did not Montgomery insist that commanders should have time to sleep and to think? Percival's judgment cannot but have been affected by the strain which he bore with such fortitude.

He made the decision that Bennett should hold the Jurong line with the three weak brigades; 12th, 44th and the remains of the Australian 22nd, such as it was; with 6/15th Brigade coming up as reserve. He then returned to his HQ and prepared a secret instruction for the eyes of Heath, Bennett and Keith Simmons alone, that if the Japanese broke through to the Bukit Timah road a perimeter was to be held around Singapore city which he designated. This step was not only psychologically disastrous, but was in fact misinterpreted by Brigadier Taylor when it reached him via Bennett with consequences which, as we shall see, only added to the generally calamitous events that day.

Whilst Taylor was patching up affairs around Bulim, Brigadier Maxwell of 27th Brigade was worried about his west flank. Some remnants of 22nd Brigade had been seen crossing the swamps and rivers; his 2/29th Battalion reserve had been taken away, and he sought permission to withdraw from the causeway area, a request which was repeated, only to be refused by Bennett as would be expected. Maxwell was told to form a reserve force by withdrawing one platoon from each company of the 2/26th and placing it to cover his rear flank between Sungei Kranji and Peng Siang. On this day also Maxwell sent Lt.-Col. Gallaghan to hospital and his second-in-command Major Ramsay took over, and if this were not enough, the commander of the 2/26th, Lt.-Col. Boyes, was replaced by Major R. F. Oakes of 2/29th to form a new battalion of reserves, X Battalion.

Artillery fire intensified during the 9th February on their front, and about 20.30 hours 4th Guards Battalion began its assault. Only one battery was available for defensive fire; following the pattern of mishap one battery west of the road had been ordered to move after dark to Mandai Road, and was out of action when needed. Nevertheless, 2/26th put up a stiff resistance, and it was not the walkover that 22nd Brigade had suffered; indeed at midnight General Nishimura had asked General Yamashita for permission to call off the attack and land behind 5th Division in 22nd Brigade area. There was no love lost between Yamashita and the Guards Division and a staff officer was sent over to check on this request.

Then it was that, by an act that has never been properly explained, Brigadier Maxwell against Bennett's orders withdrew his brigade back from Kranji and the causeway in the early hours of 10th February, and the Japanese staff officers, arriving to find pressure relaxing, ordered the Japanese Guards to persevere. This fatal order meant that the 27th Brigade was now aligned facing west from Mandai to Bukit Panjang village and had opened the causeway and trunk road leaving a gap of two miles between themselves and 11th Division and permitting the Japanese to consolidate their landing. Kirby states that Maxwell was unsure of himself and always established his HQ back near Divisional HQ on which he leant heavily, but here clearly he had acted on his own and contrary to Bennett's distinct and repeated orders. Bennett stated categorically after the war that he gave no permission to Maxwell to withdraw. Nor, it appears, was Bennett informed promptly for it was not known at Western Area HQ until about 05.00 hours on 10th February that the 27th Brigade had withdrawn, and Malaya Command was informed, although the information had reached 11th Division in a less orthodox way. At 04.30 hours a havildar of 2/2nd Gurkhas received from a 2/30th Australian runner a scrap of paper which read: "Position on Mandai Road near B.T. Mandai and 195 feature near 13 mile post." This was checked by an officer patrol and 11th Division was informed whereupon General Key asked 27th Brigade to re-occupy Mandai village, to which the reply was that there were not enough troops available, and further ordered 8th Brigade from Nee Soon in his reserve to occupy the hills bordering the main road. From now on the Indian and Gurkha troops of 11th Division were engaged in a fruitless and costly attempt to plug the gap.

212

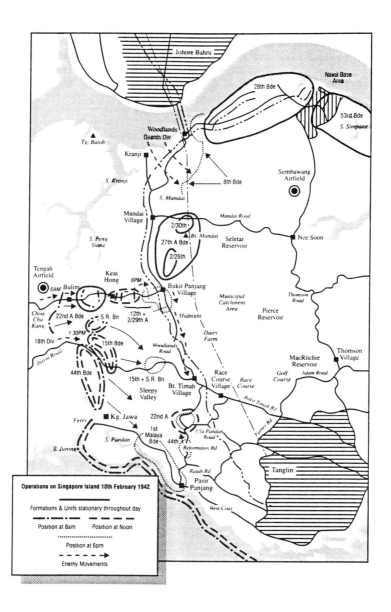

Johore Bahru

Naval Base Area

28th Bde

53rd Bde
S. Simpang

Woodlands Guards Div

Tg. Buloh

Kranji

S. Kranji

8th Bde

Sembawang Airfield

S. Mandai

Mandai Village

Mandai Road

2/30th

Bt. Mandai

27th A Bde

Seletar Reservoir

Nee Soon

2/26th

S. Peng Siang

Tengah Airfield

Keat Hong

6PM

Bukit Panjang Village

Municipal Catchment Area

Thomson Road

Pierce Reservoir

6AM Bulim

Choa Chu Kang

22nd A Bde

S. R. Bn

12th + 2/29th A

Midnight

Dairy Farm

18th Div

1.30PM

15th Bde

Woodlands Road

MacRitchie Reservoir

Thomson Village

44th Bde

15th + S.R. Bn

Sleepy Valley

Bt. Timah Village

Race Course Village

Race Course

Golf Course

Adam Road

Jurong Road

Bukit Timah Rd

Ferry

Kg. Jawa

22nd A

S. Jurong

S. Pandan

1st Malaya Bde

44th

Ulu Pandan Road

Reformatory Rd

Farrer Rd

Tanglin

Rajah Rd

Pasir Panjang

West Coast

**Operations on Singapore Island 10th February 1942**

Formations & Units stationary throughout day

Position at 8am    Position at Noon

Position at 6pm

Enemy Movements

213

Whilst the causeway front was being broken we must return to the "Jurong Line", as the evening of the first day of the landing approached. Taylor, 24 hours without sleep and subject to the constant strain of a confusing situation, on his own and lacking the support of a personal visit by his divisional commander in the crisis, received orders from Bennett to hold Bulim with the remnants of his brigade until 06.00 hours next morning, 10th February, and then to move back between 12th and 44th Brigades on the Jurong line, an area between the headwaters of the Kranji and Jurong which covered the Choa Chu Kang road to Bukit Panjang and south of the Jurong Road to Bukit Timah. The 6/15th Brigade was brought up to take a position at dawn on the left of 22nd Brigade. To defend this vital area were these four brigades, of roughly battalion strength each in numbers, and of doubtful quality. They were called upon to move in the dark to an area unknown to them, with only a vague idea of the general plan and little contact with their flank formations. The 44th Indian Brigade which was settling into its positions at 20.00 hours had orders to move south to make way for the 6/15th Brigade and take up fresh unreconnoitred positions having been on the move for twelve hours. The Kranji oil tanks had now been fired and a rain descended on the troops which blackened their faces with the condensing of the vaporized oil.

The Australian *Official History* comments aptly that "Taylor's front with its excessive dispersal of units was about as capable of withstanding a concerted assault as a sieve was of holding water."

Shortly before dawn Taylor led his brigade back from the Bulim position through the Argylls, but now it was that he received about 09.00 hours the secret instruction of Percival as passed on by Bennett, as to a provisional position on the perimeter south of Bukit Timah road, and here can be seen the failure of personal contact. Like the message written by General Airey to General Lucan at Balaclava the terms were misunderstood, and what was meant to be a reconnaissance was taken as an order: Taylor withdrew 22nd Brigade from the line to his area off Reformatory Road at Bukit Timah, and the Jurong position was left to be defended by three weak and uncoordinated "brigades". Taylor and his staff had been under heavy pressure now for several days with little respite or rest, and, they may well have felt unsupported in a hopeless task, and were undoubtedly almost at the end of their tether.

The fate of the two forces, one covering the Choa Chu Kang road and the other the Jurong road, was decided on this second day of the assault, 10th February. Lt.-Col. Stewart again in command of his Argylls, and Brigadier Paris of 12th Brigade, though a mere handful of Argylls and Hyderabads, were under orders from Bennett, but not in close touch, and had to act on their own initiative. Lt.-Col. Stewart has left his own vivid account of his battalion's experiences,* and nothing illustrates more plainly the confusion around this area as the Japanese closed in, and that what was needed was a fresh cohesive force under a vigorous commander, instead of these makeshift arrangements.

Whilst the 22nd Brigade departed, the Australian 2/29th brought over as a reserve that morning joined the Argylls in the defence of the road, and receive high marks from Lt.-Col. Stewart who in his account writes:

> The 2/29th arrived at first light, having done rearguard to the withdrawal (of 22nd Brigade), but on their heels came the Japs, who at once exerted pressure astride the road before 2/29th could get into position. The latter who were not more than half strength, behaved with great coolness, ably led by their commanding officer, Major F. Hore, who although soon wounded in the foot by a mortar shell, continued to lead his battalion. The 93rd had met this fine unit before, and in the undignified "pot calling the kettle black" recriminations that have at times occurred over Singapore, it is well to say that if the 93rd had to choose a unit with whom they would like to go into battle, they would not look beyond the 2/29th Australians."†

---

* *History of 2nd Argyll and Sutherland Highlanders, 1941–2.*
† *Op. cit.* p.198.

These were in fact three companies under Major Hore that had got split up, and headquarters with the commanding officer, Lt.-Col. Pond, and one company went astray, eventually rejoining the 22nd Brigade.

Out of contact with brigade, and with the departure of Taylor's troops, Stewart had to make a decision in the new circumstances and ordered a fighting withdrawal down the road towards Bukit Panjang village. Brigadier Paris now appeared on the scene, and out of touch with division and finding no contact, decided to retire that evening, in view of the danger from the trunk road with 27th Brigade around Bukit Panjang village. The experience, circumstances and fate of his little force are typical of others in the next few days: hastily assembled, inadequately informed, and overwhelmed. The 2/29th Australians were now at Bukit Panjang village covering the now open trunk road from the causeway, 4/19th Hyderabads were astride the road from Tengah, and Argylls in depth south of the village in a quarry to the right of the trunk road. His action uncovered the northern part of the so-called Jurong Line, but without orders or contact Paris had no option and had to use his own judgment. At 19.00 hours the tenuous contact with Western Area was resumed when a liaison officer arrived with the usual order for counter-attack at dawn. Stewart comments tersely, "It may have been a good plan off the map but it had no relation to the realities of the situation," a comment which applied to many such orders shortly to be issued by Westforce under Bennett.

Bennett records that Percival called upon him that afternoon and "seemed very worried". Poor Percival, he pondered all the perplexities of his problems, conscientiously considered all the solutions, and so often arrived at what turned out on vital matters to be the wrong one. As for Bennett, he had no illusions. Before the causeway was crossed he had informed his Chief Signals Officer (Col. Kappe) that they would be caught like "rats in a trap", but he added, "They won't get me."* Some eighty or so years before, as Michael Howard graphically records in his

---

* *The Gordon Bennett Story*, p. 222.

classic *History of the Franco-Prussian War*, on the eve of the fall of Sedan, General Ducrot had marked his maps, and uttered the single deathless sentence, "*Nous sommes dans un pot de chambre, et nous y serons enmerdes.*" Now it was the unfortunate Australians, British and Indian troops who were the victims of this process.

Kirby speaking of Bennett, and his defence of his sector of Singapore writes:

> It was most unfortunate that Major-General Bennett was placed in charge of the Western sector, where it was highly probable that the Japanese would make their initial assault, as they in fact did. Personal ambition, it appears, dominated his outlook, to the detriment of his duties as divisional commander, and he was unable to contemplate with equanimity the possibility of spending the rest of the war as a prisoner. He therefore began to make arrangements with a couple of trusted Staff Officers, through the Sultan of Johore, to escape by a boat before the final surrender.*

It seems, however, that although eventual escape had been in the minds of some individuals at HQ, it was not until the next day, 11th February, that it was discussed collectively.

At dusk the Hyderabads were attacked, and fell back through the 2/29th Australians and disintegrated; the 2/29th, attacked by tanks, were driven off the road into the hills on the east of Bukit Timah road and withdrew down the Pipe Line to the racecourse. The Argylls (some 400 strong reinforced with Marines from *Repulse* and *Prince of Wales*) now stood alone between the advancing Japanese and the road into Singapore, and between 21.00 and 22.00 hours hurriedly manned roadblocks, but without anti-tank guns which had disappeared in the confusion, were formed to face a tank threat. Lieutenant Bremner, in charge of "A" & "D" Companies, who had only reached the battalion from India a week

---

* *The Gordon Bennett Story*, page 252.

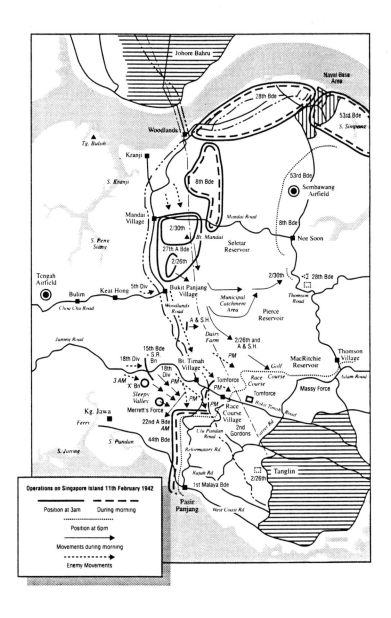

Operations on Singapore Island 11th February 1942

Position at 3am

During morning

Position at 6pm

Movements during morning

Enemy Movements

218

before, was killed in a gallant attempt to halt the tank attack that came in, but the Argylls imposed enough delay to enable the brigade major, Major Macdonald, also an Argyll, to have organized by the Australian 22nd Brigade an anti-tank defence two miles back south of Bukit Timah. Nevertheless during the night of 10/11th February the tanks reached Bukit Timah and cut off the 6/15th and 44th Brigades' communications. The Argylls were forced off the road and after a night of skirmish the remnants retired to the Racecourse area. This was the end of their saga except for the long years of imprisonment for those who remained.

The experiences of the Australians, Special Reserve Battalion, 6/15th and 44th Brigades over the two days of 9th–10th February were similar in the Jurong road area south of Bukit Panjang village covering the main trunk road to Bukit Timah. Whilst 12th Brigade was withdrawing to Bukit Panjang village, a less orderly withdrawal was taking place at Jurong. At about 13.00 hours on the 10th a portion of 44th Brigade was routed and hastily retreated over the Sleepy Valley towards Pasir Panjang, which necessitated a similar retrograde but orderly movement by the Australian Special Reserve Battalion and 6/15th Brigade which contained the much reduced British Battalion still under its stout-hearted commander, Lt.-Col. Morrison. 1st Malaya Brigade had also to pull back from the Sungei Jurong, and thus by dusk the southern part of the Jurong line was abandoned. Since the Japanese had the better part of 5th Division on the Tengah road, and a similar force of 18th Division on the Jurong road, it is hardly surprising that our weak and hastily spatchcocked forces were routed. Bennett and his Western Area HQ were out of touch with all this, and issued through liaison officers at 16.45 hours orders for counter-attack. These were the orders to which Stewart refers.* Brigadier Taylor visited Western Area HQ and protested against these wildly chimerical edicts, but they stood. Brigadier Coates did his best to comply, and placed his 6/15th Brigade at milestone 9 astride the Jurong road, and the Special Reserve Battalion without orders from 22nd Brigade

---

* *The Gordon Bennett Story*, p. 252.

prolonged its position south of the road. Taylor placed what was left of 22nd Brigade, "Merrett's Force", and X Battalion with remnants of 2/18th on the left flank reaching south to Reformatory Road. These wretched forces were intended to be poised for counter-attack, and had to carry out their final moves in the dark in unknown country preparatory to a dawn assault on the thrusting and victorious Japanese.

At 03.00 hours in the early morning of 11th February, as the Argylls were being pushed off the Bukit Timah road, the Japanese 18th Division struck the unfortunate X Battalion, which had only just reached its position, and overwhelmed it; the colonel and second-in-command were killed and the few survivors found their way back to Reformatory Road. The 6/15th Brigade in position held the attack, but meantime, as we have seen, their communications with Bukit Timah were cut, and at 05.30 hours Coates cancelled the operation only to be attacked shortly after in his own headquarters, one mile north-west of Bukit Timah, by the Japanese who had by now pierced through the Argylls on Bukit Timah road. His Brigade-Major was killed, he took refuge with the British Battalion, and when the enemy attacked along the road at 07.30 hours they were held by this much-tried and reduced unit. The Jats on the right had not received the order to cancel the counter-attack, and went forward into the blue, and having reached their objective, found themselves cut off in the open country around the headwaters of the Sungei Jurong. They comprised some 500 men, of which 300 were recruits, under Lt.-Col. Cumming who had won a VC at Kuantan, and had returned to the battle after recovery from his wounds. Here they lay up as the battle passed them by, and here when all was over they surrendered, apart from the British officers, including Lt.-Col. Cumming, the subahdar major and two jemadars, who escaped by boat and reached Sumatra and eventually India.

Cut off now from Bukit Timah, Coates disengaged and split up the parties to make their way through Sleepy Valley to Reformatory Road, but they were caught by the Japanese and only some 400 out of a brigade of 1500 reached 22nd Australian Brigade's position. Merrett's force to the east had a similar experience, and even 22nd Brigade HQ came under attack from Bukit Timah, during which fight the brigade major, Major Beale, was wounded, and the intelligence officer was killed. Major Beale, a fine regular officer, was, sad to relate, killed by the Japanese in the atrocities when the Alexandra Hospital was overrun a few days later.

From afar Winston Churchill cabled Wavell who was in Singapore on his last visit on this black day, 10th February, that "there must be no thought of saving the troops or sparing the population... commanders and senior officers should die with their troops." This exhortation was in the spirit of Churchill in the charge of the 21st Lancers at Omdurman. As regards the commanders and troops the facts speak for themselves, but we might spare a thought for the wretched population now swelled to near a million, ill protected against the constant air and artillery attacks. The Chinese who formed the bulk exhibited their usual stoicism; indeed they needed it all for their sufferings were not to end with the capitulation but to continue another long three-and-a-half years of brutality and privation. Many prisoners of war will recall with gratitude their courage and kindness during those years.

But the stage of such exhortations was past. The battle was now irretrievably lost, with the failure to use 18th Division for counter-attack. All the Western Area was now in Japanese hands, and hurriedly-assembled forces from 18th Division – "Tom Force" and "Massy Force" – were brought in to plug gaps. The end could not now be long delayed.

Major Moses, liaison officer from Bennett with 15th Brigade, described his experiences as the Japanese closed in on the mixed force of Australians, British and Indian from front and rear in the early hours of 11th February. He made his way after many adventures to Malaya Command HQ and in its dugout at Fort Canning, reported to the tired Percival who said to him, "What do you think we should do, Major?"*

The fighting core of a fine division, 8th Australian, had now been consumed by the flames in forlorn hopes and tasks beyond human

---

* *The Gordon Bennett Story*, p. 241.

capacity, first the attempt to salvage the position at Bakri, then in the hopeless defence of the Tengah area, but those that remained took their place in the perimeter to carry on the next few days of diminishing resistance. The casualties of the division were at the end 3095 killed and wounded, out of two brigades, in a little more than a month. For the Australians in World War II such casualties are only comparable with the famous élite 9th Division under General Morshead at Alamein where the casualties, killed and wounded, were 4800 in under a fortnight.

It was now the morning of 11th February and at dawn the indefatigable Wavell flew back to his HQ at Batavia after his final visit, now aware that the end could not be far away. He reported to Churchill that "Morale of some troops is not good and with none is it as high as I should like to see." He left behind a message for General Percival which read:

> It is certain that our troops in Singapore Island heavily outnumber any Japanese who have crossed the Straits. We must delay them.
>
> Our whole fighting reputation is at stake and the honour of the British Empire. The Americans have held out in the Bataan Peninsula against far heavier odds. The Russians are turning back the picked strength of the Germans. The Chinese with an almost complete lack of modern equipment have held the greater part of their country against the full strength of the Japanese for four-and-a-half years. It will be disgraceful if we yield our boasted Fortress of Singapore to inferior enemy forces.
>
> There must be no thought of sparing the troops or civil population and no mercy must be shown to weakness in any shape or form. Commanders and senior officers must lead their troops and if necessary die with them. There must be no question or thought of surrender. Every unit must fight it out to the end in close contact with the enemy.

Please see that the above is brought to the notice of all senior officers and by them to the troops.

I look to you and to your men to fight to the end and to prove that the fighting spirit that won our Empire still exists to enable us to defend it.

It will be noted this incorporated the gist of a message from Churchill, and in a covering note to Percival, Wavell asked that it should not be published or communicated to the Press, as his intention was that the spirit should be communicated to the troops by the commanders, although he gave him permission to publish it as a general order, which Percival did. It seems few troops knew of it, some not until after the capitulation.

When it comes to comparisons none better could be made than with the Japanese themselves, who as the Americans and British found later literally died to the last man: Japanese prisoners of war were a rarity. Mr Gavin Long, the Australian historian, points out however, that "it cost a far stronger Japanese Army as many days of actual combat to take Malaya as it cost the Japanese to take Bataan and Corregidor." The Japanese transferred their 48th Division to speed up their conquest of the Dutch East Indies and prolonged the operations in the Philippines.* In the light of other days Singapore will be remembered as a shambles, and one of the pages of military history to be remembered by soldiers not perhaps with shame but certainly with chagrin; as to Churchill's assertion in the House of Commons that 100,000 British troops surrendered to 30,000 Japanese, this bald statement must be considered against the stark facts we have had to record.

His own share in the sequences of events has been described, and whilst he has suffered sometimes as much from adulation as denigration, perhaps the best verdict on him is that of A. J. P. Taylor (*English History, 1914-1945*):

He never drew breath. In this turmoil of activity he made some

---

* Gavin Long, p. 83.

great mistakes and many small ones. The wonder is that he did not make more. No other man could have done what he did, and with a zest which rarely flagged.

No one who lived through 1940, and heard his noble voice, can be impartial about Winston Churchill, but since he dominated the War Cabinet, he bears, and never sought otherwise, the responsibility for much that went wrong in these years. Lloyd George said that his powerful mind and personality needed the corrective of the judgements of men around him, but since his experiences of Admiral Fisher he seemed to prefer those who did not argue with him, though he out-argued Fisher. In his War Cabinet, of the principal members, Anderson, Bevin and Morrison devoted their time to civil affairs; Attlee, whom one may have thought would have something to say on the strategy of the war, appears to have been a nonentity, except for a protest at his monologues; and Eden reinforced his military misjudgments over Greece and the dispatch of *Prince of Wales* and *Repulse* to Singapore. Eventually he caught a tartar in General Sir Alan Brooke, and another in Admiral Cunningham whom he tried to avoid, but could not.

When Wavell left in the morning of 11th February "without much confidence in any prolonged resistance", he little knew that the events around Bukit Timah of the night of 10th–11th he had spent in Singapore were such that the Japanese might well have penetrated to the city with consequent chaos and slaughter if it were not for their need for a pause to bring up their supplies.

Bennett at Western Area HQ had not become aware of the break-up of 12th Brigade on the main trunk road until the early hours of 11th February. Percival had anticipated the need for a reserve in the Bukit Timah area, and a force from 18th Division had been organised under Lt.-Col. L. C. Thomas – "Tomforce" – comprising 18th Battalion. Reconnaissance Corps, 4th Norfolk and 1/5th Sherwood Foresters, with artillery and signals, and this was ordered to attack and regain Bukit

Panjang, but by this time the Japanese 18th and 5th Divisions had two regiments forward, and after fighting in which they admitted to heavy casualties, the attack had failed by midday. At the point of impact we were never able to bring to bear sufficient forces, and now the end was near.

Yamashita had expected greater resistance in his attack through to Bukit Timah, and whilst our artillery was considerable and effective the condition and state of the forces assembled to oppose him in muddle and confusion had given him a quick and unexpected success.

Whilst all this was taking place, the 27th Australian Brigade lay out on a limb around Bukit Mandai, and 8th and 28th Brigades essayed to close that gap in the hills to the north of the Mandai road. The elusive Maxwell moved back his HQ in the afternoon of 10th February to Holland Road, and Key endeavoured to get in touch and urge him to re-occupy Mandai village. When finally the order was received and passed on to 2/30th Battalion it was not in fact accomplished, and, moreover, Maxwell by now having received the famous "secret" orders regarding the positions on the perimeter of Singapore, informed his two battalion commanders that should they be unable to hold their positions around Bukit Mandai they should withdraw east of the road down the Pipe Line to the vicinity of the Singapore racecourse, an order that failed to reach the 2/30th.

With the western flank around Bukit Timah in disarray in the morning of 11th February it appears, though the origins are obscure, that Bennett ordered Maxwell (who was still nominally under the command of Key of 11th Division) to attack not north to Mandai village but south to Bukit Panjang, in conformity with the operations of Tomforce. This may have made sense, but it was unknown to Key and to Percival, who only that evening at 20.00 hours issued an order that "27th Brigade will revert to the command of AIF when it can be released by III Corps," and is sadly typical of the reigning confusion.

This attack went the way of most these last two days. The 2/30th received the orders for attack about 09.00 hours on the morning of

February 11th, but themselves were attacked by the Japanese as they were disengaging from Bukit Mandai; the 2/26th commander, aware of the breakthrough at Bukit Timah, decided now to act on the secret instructions and the order for the counter-attack on Bukit Panjang arrived too late. Both battalions made their way with difficulty through the jungle and hilly country of the municipal catchment area, not without clashes with the Japanese en route: the 2/26th to their new rendezvous near the racecourse, and 2/30th past Pierce Reservoir to Thomson Road, on fresh orders from Maxwell, to protect the communications of 11th Division.

Heath realized now that there was no alternative but to withdraw from the north coast; the naval base was abandoned by nightfall after demolition by the Gurkhas. To these stout troops who had borne so much since Jitra – as the histories of 2/9th Gurkhas relates – "it was a numbing moment. After weeks of buffeting from position to position the Gurkha Brigade had won the right to defend a citadel in which every massive installation bespoke the power of the Raj – the symbol of mighty and ordered authority to which they had sworn fealty. This was the place to stand to the last man. Yet, they were marching out relinquishing it to the enemy as though it were no more than a patch of jungle."*

A new force – Massy Force – from 18th Division was formed to come in on the right of Tomforce, and during the day, despite much confusion and difficulty of deployment, a line was established that ran from Pasir Panjang on the south coast across the Bukit Timah road at Racecourse village to the MacRitchie Reservoir and Thomson village.

On this evening of 11th February General Yamashita dropped a message by aircraft calling upon the garrison to surrender, to which Percival rejoined with a refusal, but he also issued instructions to prevent military material falling into the enemy hands, not in the end destined to be fully accomplished, as the American Marines found in their epic assault on Tarawa in 1943 which was defended by British

---

* *History of 9th Gurkha Rifles.*

guns brought from Singapore.

The next day, 12th February, the cruiser *Durban*, two destroyers and an armed patrol vessel left with air force and naval personnel, nursing sisters and selected officers, and despite bombing attacks reached Batavia safely with few casualties. This was the last convoy; further small coasters left independently on the next day with men and women and were not so fortunate.

Before dawn on the 12th February it was the turn of the Imperial Guards Division to attack 11th Division with its reinforced remnants of the battalions who had fought down the country from Jitra and were now over in the north-east near Paya Lebar, and whilst the raw reinforcements did disintegrate the old stalwarts restored the situation. The attacks nevertheless caused Percival to abandon Changi and the north-east and pull back his troops to a shorter perimeter of some 28 miles around Singapore city, and this was done by dawn on Friday 13th February.

The city was by now a depressing sight. Prisoners had been released from the gaols to savour the freedom of being bombed and mortared. Stragglers appeared in the town and parties were formed to round them up, but ugly scenes occurred at the docks. Anti-looting squads led by old veterans of World War I went about their patrols calmly. There was an air of dissolution in the once gay and imperial city.

On the night of 13th–14th all remaining seagoing craft left with some nurses and selected service and civilian personnel, in which was included Rear Admiral Spooner and Air Vice-Marshal Pulford, the senior naval and air officers, the latter on the particular insistence of Percival, with whom he had always worked in mutual trust and friendly co-operation. The Japanese fleet had now interposed itself between Singapore and Java, and in the resultant clashes and losses these two officers were stranded with others on an island and died of their privations.

On these days also there were telegraphic exchanges with Wavell seeking discretionary powers to which Wavell replied:

You must continue to inflict maximum damage on enemy for as
long as possible by house-to-house fighting if necessary. Your
action in tying down enemy and inflicting casualties may have
vital influence in other theatres. Fully appreciate your situation
but continued action essential.

The 13th February was noteworthy in that the Malay Regiment,
formed in the early thirties, had its first introduction to the battle. The
Japanese 18th Division having been held by the Australian 22nd Brigade
on the 12th, the Japanese attack switched south and the 1st Malayan
Brigade which included the 1st Malay Regiment and the Loyals put up a
stout defence. The Malay Regiment, with its regular British officers
reinforced by some Volunteer officers, exhibited qualities that make it
all the sadder that their display was delayed until the battle for Singapore
was really lost, and no valour on their part could retrieve it. The brigade
was forced back by superior forces on the sector of Pasir Panjang and
the Gap in constant fighting during 13th–14th February until they were
by the morning of 15th February at the city's edge. The Australians,
now with 2nd Gordons attached, held a bulge in the perimeter to the
north beyond Tanglin, and had good observations of the Japanese
advancing south across open land, but Bennett had ordered with the
shortage of ammunition that the guns should only be used in defence of
the perimeter or for observed targets, and so they were no help to the
sorely pressed 1st Malaya Brigade. Further to the north and north-east
pressure continued and small gains were made in the perimeter but not
any of significance.

In the morning of 15th February Percival took stock of the position,
and at 09.30 hours held a conference of all commanders, summarizing to
them the situation: ammunition adequate for small arms but short of all
field and anti-aircraft; little petrol for transport left; water for twenty-
four hours; a population of about one million compressed into this small
perimeter and in peril from hunger, disease, and bombs. He posed the
only alternatives: to counter-attack and regain the reservoirs and stores

at Bukit Timah, or to capitulate. The commanders were unanimous that a counter-attack was impracticable, and so Percival took the only decision possible, Wavell's permission having arrived during the morning, and at 11.30 hours a senior staff officer, the Colonial Secretary and an interpreter drove in a motor car bearing a flag of truce towards the Japanese lines to propose capitulation at 16.00 hours, although Heath protested strongly that it should be 20.00 hours. The party returned at 13.00 hours with instructions that Percival was to present himself at the Ford Motor Works at Bukit Timah at 17.15 hours where he was received by General Yamashita. At 18.10 hours the terms were signed. Hostilities were to cease at 20.30 hours.

During the day there were penetrations in various parts of the perimeter, and in the east by evening units were ordered back to the Kallang bridge for a last stand in ignorance of these events. Heavy air attacks continued and gunfire, and for many the first intimation that all was over was a deathly silence that descended on the city as night fell. With others there was confusion over the time and terms of the capitulation, and cynics had their last say that even this was mismanaged.

The Japanese had beaten their target by 30 days, and a large army of prisoners marched to the old barracks at Changi for their long years of captivity.

MacRitchie Reservoir
Japanese Guards Div
Thomson
Paya Lebar
53 Brit Bde
11 IND DIV
Woodleigh
BRADDELL RD
PAYA LEBAR AIRSTRIP
SINGAPORE GOLF CLUB
Japanese Div
5
Racecourse
ADAM PARK
ADAM RD
55 Brit Bde
Mt. Pleasant
54 Brit Bde
RAFFLES COLLEGE
MANOR HOUSE
OLDHAM HALL
2 Malaya Bde
8 AUST DIV
HOLLAND ROAD
Tanglin Bks.
KALLANG
GOVT HOUSE
ORCHARD ROAD
Singapore
Mt. Echo
18 Jap Div
44 Ind Bde
FT CANNING
Alexandra Bks
1 Malaya Bde
Buona Vista
Mt. Faber
KEPPEL GOLF COURSE
Harbour
Keppel
YARDS 1000 0 1000 2000 3000 4000 5000 6000 7000 YARDS

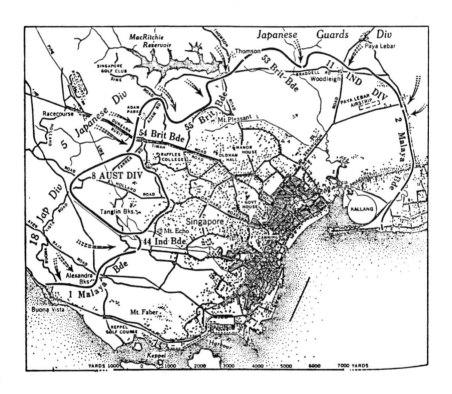

# CHAPTER XIV

## Lookback

Great Britain emerged from World War I victorious and with an extended Empire, but in every other respect impoverished. There was not only the grievous loss in human terms, but soon she was faced with serious economic decline, and the story of the years between the wars is one of an unsuccessful struggle by our defence chiefs to cope with this decline and at the same time find the means to sustain a great and widespread Empire. This story is nowhere better told than in the volumes of the eminent historian Captain Stephen Roskill, in *Naval Policy Between The Wars* and in *Maurice Hankey – Man of Secrets* in particular. In perhaps more moving terms, in his latest biography, *Admiral Of The Fleet, Earl Beatty: The Last Naval Hero*, it is epitomized most vividly.

Beatty, in his last years as First Sea Lord striving to maintain an adequate naval defence, declared that the name "Singapore" would be graven on his heart. He did not live to see its fall.

In 1924 Beatty had to face a Cabinet Committee of the Labour Government under Ramsay Macdonald, and Roskill has recorded, in *Naval Policy Between The Wars*, his

> concise but masterly statement in which he first outlined British Naval policy up to renewal in 1905 of the Anglo-Japanese Alliance. He then described the changes in our dispositions brought about by the rise of German naval power, and the

equally important changes wrought twenty years later by the Washington treaties. He said that in present conditions we "existed in the Far East on the sufferance of another power" – a fact which had been pointed out to no less than three Cabinets and two Imperial Conferences all of which had accepted and confirmed the decision that a base should be established at Singapore. If, he continued, we failed to carry out that intention Japan could not only seize and establish herself at Singapore, she could "destroy our oil fuel storage and the ports of Colombo, Trincomali, Madras, and Rangoon. She could exercise complete control of the sea communications in the Indian Ocean for 42 days, and (for) at least a year in the Pacific. All trade in the Indian Ocean would cease...and the coast of India would be open to attack.

It would scarcely have been possible to make a more accurate forecast of the events of 1941-42. Though the Empire had been maintained and extended, the fact that the Japanese were allies and not enemies had ensured this, and the subsequent Japanese expansion, together with the ending of our treaty alliance with them, increased heavily our imperial responsibilities.

No man perceived more comprehendingly the whole scene than Sir Maurice Hankey, Secretary to successive War and subsequent Cabinets; a unique civil servant, tireless, omniscient, and powerful in the influence he exerted, based on a reputation that reached beyond the leading men in Great Britain to those in the Empire and in Europe.

There is a revealing diary entry by Hankey on 6th September 1931 which summarises the malaise that afflicted British society as seen by a leading member of the Establishment. The diary analyses the causes of our exhaustion and economic weakness, and there is a passage designed to give apoplexy to a young student of today which states:

whilst our fighting strength has been reduced by repeated "cuts"

– relative to foreign nations – there has been an orgy of extravagance on social reform."*

Inadequate as the expenditure on social needs is regarded today, the competing demands of defence and social reform bedevilled the harassed politician of those years in a pre-Keynesian climate of economic thought.

Baldwin and Chamberlain were indeed alive to the need for social expenditure, and grudged the money spent on defence. In 1921 the King, through Hankey, had conveyed his concern at the problem of unemployment, and his private secretary, Lord Stamfordham, wrote:

> It is impossible to expect people to subsist upon the unemployment benefit of 15/- for men and 12/- for women.†

and this for the ear of Lloyd George, whom no one could accuse of lack of sympathy with the underdog.

Though deficient "by present-day standards" in sympathy with the urge for social reform and the lot of the ordinary man and woman, no one strove harder than Hankey, but with only limited success, to ensure during those years "when he was in a position of signal influence" the essentials of imperial defence, and to bring them to the notice of his masters. Chamberlain placed him in his War Cabinet, but he had fallen out with Churchill in 1937 at the time of the abdication crisis and was critical of his conduct. After the fall of Singapore Hankey was dropped from his minor post of Paymaster-General in the Cabinet, where he was concerned with post-war reconstruction problems.

The extent to which Great Britain bore the main burden of imperial defence is illustrated by figures submitted by the Admiralty at the 1926 Imperial Conference on defence expenditure per head of the population:

---

* S. Roskill, *Maurice Hankey – Man of Secrets*, pp. 544–5.
† Harold Nicholson, *King George V*, pp. 341–2.

| | | |
|---|---|---|
| Great Britain | - | 25/7d. |
| Australia | - | 17/2d. |
| Canada | - | 0/8d. |
| South Africa | - | 0/2d.* |

The power of any empire is based on its economic success, and this applied to the British Empire as much as any. Although the British Empire was a victor in the First World War, the economic debilitation created by the military effort was too great for Britain to sustain if its ambition was to retain the same position of power as before the war. Yet being a victor only reinforced the desire of its rulers and a large proportion of the inhabitants to maintain the Empire intact with all its corollaries, a very expensive navy, outdated notions of economic theory which applied at the time when Britain had a growing empire, delusions of grandeur in politics with a consequent ossification of thought and initiative in government, frequent slump at home and an empire which had to pay its own way abroad.

Britain's weakness was illustrated soon after the war by Ireland's successful bid for self-government for most of its area. The moderate boom period 1923–9, combined with relative international peace, relieved the Empire of either considering its weakness or testing its strength. But when the great slump came the foundations of Britain's economic power were shown to be very shaky, and this was particularly illustrated by the humble way Ramsay Macdonald had to approach the New York financiers for a loan to prop up Britain's Gladstonian financial system, which only perpetuated the economic distress of the nation and thus its weakness.

For its subject peoples, Britain maintained an elaborate façade of power which she was reluctant to put to the test with anything looking like a strong aggressor. Thus we got Japanese intervention in Manchuria in 1931 and China in 1937, German invasion of Austria in 1938, and Italian of Abyssinia in 1935, all passing off without any military sanctions or even threat of sanction. Yet maintaining this façade made certain

---

* S. Roskill, *Maurice Hankey – Man of Secrets*, page 430.

intellectual demands on Britain's rulers at home and in the colonies. Since they, at least subconsciously, were dubious of Britain's real military might, they had to compensate for this with the relative writing-down of their potential opponent's capabilities. This was especially true of the Japanese. Japan's successful invasion of China from 1937 onwards did not dispel any such illusions because the Chinese were regarded as even lower beings, despite the occasional very tough resistance of Kuomintang troops. Yet to see reality would have to have given up hope – or almost. In Malaya people buoyed themselves up with the concept of "Fortress Singapore" as a bulwark against invasion. Yet no such fortress existed, and the white inhabitants of Malaya did not realise this.

The troops of the Empire in Malaya were quite insufficient to resist Japanese invasion for long, however well led they were or however badly led were the Japanese. In the event, the Japanese were well led, their regiments greatly over complement and including crack troops. The British imperial troops suffered from the errors of the High Command, and a prime factor was the state of inaction imbued in the military leadership by the self-indoctrination of the impossibility of defeat, which, when defeat came near, turned to that other side of the coin: fatalism.

There are circumstances in history when the very completeness of a collapse carries with it some countervailing effect. The events in France in 1940 in their consequences for Great Britain are a case in point. The fall of France was so swift that our own small, highly trained, professional army, with its skilled corps of officers, the seed-bed of future victory, was saved at Dunkirk by an evacuation that was described as a miracle. It may be surmised that more prolonged defence by France would have meant that our army would have been enmeshed and swallowed up in the débâcle, with incalculable consequences. Dunkirk at least gave us a breathing space to train up a vastly expanded army and air force. It is tempting, even if useless, to speculate on what might have been the course of events if our defence of Malaya and the requisite delaying strategy had been conducted with skill and resource comparable to the rearguard action in France under Gort, Brooke, Alexander, and Montgomery.

A more stubborn defence would doubtless have delayed the Japanese invasion of Burma, Java, and Sumatra, but it must be remembered that in the event the Japanese captured Singapore thirty days before their own target date, and had a division in reserve which was not needed for Malaya. It is questionable whether a more prolonged defence might have swallowed up in Malaya or Java the two Australian divisions which were on their way back from the Middle East. The control of a lifeline along the Dutch Islands to Australia or retention of Burma would have been a formidable task for the Allies. Either might have been done, and rendered less costly and arduous the long haul back.

On the morrow of the fall of Singapore, Wavell in a dispatch to the Prime Minister (16.2.42) summed up:

> Burma and Australia are absolutely vital for war against Japan. Loss of Java, though a severe blow from every point of view would not be fatal. Efforts should not therefore be made to reinforce Java, which might compromise defence of Burma and Australia.*

There would have been agonizing decisions to make but with the fall of Singapore, the Australian Government (rightly, it seems, in retrospect) refused to let these two valuable divisions that remained to them be diverted to what seemed a hopeless cause in Burma, and they were brought back to Australia. The case might have been different with an Australian 8th Division in Malaya still holding out in Johore with the British 18th Division. Would they have been added to the other forfeits?

The Japanese Admiral, Yamamoto, predicted success only "for a year or so"†, but the vigour and valour of their armed services were still being underrated long after the fall of Malaya and Burma. An Allied

---

* Winston Churchill, *The Second World War*, vol. IV, p. 125.

† John Toland, *The Rising Sun*, page 90.

naval force was caught napping on the night of the 8th–9th August 1942 after a successful and almost unopposed landing in Guadalcanal, and suffered a humiliating defeat with the loss of four cruisers, three American and one Australian, and 1023 killed and 709 wounded, with trifling damage to the Japanese. Guadalcanal was a "close-run thing" and the American naval historian, Samuel Elliot Morrison, writes:

> When they (the Japanese) finally "threw the book" at Guadalcanal, it was too late; if they had done so in August or the first week in September they could hardly have failed to clean up.*

Even later, the British offensive in Arakan in Burma in early 1943 was a disaster, on which Winston Churchill commented in a minute to the Chiefs of Staff (8.4.43):

> The campaign (in Burma) goes from bad to worse, and we are being completely outfought and outmanoeuvred by the Japanese. Luckily, the small scale of operations and the attraction of other events has prevented public opinion being directed upon this lamentable scene.†

The local white population and civil service came into much criticism, largely from ephemeral journalistic sources, and as a member of that body it is difficult for one to be objective in regard to the charges of general complacency to which I have referred earlier. It is interesting to record the observations in his memoirs of Field Marshal Viscount Montgomery regarding the attitude he found in the south of England when called upon to defend the coast against the imminent prospect of invasion after Dunkirk:

---

* *The Struggle for Guadalcanal*, History of United States Naval Operations in World War II, Samuel Elliot Morrison, p. 117.
.† Winston Churchill, *The Second World War*, vol. IV, p. 841.

...so we moved to the south coast and descended like an avalanche on the inhabitants of that area; we dug in the gardens of the seaside villas, we sited machine-gun posts in the best places, and we generally set about our job in the way we were accustomed to do things in an emergency. The protests were tremendous. Mayors, County Councillors, private owners, came to see me and demanded that we should cease our work; I refused, and explained the urgency of the need, and that we were preparing to defend the south coast against the Germans.

The real trouble in England in the early days after the fall of France was that the people did not yet understand the full significance of what had happened, and what could happen in the future.

It is doubtful whether this last generalisation is just. In Malaya, where the nature of the Japanese threat was more obscure, there was, as I repeat, more ignorance than complacency.

Recently, on the death of a former head of a large mercantile firm and a member then of the Singapore Legislative Council, his daughter discovered a pass issued by the Governor permitting him to leave the island. He did not use this pass, deciding to stick at his post along with the Governor, Sir Shenton Thomas, and his wife, and indeed this was not unrepresentative of the senior members of the white community whose conduct, with few exceptions, was a credit to their race.* It was a military defeat, on which the actions or supposed inactions of the local government had insignificant effect.

The Governor, Sir Shenton Thomas, of course, came in for criticism,

---

* This was Mr E. C. H. Charlwood, Chairman of Adamson Gilfillan Ltd., Singapore. Recently Mr Gerard Moxon who was at the time a junior member of the firm, later a POW, told me that at a meeting in Singapore Mr Charlwood told his expatriate staff about the permit which he had resolved not to use and offered it to any of the staff who felt the need to leave. All refused.

but it deserves to be recorded that before marching into captivity at Changi he is reported to have said to his Colonial Secretary, Hugh Fraser, later murdered by the Kempetei:

> It doesn't matter about us. It's the people I'm sorry for. It's their country – and somehow we've let them down.*

Thus spoke a man who conceived his first duty was to the people of Malaya.

It has, however, to be said that Shenton Thomas was dependent on military intelligence, and his private secretary, Hugh Bryson, MC, told me in the last year of his life that a month before war broke out a member of the service was due on a mission to Hong Kong, and, in the light of the impending threat which was then evident, asked the Governor whether he should proceed. The Governor consulted the military and was told that there was no likelihood of any Japanese attack before the next spring. This opinion was despite the forecast made by Dobbie, when Percival was his Chief of Staff, that the most likely time for an invasion would be in the autumn monsoon when cloud cover would impede detection.

How can one sum up the military defeat that took place with such catastrophic speed? It surprised even the Japanese themselves.

It is pertinent to point out that as regards the British forces the men who served in Malaya were a cross-section of those who later achieved victories in the desert, Italy, north-west Europe, Burma and the Pacific, the only difference being that the latter were more experienced, had profited by past mistakes, were considerably better equipped, had tried and competent commanders and were sustained in their morale by the prospect and confidence of victory. It has to be remembered that at that time in 1941 and even later, the Army, about whom the narrative is principally concerned, was still searching for commanders, and names

---

* Noel Barber, *Sinister Twilight*, page 218.

such as Alexander, Montgomery, Slim, Leese, Horrocks, Dempsey, and many others were then barely known or were unknown to the public, and were only to emerge later, although their worth had been valued and noted in their profession during the period of retreat and defeat when resources were slender.

Comparisons have been made by military historians, such as Captain Cyril Falls, between the veterans of World War I and their sons of World War II, to the disparagement of the latter. The sombre sacrifices stoically accepted by the troops on the Western Front are a matter of history and never likely to be repeated, but there is a significant entry in the diary of General Sir Douglas Haig on 4th December 1914, germane to this whole question of morale, which was evoked by a visit to the front by King George V. Haig makes the illuminating remark after this visit that:

> ...the King seemed very cheery, but inclined to think that all our troops are by nature brave and is ignorant of all the effects which commanders must make to keep up the "morale" of their men in war, and of all the training which is necessary in peace in order to enable a company for instance to go forward as an organised unit in face of almost certain death. I told him of the crowds of fugitives who came back down the Menin Road, from time to time during the Ypres battle having thrown everything they could, including rifles and packs, in order to escape, with a look of absolute terror on their faces, such as I have never before seen on any human being's face.*

There was a tendency at that time to equate forces and formations merely numerically, without regard to their fitness for battle. Certain forces were estimated to be necessary to defend Malaya, and these were not available, but those that were had serious deficiencies in training. Brigadier Selby has said that his original trained battalion of 2/9th

* Robert Blake (ed.), *The Private Papers of Douglas Haig, 1914-19*, page 79.

Gurkhas would have been of more effective use than his much-milked brigade. It was Paget, Alexander, Montgomery, Giffard, and Slim who exerted the necessary drive to ensure that the troops were fit for battle. Some of the reinforcements sent to Malaya were useless and merely swelled the numbers of prisoners of war. In the circumstances it may have been unavoidable, but a more realistic appraisal of their capabilities might have prevented some of the mistakes referred to in this account, such as the allotment of the 45th Brigade to a task for which it was manifestly unfit, which courted disaster.

Montgomery has affirmed that "The morale of the soldier is the greatest single factor in war,"* and preparatory to the Battle of Alamein devoted a section of his directive to "Orders about Morale". He frequently returns to it, and his often criticised "showmanship" was a shrewd recognition of the human material he commanded and the need to work on their imaginations. "It seemed to me," he said, "that to command such men demanded not only a guiding mind but also a point of focus."† He also laid great stress on careful selection of commanders.

It is understandable that Percival wished to hold the Japanese as far forward as possible to protect and deny the aerodromes whilst reinforcements were arriving, but it will be seen that this involved the 3rd Indian Corps in tasks beyond their capability and led to a serious series of disastrous encounters which accelerated, instead of delaying, the Japanese advance.

The lack of confidence in the relations between Percival and Heath, who with recent battle experience appears to have been more in touch with the realities of the situation, affords another lesson. There was none of that trust and confidence which in similar desperate circumstances in France in May 1940 existed between Brooke and his subordinates, Montgomery and Alexander, and the same pattern ran through the whole picture of high command. The Australian Commander was a difficult personality, and this had become apparent to Percival before the campaign.

---

* *Memoirs*, p. 83.
† Ibid., p. 111.

When the Australian Chief of General Staff, Lieut.-General V. A. Sturdee (who had his own reservations), visited Malaya in the autumn of 1941, it appears the matter of his replacement was discussed, but Percival felt that as Bennett was then on a visit to the Middle East it was not "cricket" to take action.*

In all the affairs of man the selection of leaders is crucial, and Malaya seems to have been singularly unfortunate in this respect, for on the evidence available the appointments by Whitehall of Brooke-Popham, Duff Cooper and Percival appear to have been ill-judged.

Wavell's intentions, with his under-estimation of the Japanese, were no more fortunate. Traditional rallying cries were no substitute for a sober appraisal of realities. When General Pownall, by then Wavell's Chief of Staff, visited Australian HQ in Johore, the GSO1, Colonel Thyer, records that:

> Pownall had half-an-hour with me in my office in Johore Bahru.
> He said that we should now "Drive the Nips back and give them
> a bloody nose". He did not seem to have grasped the situation
> at all."†

Even in the appointment of Admiral Sir Tom Phillips we see the same fatality. In an anniversary broadcast by the BBC (December 1971), an Admiralty spokesman related that Phillips' selection was largely at the insistence of Churchill who had had several differences of opinion with him as Vice-Chief of the Naval General Staff, and this provided a neat solution. Alas for such neat solutions! Rear-Admiral Phillips, as he was then, was an accomplished staff officer but had never commanded a fleet at sea, and there was another factor recorded by a colleague in the early days of the war and before:

Tom Phillips was a splendid Naval officer and a staff officer of

---

* Smyth, *Percival And The Tragedy Of Singapore*, p. 262
† Ibid., p. 263.

exceptional calibre. It was perhaps one defect of his outstanding qualities that he was quite irrational on the subject of air power in relation to navies. He was my opposite number in the Admiralty during my first year as Director of Plans and, though we were personal friends and I had the highest regard for him as a colleague in the Joint Planning Committee, we had to have a sort of pact not to discuss aircraft versus ships except when our duty made it inevitable in committee when there was usually a row. Tom resolutely and sometimes violently rejected the idea that an aeroplane could be any real threat to a man-of-war.*

So speaks Marshal of the Royal Air Force Sir John Slessor, who after the war became Chief of the Air Staff. He also quotes a jocular farewell by "Bomber" Harris to Phillips which is almost macabre in the terrible fidelity of its prophecy of the tragic fate of this gallant commander of Force "Z".

As regards the commanders in the field, the roll of names is an honourable one: Murray Lyon, who courageously salvaged a desperate situation in Kedah in circumstances largely not of his own responsibility; Major-General Barstow, killed going forward on foot to save his 22nd Brigade; Brigadier Duncan and Colonel Moorhead, who fell leading forlorn hopes in Johore; Stewart of the Argylls; the two VCs Colonels Cumming and the Australian Anderson; and Major-General Key, Brigadier Selby and Colonel Allsebrook of the Gurkhas, Colonel Morrison of the Leicesters, and Colonel Parkin of the Sikhs, to name some of those who upheld the traditions to which they had been trained. Major-General Key, who had led the 8th Brigade in Kelantan with calm competence and skill and who was later placed in command of the 11th Division, had good reason to know the score, and illustrates in a recent comment that divorcement from reality of the supreme command:

---

* Sir John Slessor, *The Central Blue*, p. 277.

Wavell had been a wonderful soldier and I had the greatest regard for him but in Malaya he hardly uttered and was not inspiring. He was inclined to adopt the attitude that the Japs were a rabble – and why couldn't we stop them? But you and I know that they were fine soldiers and fanatics. When the Japs had landed in Singapore Island and were approaching the Ford Works Wavell issued an "Order of the Day" saying it was time for the commanders to get out in front of their troops and lead them, etc. In 11th Division, I refused to send it out to my commanders as they were first class.*

When one talks of leading one's men, let it be remembered that during the campaign one divisional commander, one brigade commander and seventeen battalion and artillery regimental commanders were killed doing just that.

When finally all was over, Japan defeated, and the prisoners of war freed, and they met for the first time such commanders as Mountbatten and Slim, saw in Rangoon and elsewhere the masses of modern arms and equipment – although Burma veterans assured them that compared to the prodigal supplies and support of the British Liberation Army in 1944–5 they had crossed the Irrawaddy on "bamboo and bloody bootlaces" – the effect on them was electric. It was a vision of plenty and splendour and success.

The responsibility, therefore, must be placed, as it has been, fairly and squarely on Whitehall, who selected the men to command and by their actions or inactions denied them the means to do so even within the limitations of other more pressing commitments. With such a dominating leader as Winston Churchill, responsibility reaches to its source. His great achievements can sustain it, and given his character and personality it is not surprising that with all his tremendous problems and responsibilities he should, by force of circumstances, and even by instinct, have concentrated his capacious mind and formidable energies on the

---

* Letter to author quoted in General Smyth, op.cit., p. 264.

urgent matters nearer home. He gazed only fitfully at the Far East, of which he knew little, and that more romantic than realistic, of the days in the time of Queen Victoria when he was a cavalry subaltern in India and fought on the North-West Frontier against Afghan tribesmen.

One of his greatest admirers, Sir (then Mr) Robert Menzies, who had visited Cairo and London at the time of the Desert setbacks and of Greece and Crete in the spring of 1940, as Prime Minister of Australia, looked with a critical eye on the War Cabinet, and is quoted by the Director of Military Operations (Major-General Kennedy, *Business of War*, p. 115) as declaring that Churchill "...does not seem to realise that men without proper equipment and with nothing but rifles do not count in modern war – after all we are not living in the age of Omdurman," and that only "his magnificent courage and leadership compensated for his deplorable strategic sense."

Liddell-Hart has described the efforts made by General Dill, the CIGS in May 1941, to bring home the risks we ran in Malaya and the time needed to reinforce, and how he was brushed aside by Churchill, and concludes:

> It is clear the responsibility for the failure to reinforce Malaya's inadequate defences rests principally with Churchill himself.*

He has this to say about Churchill's fierce concentration on the Middle East to the detriment of the Far East:

> The frustration of the mid-summer effort of 1941 to gain a decisive victory in Africa, and sweep the enemy out of that continent, made Churchill more intent than ever to achieve that aim. He was determined to renew the effort as soon as possible, with stronger forces. To this end, he poured reinforcements into Egypt and brushed aside his military advisers' reminders about the longstanding decision that the defence of the Far

---

* *History of the Second World War*, p. 231.

East, and particularly of Singapore, was the second priority after the defence of Britain itself, and before the Middle East. The Chief of the Imperial General Staff, Sir John Dill, tried to remind Churchill of the carefully weighed decision, as between the two regions and risks, but was too gentle a personality and too deferential by habit to maintain it in face of Churchill's force of personality, argument and position.

Yet the danger in the Far East had now become acute, while the British forces there remained pitifully weak. Although Japan had stayed out of the war hitherto, the steps which Roosevelt and Churchill took in July to cut off economic resources were bound to make her strike back in the only way possible for her – force of arms. Her hesitancy allowed America and Britain more than four months' grace for developing their defence in the Pacific, but they failed to profit by it and in Britain's case that neglect was largely due to the way that Churchill's interest and efforts had become focused on North Africa. Thus Rommel indirectly produced the fall of Singapore – and as much by personal impression he made on a personality-minded Prime Minister as by his potential threat to the Nile Valley and the Suez Canal.*

Lloyd George wrote of his old friend and comrade that his "ardent temperament and powerful mentality needed exceptionally strong brakes."†

These brakes were then in 1941 missing. General Dill was weary and overburdened by now, and soon to give way to General Brooke just before the Japanese attack. It is interesting to note that Churchill's first choice or thought was an able but comparatively junior officer, General Nye. One notes an ambivalence in Churchill's attitude to strong

---

* *History of the Second World War*, p. 182.
† *War Memoirs*, vol. 1, pp. 635–6.

characters; he was later to hesitate before appointing that famous sailor Admiral Cunningham to replace Admiral Pound as First Sea Lord.

Whilst the criteria which Montgomery lays down for successful command – training, good morale, careful selection of commanders, etc. – were largely wanting, this is not to say that the picture of preparation is all black. Brigadier Selby of 28th Gurkha Brigade has been mentioned. He was one of that small but staunch band of regular professional soldiers, experienced in the test of World War I, whose qualities saved the 11th Indian Division from complete disaster after the terrible events of Jitra, and his post-war and private narrative is illuminating. He was in command of 2/9th Gurkha Rifles when the brigade arrived in Malaya from India on 3rd September 1941, a bare three months before the outbreak of the war. The brigade proceeded to Taiping, and he relates:

> Platoon and company training was started after our arrival, but individual training of MT drivers, the mortar platoon and the carrier platoon still went on.
>
> In October battalion schemes were started and during this month the battalion, less two rifle companies, went in MT to Grik for five days intensive training in jungle warfare, bamboo raft construction for river crossings and the construction of defended company camps in the jungle. The return journey was opposed by the two remaining companies from Taiping and from this exercise the chief lesson learnt was the difficulty of maintaining control in close country and the consequent need for great initiative on the part of rifle section leaders – a hard lesson to teach having regard to the complete inexperience of our very young and immature section leaders. The contrast between the present and the state of the battalion in 1940, when all section leaders and many men had considerable frontier experience and were used to the responsibility of acting independently in section piquets of ten under fire, made one wonder whether the triple expansion and consequent lack of

247

experienced section leaders had perhaps resulted in greater weakness. A battalion experienced in active frontier conditions, used to sniping and the methods of the Pathan, might well be far more valuable in the Malayan jungles than a brigade composed mainly of very young recruits, who, though keen and willing, had most things still to learn and had never been tested under fire.

In November the battalion acted as enemy in an attack on a brigade of the 9th Division during a four-day scheme south of Kuala Lumpur. During this exercise a sudden attack by our carriers straight down the road completely surprised the brigade. The carriers got through unscathed to the harbour some three miles in the rear of the brigade position. This attack was disallowed by the umpires as being "unreal", and the carriers were ignominiously turned back. Little was it realised that during the coming two months very similar attacks would be made and succeed – but then there would be no umpires to say such things could not be done.

A similar exercise was carried out later in the month with the 12th Brigade. This time the battalion occupied a defensive position and was attacked. It then withdrew occupying successive delaying positions. Valuable experience was gained by all ranks during this three-day exercise and sections were beginning to shake down and develop a team spirit – but there was still all too much to learn. Another six months' training would have seen the battalion becoming more seasoned and the leaders with more confidence bred of experience. All the intelligence reports pointed to the impossibility of any Japanese attack during the Monsoon so it was hoped that we would have until the end of February at the earliest in which to continue our training.

It will be seen there was no lack of urgency to train on the part of some units such as the 28th Gurkha Brigade and the 12th Brigade, but by no means all – and these seem to have been exceptions. Despite General Dobbie's accurate appreciation of Japanese moves in 1937, in which Percival as his principal Staff Officer participated, there was the unfortunate misapprehension that we had time, and the Army was not vouchsafed those precious few more months to prepare.

The optimistic Matador plan was moreover inhibiting to defence works. Lieutenant-Colonel Selby, as he then was, visited the Singora area in Siam in civilian clothes and with a civilian passport to reconnoitre, and there met Japanese on similar missions but far more openly and apparently assisted in every way by obliging officials.

When all was over and the captured British troops were sorting themselves out on the day following the capitulation preparatory to marching out to Changi, a soldier entered a room in the customs house in search of some blankets and found a Japanese officer, booted and spurred with a sword, asleep in a chair. The officer awoke on the sound of his entry and appeared to be not a little intoxicated. The soldier indicated his mission by gesturing to some blankets in a corner and the officer, rousing himself from his drunken stupor, in halting English said huskily; "You have lost Singapore; you have lost the Empire," and having delivered himself of this oracular pronouncement relapsed into sleep again.

We had lost Singapore, and notwithstanding all the sacrifice and skill of the 14th Army in Burma, only American might could ensure that we regained our lost possessions. We were witnesses of the climax of an era, but few realized at the time that the assertion that we had lost our Empire was on its way to fulfilment.

The independence of India eventually and at no distant date was inevitable after the war, and we had depended, to an extent that surprised some when they came to realize it, on Indian soldiers to defend both Hong Kong and Malaya. Their losses and sufferings were grievous, and we should never lightly forget this. There were defections, not surprising in the circumstances. The Gurkha prisoners of war, of course, remained staunch to the Raj to a man, and whenever in Singapore they were seen by the British or Australians they always evoked a warm cheer of affection.

It is an almost uncanny experience for anyone who was in Singapore in 1942 to read Evelyn Waugh's account of the disaster of Crete in 1941, in which he was a participant, both in his diaries and in *Officers and Gentlemen*, part of his famous war trilogy. According to his biographer, Christopher Sykes, he was particularly harsh in his judgment of the behaviour in general of the British and Empire forces. Whether that may be, it is a masterpiece of description, as one would expect from him, of human behaviour in a debâcle not dissimilar from Singapore, where there were errors of command, and much hasty improvisation, much valour, and some the reverse, but where the bulk of the garrison was, unlike Singapore, evacuated, at grievous cost to the Navy, who thus had little to spare next year for the Far East.

One can only say that it shows that in such emergencies some behave well, and others badly, and there is nothing new or surprising about that.

Anyone visiting Singapore today, forty years on, will find it almost unrecognizable as it then was, and perhaps the same could be said of much that was written at the time regarding the fall of Singapore.

There are some memories "photographically lined on the tablets of my mind." Major Kidd MC, walking in the evening with his family in the Lake Gardens of Kuala Lumpur when Resident of Selangor; he was nearing retirement, but he was to die with the Australians around Bakri. Douglas Fraser MC, a gunner of the First World War, leading a small Asian squad of an anti-looting patrol in Raffles Square during the last days of Singapore, and the same cheery fellow who dispensed hospitality in his rubber estate bungalow at Kuala Kubu, after rafting picnics on the Bernam River; he was not to survive internment. Another planter, H.V. Puckridge DFC, one of the First World War fighter pilots, emerging from a shelter after one of the raids on Singapore as the Japanese closed in, with some jaunty, amusing comments for which he was famous. Gerald Hawkins MCS, another veteran of the First World War, who had rushed back from leave in Australia and whom I met at Segamat Rest

House as the Australians were taking over. Mr Cherry, head of Boustead, bidding farewell to his Asian staff in Union Building, on the day after the fall, and telling them that we would be back, and this was but a phase.

It seems fitting, therefore, that one should conclude this account, which seeks to do justice to the soldiers who fought, with a tribute to these men and women of my own race, as well as to the unfortunate local population who bore stoically their trials under the Japanese occupation over the next three-and-a-half years, and welcomed us back so generously when we returned in 1945, considering the circumstances of our departure.

# APPENDIX 1

## Order of the Day Issued on

## 8th December 1941

Japan's action today gives the signal for the Empire Naval, Army and Air Forces, and those of their Allies, to go into action with a common aim and common ideals.

We are ready. We have had plenty of warning and our preparations are made and tested. We do not forget at this moment the years of patience and forbearance in which we have borne, with dignity and discipline, the petty insults and insolences inflicted on us by the Japanese in the Far East. We know that those things were only done because Japan thought she could take advantage of our supported weakness. Now, when Japan herself has decided to put the matter to a sterner test, she will find out that she has made a grievous mistake.

We are confident. Our defences are strong and our weapons efficient. Whatever our race, and whether we are now in our native land or have come thousands of miles, we have one aim and one only. It is to defend these shores, to destroy such of our enemies as may set foot on our soil, and then, finally, to cripple the power of the enemy to endanger our ideals, our possessions and our peace.

What of the enemy? We see before us a Japan drained for years by the exhausting claims of her wanton onslaught on China. We see a Japan whose trade and industry have been so dislocated by these years of reckless adventure that, in a mood of desperation, her government has flung her into war under the delusion that, by stabbing a friendly nation in the back she can gain her end. Let her look at Italy and what has happened since that nation tried a similar base action.

Let us all remember that we here in the Far East form part of the great campaign for the preservation in the world of truth and justice and freedom: confidence, resolution, enterprise and devotion to the cause must and will inspire every one of us in the fighting services while from the civilian population, Malay, Chinese, Indian, or Burmese, we expect that patience, endurance and serenity which is the great virtue of the East and which will go far to assist the fighting men to gain final and complete victory.

R. Brooke-Popham,
Air Chief Marshal
Commander-in-Chief, Far East.

G. Layton,
Vice-Admiral,
Commander-in-Chief, China.

# *APPENDIX 2*

## *18th British Division*

Major-General M.B. Beckwith-Smith

> 118th Field Regiment, R.A.
> 135th Field Regiment, R.A.
> 148th Field Regiment, R.A.
> 125th Anti-Tank Regiment, R.A.

> 287th Field Company, R.E.
> 288th Field Company, R.E.
> 560th Field Company, R.E.
> 251st Field Park Company, R.E.

> 9th Northumberland Fusiliers
> (Machine-Gun Battalion)

> 18th Bn. Reconnaissance Corps

| 53rd Infantry Brigade | 54th Infantry Brigade |
|---|---|
| (Brigadier C.L.B. Duke) | (Brigadier E.H.W. Backhouse) |
| 5th Royal Norfolk | 4th Royal Norfolk |
| 6th Royal Norfolk | 4th Suffolk |
| 2nd Cambridgeshire | 5th Suffolk |

55th Infantry Brigade
(Brigadier T.H. Massy-Beresford)
5th Bedfordshire and Hertfordshire
1/5th Sherwood Foresters
1st Cambridgeshire

# APPENDIX 3

## The Fate of the Indian Immigrant

## Labourers in Malaya

In this account of the Malayan tragedy a reference is due to the unfortunate Indian estate labourers. The vast acquisitions of rubber by the Japanese were far beyond their needs, and the Indians first found themselves without work or pay, hungry, forlorn and leaderless. Thus they were sent in droves in 1942 to the Siam Railway. Some 73,000, mainly Indian, were disposed of in this way, and their subsequent plight in 1943 was piteous in the extreme. Many were assembled prior to dispatch in the Selangor Club in Kuala Lumpur, attired, according to an eyewitness,* in bizarre fashion, wearing abandoned European clothes, flowered hats and coloured dresses – a sort of zany air of carnival preceded their Nemesis. In Siam they met and sometimes worked as fellow-coolies with their former European masters. Presents of tobacco and other little comforts were exchanged, often freely offered by the Tamils, and the talk was of happier days. In 1943 they were decimated by the horrible scourge of cholera.

Contemporary critics† are censorious of the pay and conditions on rubber estates pre-war, but on the whole the European planter had an affection for his "Narlakis". The better employers were improving housing and amenities, such as replacing the old back-to-back lines with

---

* Mr. R.H. Beins, a leading Eurasian in the K.L. community.
† cf. *Industrial Conflict in Malaya* by M.R. Stenson, 1970.

semi-detached cottages and providing a nutritious meal each day for the children, and it is pertinent to recall that Mr Srinivasa Sastri, the great Indian Liberal, who was sent by the Indian Government in the late thirties to report on conditions, told a large multitude that they achieved in Malaya a far higher standard of living than would be possible in their Indian villages.*

However this may be, shared misfortune and hardship produced the unusual spectacle (which might have confounded Kipling) of former master and servant, each naked except for a loincloth, working side by side on the railway, and in the rest period sharing a joke at the expense of the 'little monkeys', the Korean guards.

The forced abandonment of the Indian labourers on the estates is not to be recalled except with bitter regret and shame but it should be said that when all was over some senior Malayans, led by Lt.-Col. W. M. James MC, DCM, and Major A. Arbuthnott of the Selangor Volunteer Battalion, stayed behind in Siam to see to the repatriation of the remnants of those Indians, much emaciated, who had survived the cholera, dysentery and other diseases which took the lives of so many.

Major Arbuthnott, a young regular gunner, was badly wounded in the 1st World War, losing one arm, and was invalided out of the Army. He was a leading member of the commercial community in Kuala Lumpur, an accountant and director of rubber companies. Despite his disabilities he insisted on joining a party going to the Siamese Railway where he suffered much. When the Japanese capitulated he should have been repatriated immediately, but saw it as his duty to give succour to the Indian labourers, some of whom, of course, were in effect his own employees. The same sense of duty impelled Lt.-Col. James, and Major Crawford who was a well-known estate medical officer in Johore.

---

* The writer was present at the meeting in Kuala Lumpur.

257

# BIBLIOGRAPHY

| | | |
|---|---|---|
| Louis Allen | Singapore 1941-42 | Davis Poynter, 1977 |
| Noel Barber | Sinister Twilight | Collins, 1968 |
| Robert Blake *ed* | The Private papers of Douglas Haig, 1914-1919 | Eyre & Spottiswoode, 1952 |
| Brian Bond *ed* | Chief of Staff: the diaries of Lt. General Sir Henry Pownall | Leo Cooper 2 Vols. 1972 and 1975 |
| Russell Braddon | The Naked Island | Werner Laurie, 1951 |
| Arthur Bryant | The Turn of the Tide, 1939-43 | Collins, 1957 |
| Winston Churchill | The Second World War. Vol. 3 The Grand Alliance | Cassell, 1950 |
| John Connell | Wavell, Supreme commander, 1941-43 | Collins, 1969 |
| Ronald Lewin | The Chief | Hutchinson, 1980 |
| Duff Cooper | Old Hen Forget | Hart-Davis, 1953 |
| C.A. Fisher | South East Asia | Metheun |
| Michael Foot | Aneurin Bevan, Vol. 1 1897-1945 | McGibbon & Kee, 1962 |
| Andrew Gilchrist | Malaya 1941: the fall of a fighting empire | Robert Hale, 1992 |
| Russell Grenfell | Main fleet to Singapore | Faber & Faber, 1951 |
| Francis de Guingand | Generals at War | Hamish Hamilton 1964 |
| G.M.A. Gwyer | British hisroty of the Second World War. Grand strategy vols. 1 & 2 | H.M.S.O. |

| | | |
|---|---|---|
| H. Egmont Hake | The new Malaya and you | Lindsay Drummond, 1945 |
| Nigel Hamilton | Monty. Vol 1. the making of a general, 1887-1942 | H. Hamilton, 1981 |
| Kenneth Harrison | The Brave Japanese | Angus Robertson, 1996 |
| Michael Howard | The Franco-Prussian War: the German invasion of France, 1870-71 | Hart-Davis, 1961 |
| D.H. James | The Rise and Fall of the Japanese empire | Allen & Unwin |
| Sir John Kennedy | The Business of War | Hutchinson, 1957 |
| Cecil King | With malice toward none | Sidgwick & Jackson, 1970 |
| S.W. Woodbury Kirby | The War against Japan. vol 1 the Loss of Singapore | H.M.S.O., 1957 |
| S.W. Woodbury Kirby | Singapore: the Chain of Disaster | Cassell, 1971 |
| Frank Legg | The Gordon Bennett story. | Angus & Robertson, 1965 |
| R. E. Lidell Hart | History of the Second World War | London, 1970 |
| Compton Mackenzie | Eastern Epic | Chatto & Windus, 1951 |
| Arthur Marder | Old enemies, New friends | Clarendon P. Oxford, 1981 |
| R.P. Masani | Britain in India: An account of British Rule in the Indian Sub-Continent | O.U.P., 1961 |
| Henry Maule | Spearhead General (Messervsy) | |
| Sir George Maxwell | Civil defence of Malaya | Hutchinson, 1944 |
| Bernard L. Montgomery | Memoirs | Collins, 1958 |
| Ian Morison | Malayan postscript | Faber & Faber, 1943 |

| | | |
|---|---|---|
| Samuel Elliot | The struggle for Guada canal History of U.S. naval operations in WWII, Vol. 5 | Little Brown, 1949 |
| Harold Nicolson | Dairies and letters 1939-45 | Collins, 1967 |
| Harold Nicolson | King George V | Constable, 1952 |
| Chris Noble | Journal of British Association of Malaya | March 1972 |
| Frank Owen | The Fall of Singapore | Michael Joseph, 1960 |
| A.E. Percival, Gen. | War in Malaya | Eyre & Spottisoode, 1949 |
| A.E. Percival, Gen. | Operations in Malaya | H.M.S.O. |
| Victor Purcell, M.C.S. | Memoirs of a Malayan official | Cassell, 1965 |
| S. Roskill | Maurice Hankey: man of secrets vol 1 1877-1918 vol 2 1919-31 vol 3 1931-63 | Collins 1970 1972 1974 |
| S. Roskill | Naval policy between the wars vol 1 vol 2 the period of reluctant rearmament1930-39 | Collins 1976 |
| Ivan Simson | Singapore: too little, too late: some aspects of the Malayan disaster in 1942 | Leo Cooper, 1970 |
| Sir John Slessor | The Central Blue | Cassell, 1956 |
| J. Smyth, V.C., Brig., M.C. | Percival and the Tragedy of Singapore | MacDonald, 1971 |
| M.R. Stensen | Industrial conflict in Malaya | O.U.P., 1970 |
| G.R. Stevens | The 9th Gurkha rifles 1937-47 vol 2 | 1953 |
| Frank Swettenham | British Malaya | Allen & Unwin |
| John Toland | The Rising Sun: Decline and Fall of the Japanese Empire 1936-45 | Random House, 1970 |

# Bibliography

| Lionel Wigmore | Australia in the War of 1939-45 (Army) The Japanese Thrust | Griffin P. Adelaide, 1957 |
|---|---|---|
| Angus Wilson | The strange ride of Rudyard Kipling: his life & works | Secker & Warburg, 1977 |
| Callahan Raymond | The Worst disaster: The Fall of Singapore | Associated University Press London, 1977 |
| I.M. Stewart Brig. | Malayan Campaign 1941/2 The 2nd. Battalion Argyll and Sutherlands Highlanders | T. Nelson, 1947 |
| Brian Montgomery | Shentor of Singapore | Leo Cooper, 1984 |

My sources are mainly secondary; that is, the official histories and the subsequent stories of Major General Kirby and Brigadier Simson, and I rely principally on these. I have been able to secure comparatively few original sources, apart from some personal recollections and information which seemed to me significant, and certain regimental records which are used and are of considerable value, in particular those for which I am indebted to Brigadier Selby of the Gurkha Brigade. As regards Japanese sources, I have relied mainly on Major Swinton who based his revealing story of four of the most distinguished Japanese generals, including General Yamashita, who commanded in Malaya, on an extensive reading of Japanese sources which he records in full in an Appendix to his book *The Four Samurai.*

# *Index*

Notes
1. *Page numbers in italic indicate illustrations*
2. n denotes references to footnotes

Anti-Tank
  2/14th, 171
  80th, 115
Argyll and Sutherland Highlanders, xvi, 39, 115, 116, 120, 121, 195-6, 210, 214, 215, 216, 217, 219, 220, 243
    2nd, 61, 100, 118, 119, 148, 150, 151, 156
Artist Rifles, xv
Baluchs: 2/10th, 93, 132, 195
X Battalion, 211, 220
Bedfordshire and Hertfordshire: 5th, 255
British Battalion, 110, 122, 125-30, 175, 189, 219, 220
Cambridgeshire, 192
  1st, 255
  2nd, 175, 189, 254
  52nd, 172
Dogras: 3/17th, 93, 132, 160, 186
East Surreys
  2nd, 104, 105, 110, 111-12, 113
    *see also* British Battalion
Frontier Force
  1/13th, 93, 132
  2/12th, 93, 132-3, 134, 135
Garhwalis, 134
Garwhalis, 5/18th, 168, 171, 173
Gloucestershire Regiment, xvi
Gordons, 194, 202
  2nd, 228
Grenadier Guards, 52, 55
Gurkhas
  2/1st, 95, 96, 103, 106, 112, 113, 114, 152-3, 156
  2/2nd, 97, 98, 103, 104, 106, 114, 152, 154, 156, 212
  2/9th, 97, 103, 105, 106-7, 112, 114-15, 148, 152, 154, 156, 226, 240-1, 247-8
  9th, 39
Hyderabads, 210, 217
  4/19th, 120, 133, 148, 150, 151, 156, 215, 216
Jat/Punjabi Battalion, 122, 126, 130, 186
Jats, 160, 220
  2/9th, 102, 103, 104-5, 106
  4/9th, 168, 171, 173

215th Anti-Tank, 103
273rd Anti-Tank, 94, 98
336th Field, 190
Companies
28th Bombay Sappers and Miners, 96
251st Field Park RE, 254
287th Field RE, 254
288th Field RE, 254
560th Field RE, 254
"C" (British Battalion), 125, 126, 130
"C" (Gurkhas), 105
"D" (British Battalion), 125, 126, 128, 129, 130
"D" (Jats), 104
"A" (2/9th Gurkhas), 107
"A" (British Battalion), 125, 126, 128, 130
"B" (2/9th Jats), 115
"B" (British Battalion), 125, 126, 130
Gujar and Sikh (Jat/Punjabi), 122, 124
*see also* Royal Air Force; Royal Navy
Allies *see* ABDA
Allsebrook, Major (later Colonel), 105, 106-7, 148, 243
Alor Star, 8, 105, 106, 107
airfield, 94, 103
bridge, 108
Ama Keng village, 209
Amery, Mr Leopold (Indian Secretary of State), 36
Anak Bukit station, 18, 94
Anambas, 203
Anderson, Lt.-Col. (1/14th Punjabis), 160
Anderson, Lt.-Col., VC (2/19th Battalion), 174-5, 178, 180-2, 184, 207, 243
Andrews, Major, 94
Annan, Lord Noel, 69
ANZAC forces, 37, 39, 71, 128, 135, *136*, *138*, 161
*see also* Allied forces
Arakan offensive (Burma), 64, 65, 237
Arbuthnott, Major A., MBE, xv-xvi, 257
Asdic detection, xxix
Asquith, Lady Cynthia, 52
Assam hills, 64

Baxter, Lt., 115
BBC broadcast, 242
Beale, Major, 221
Beatty, Earl David, 231
Beaverbrook, Lord, 53, 59
Beckwith-Smith, Major-General M. B., DSO, MC, 201, 210, 254
Behrang, 153
Bennett, Major-General Gordon, 16, 62, *138*, 242
  defence of Singapore, 201, 203, 206-7, 209-10, 211, 212, 214, 215, 216-17, 219,
    221, 224, 225, 228
  Johore battle, 164-8, 170, 171, 172-3, 174, 175, 178, 179, 180, 182, 183-4, 194, 196
Bentong, 135
Benut, 190, 192, 193
Bernam River, 250
Beserah, beaches at, 131
Betong, 98, 100
Bevan, Aneurin, 13
Bidor, 9, 121
Bisseker, Mr, 36
Blamey, General (later Field-Marshal), 165
Blanja Bridge area, 119
Bobe, Lt., 127
Bond, Lt.-General L. V., 7-9, 11, 28, [U]138[u], 186
Borneo, protection of, xxi
Bourne, Major, 112
Bowden, Mr (Australian High Commissioner), 35, 57
Boyes, Lt.-Col., 211
Bracken, Brendan, 55
Braddon, Russell, 182
Bremner, Lt., 217, 219
Briggs, General, 40
British Army *see* Allied forces
Bron, Midshipman A. C. R., 81
Brooke, General Sir Alan (CIGS), 12, 13, 15, 45, 50, 51, 65, 69, 117, 118, 181, 224,
  236, 241, 246
Brooke-Popham, Air Chief Marshal Sir Robert, xviii, xxiii-xxiv, 42-51, 57, 72, *137*
  appointment, 11, 30, 242
  and Force Z, 75, 76, 78-9
  and "Matador", xxvi-xxviii, 17, 45, 46-7, 48, 49, 73-4, 77, 89, 90

Noble, Mr Chris, 37-8
Noble, Admiral Sir Percy, 34
Norfolk, Virginia, xxv
Norway: campaign, xxv, 32
Nyasaland, 34
Nye, General, 246

Oakes, Major R. F., 211
Ozawa, Admiral, 89

Padang, 105
Padang Besar, bridge at, 95
Page, Mr (HMS *Repulse*), 81
Paget, General, 19, 45, 241
Pahang, 2
  airfield defence, 7
  Kuala Lipis, 5, 24, 93, 131, 133
  River, 131, 135
  Volunteer Battalion, 27
Painter, Brigadier, 133, 134-5, 194, 195
Pangkor Island, 122
Paris, Brigadier (later General), 62, 100, 119, 120, 122, 124, 147, 148, 150, 154, 215,
    216
Parit Buntar, 115
Parit Java, 168
Parit Jawa, 173
Parit Sulong, 173, 175, 179, 181, 183, 193
Parkin, Colonel, 195, 243
Pasar Panjong ridge, 199
Pasir Panjang, 219, 226, 228
Patani, 7, 45, 73, 78, 88, 90, 103
Paya Lebar, 227
Pearl Harbor, xxv, xxx, 46, 72, 87, 117
Pekan, 131
Penang, 2, 4, 26, 88, 98, 124
  evacuation, 25, 36, 109, 114, 197
  fall of, 59
  Legislative Council, 36
Peng Siang, 211

Pontian Besar, 7
Pontian Kechil, 187, 189, 190, 193
Port Swettenham, 26, 118
Porter, Mr A. W., 29
Pound, Admiral of the Fleet Sir Dudley, xxii, xxiv, xxv, xxviii, 68, 69, 70, 75, 83, 247
Pownall, Lt.-General Sir Henry, 45-6, 49-51, 70, [U]138[u], 242
Prai, 120
prisoners-of-war, 17, 84, 156, 238n, 244
  brutal treatment towards, xv, 63, 152, 153, 221
  Burma-Siam railway, xvi, 256, 257
  few Japanese as, 223
  Gurkhas as, 249-50
  and Indian immigrants, 256-7
Province Wellesley, 2, 9
Public Record Office, 36
Public Works Department, 13, 16
Puckridge, H. V., DFC, 250
Pudu gaol, Kuala Lumpur, xv
Pulau Ubin, 206
Pulford, Air Vice-Marshal, xxix, xxx, 11, 74, 77-8, 79, 227
Purcell, Mr Victor, 30-1

Ramsay, Major, 211
Rangoon, 232, 244
Raub, 146
Rawang, 154
Reformatory Road (Bukit Timah), 214, 220
Rengam, 194, 195
Rengit, 189, 190, 192, 193
Ridout, Captain, 107, 108
Robertson, Lt.-Col. (Argylls), 151
Robertson, Major (later Lt.-Col.: 2/29th), 174, 182, 207
Roosevelt, President Franklin D., xxi, xxii, 46, 85, 87, 246
Roskill, Captain Stephen, 69, 231
Ross, Sir Malcolm, 4
Rothermere, Lord, 53
Royal Air Force, xxviii, xxx, 33, 51, 103, 131-2, 159
  and fighter defence, xxii-xxiii, 44
  and Force Z, 82